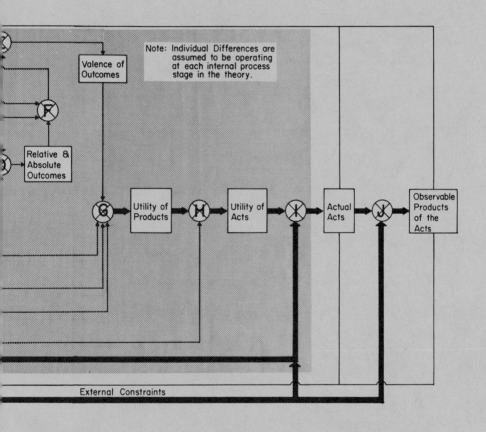

Note: Individual Differences are assumed to be operating at each internal process stage in the theory.

Valence of Outcomes

Relative & Absolute Outcomes

Utility of Products

Utility of Acts

Actual Acts

Observable Products of the Acts

External Constraints

A Theory of Behavior
in Organizations

A Theory of Behavior in Organizations

James C. Naylor

Department of Psychological Sciences
Purdue University
West Lafayette, Indiana

Robert D. Pritchard

Department of Psychology
University of Houston
Houston, Texas

Daniel R. Ilgen

Department of Psychological Sciences
Purdue University
West Lafayette, Indiana

ACADEMIC PRESS 1980

A Subsidiary of Harcourt Brace Jovanovich, Publishers

New York   London   Toronto   Sydney   San Francisco

ACADEMIC PRESS, INC.
111 Fifth Avenue, New York, New York 10003

United Kingdom Edition published by
ACADEMIC PRESS, INC. (LONDON) LTD.
24/28 Oval Road, London NW1   7DX

Library of Congress Cataloging in Publication Data

Naylor, James C
  A theory of behavior in organizations.

  Includes bibliographical references and index.
  1. Organizational behavior. I. Pritchard,
Richard D. , joint author. II. Ilgen, Daniel R. ,
joint author. III. Title.
HD58.7.N39   302.3'5   79–6798
ISBN 0–12–514450–4

PRINTED IN THE UNITED STATES OF AMERICA

80 81 82 83   9 8 7 6 5 4 3 2 1

To Georgia, Pam, and Barbara

Contents

8. Organizational Climate   251

9. Some Concluding Comments   269

Preface

There is an inevitable point in the careers of all scholars at which they feel compelled to somehow justify their work in terms of its rightful and logical place in a larger scheme of scientific thought. At that critical junction, the protective armor created by the strategy of specialization and by the rigors of careful empiricism becomes much less assuring. One feels immensely vulnerable—it is a time to scrutinize closely one's scientific values and scholarly objectives.

This book is the product (a precise term of much importance in the chapters that follow) of three people who came together 5 years ago with a mutual need to fit their scholarly activities into a larger frame of reference. Each of us came from a different tradition; each of us had a different perspective. Jim Naylor represented a decade of research in human judgment: how people cope with uncertainty; how they learn probabilistic relationships. Bob Pritchard brought more than a decade of experience in work on human motivation and satisfaction. Dan Ilgen contributed similar experience as well as considerable background in the investigation of roles and role behaviors.

The theory of behavior developed in the book is the result of our 5 years of intensive discussion and interaction in which we persistently sought to develop a theory that could accommodate our individual needs to integrate our specialized interests into an overall concept of human behavior. At last we feel that we have accomplished that goal to our own satisfaction. At the very least, we have developed a point of view concerning behavior that accommodates each of our research interests. This book is an attempt to share this point of view.

The hours spent in developing the ideas presented in the book were some of the most interesting, frustrating, exciting, and rewarding hours that we have experienced. We hope they will prove to have some value and interest for others as well.

Acknowledgments

We wish to acknowledge Mats Björkman, Berndt Brehmer, Lars Nystedt, Ola Svensen, and Howard Weiss, who provided helpful comments and suggestions relative to portions of the manuscript. Their contributions were greatly appreciated.

A Viewpoint Concerning Organizational Behavior

This book presents a theory for organizational behavior, or, more accurately, a theory of individual behavior within organizations. The term *theory* seemed the most appropriate one to describe what will be presented in the following pages since the material seems to fit the general definition of theory as presented by Marx (1963), namely that a theory is: (*a*) in the general sense, any more or less formalized conceptualization of the relationship of variables; or (*b*) any generalized explanatory principle.

A model, on the other hand, is more of an analogy, being defined by Marx as "A conceptual analogue, generally brought in from some other field, whose function is to direct empirical research: differing from other types of theory in that its modification or improvement is not involved [1963, p. 42]."

Now, since the authors would be the first to admit that there is room for improvement and modification of the ideas concerning individual behavior presented within these pages, it seems inappropriate to use the term *model* as formally defined by Marx (1963). Basically, we have tried to propose a detailed, schematic representation of behavior that unites, in a logical way, the many different variables that contribute meaningfully to individual behavior in organizations. We have attempted to be quite detailed in our theory since we believed that lack of specificity was a major limiting factor with most current organizational behavior theories. In addition, since we were bothered by the lack of completeness of other theories and models, we have attempted to be complete in the sense of dealing with as many different variables or variable "types" and as many different psychological processes as we felt were relevant.

From the beginning, we sensed that any theory of behavior should "admit" to the fact that human behavior can be and is a very complex matter and that any explanatory system developed to study behavior more realistically must itself be complex. There are many different classes of variables that can either influence or determine behavior. Furthermore, behavior is a composite or end product of a number of different psychological "processes," such as learning, motivation, and perception. To develop a theory of behavior without any one of these classes of variables or types of processes would result only in another incomplete theory. The theory we have proposed is, therefore, one in which a deliberate attempt has been made to be as encompassing as possible in the inclusion of variables and processes.

One point needs stressing. This theory is intended to deal with *individual* behavior. That is, our point of reference has been that of the psychologist, namely, the understanding and explanation of the behavior of a single individual. We do not feel that what we have developed is appropriately labeled "organizational theory." In fact, we are not sure what such a term means, except that the primary unit of interest, or focus, is *not* the individual but is instead some macro entity. In fact, we are somewhat uncomfortable with the notion that we have a theory of organizational behavior—a term that Karl Weick once referred to as being "utter nonsense."

A second point worth remembering is that whereas the theory was developed with the intent of creating a theory of individual behavior in organizations, it soon became clear that such a theory inevitably becomes a general theory of behavior. That is, work behavior is not idiosyncratic; it does not require a theory that would apply only to that specific context or environment. If a theory is capable of dealing with individual behavior in an organization, it should be as capable of dealing with individual behavior outside the organization. What is unique about the environment in any type of organization that would call for a special "theory" of behavior peculiar only to that setting? Therefore, the theory presented here is proposed as a general theory of behavior applicable to the behavior of an individual in any context, within or outside the work environment, although admittedly our contextual emphasis will be that of the work setting.

The theory presented in the following pages is a cognitive theory of behavior. It assumes that man is rational (or at least nonrandom) for the most part, and that as a systematic or nonrandom generator of behavior, man's actions are explained best in terms of conscious, thinking acts on the part of the individual. Furthermore, the theory is founded upon the concept that the basic conscious action of the individual is the action of choice, or the process of choosing among alternatives. The theory deals with why the individual chooses certain alternative courses of action in preference to others, and thus it might properly be called a theory of choice behavior. Whereas the emphasis is clearly upon the cognitive aspects of behavior, considerable attention has been devoted to external, noncognitive variables in the system that play meaningful roles in the determination of individual behavior.

Perhaps the best way to approach an understanding of the proposed theory is to view it as an elaboration of the traditional and time-honored $S \rightarrow O \rightarrow R$ sequence familiar even to those who have been exposed only casually to behaviorism. We have made the basic sequence considerably more elaborate, but the sequence itself remains inviolate. If a feedback loop is added, $S \rightarrow O \rightarrow R$ becomes $S \overset{\frown}{\rightarrow} O \rightarrow R$; and if the O in the sequence is separated into two major parts, one a detailed and dynamic cognitive component, and the other a stable individual difference component; and if the R term in the sequence is defined explicitly, the essential characteristics of the theory to be presented on the following pages begin to emerge. It is not quite that simple, but it is a first approximation. A second or closer approximation requires delineation of the basic processes of learning, motivation, and perception, working within the O part of the theory. Finally, a third phase of elaboration, one that shows how the many individual cognitive components can be structured into a cognitive system, is required for an adequate explanation of behavior. The reader may be, at first, a bit hard pressed to see the similarity between the simple sequence $S \rightarrow O \rightarrow R$ and the theory presented in complete schematic form on page 24. Yet the similarity is there and will become apparent as one follows the textual explanation of the theory.

As we mentioned previously, our attempts to develop a theory of behavior were generated by a number of antecedent conditions and concerns. First, we found ourselves dissatisfied with the limited explanations of behavior offered by most current organizational theories or models. Some were too specific and narrow, others so broad and general that they were almost completely useless. Second, there seemed to be no coherence among the current theories—that is, some theories explained behavior in terms of need systems, others in terms of force or valence notions whereas still others used equity or balance explanations. Now it is important to point out clearly that we do not wish to quarrel with any of these various explanations of behavior. Indeed, we acknowledge that a body of literature supports each of the positions mentioned, as well as half a dozen or more other viewpoints. There is compelling evidence that it is possible to explain some systematic variance in behavior, under certain specified conditions, with any one of a wide variety of current

models or theories of behavior. We also believe that it is not particularly
fruitful or even intellectually interesting to argue the relative merits of
these theories—that is, pitting or testing one theory against another is
difficult both experimentally and conceptually. They are sometimes so
diverse in terms of basic explanatory mechanisms and/or in terms of level
of specificity that tests of relative merit become meaningless. How, for
example, does one construct a test to determine whether an
expectancy–valence theory of behavior is "better than" or "worse than" a
need–hierarchy theory? Is it not more likely that both types of mechanisms play their individually important but not necessarily exclusive
parts in determining behavior?

Therefore, we concluded that the best approach would be to develop a
theory incorporating within it most, if not all, of the current theories or
models of organizational behavior as well as the data generated in support of those theories. In fact, we felt that the ability of the theory to do
exactly that would be one major test of the value of the theory. It is,
therefore, a *very* broad theory. At the same time, it is in many ways quite
specific in that it postulates explicitly the interrelations among the many
different components of the theory and the way in which certain mechanisms operate.

In developing the theory, we began with the premise that a useful view
of behavior must include a variety of different ingredients including a
functional definition of behavior itself, something lacking in most current models or theories of organizational behavior. The essential elements incorporated into our theory or understanding of behavior are as
follows:

1. A useful and meaningful definition of behavior.
2. The role of the environment upon behavior, including such external factors or influences as the physical context and the social context within which the behavior takes place. Furthermore, an explicit
   conceptualization of the means by which the environment influences behavior.
3. The role of individual differences (ID) in the determination of
   behavior. Regardless of personal prejudices concerning individual
   difference variables, no theory of behavior can be complete without
   recognizing the important and obvious ways in which these individual parameters affect behavior.
4. The role of perceptions. The theory particularly emphasizes the
   perceptions which form what we will call roles, which, through the
   mediating mechanisms of other perceptions, called contingencies
   and valences, perform an exceedingly important function in determining behavior.

5. The role of motivation, including the way in which an individual's present affective state, temporary and basic needs, and perceived outcomes influence the anticipated attractiveness of future outcomes, products, and acts.
6. The role of learning, primarily in terms of how it permits change in individual abilities and in the perceptions of expectancies, valences, outcomes, and roles.
7. The role of affect and its place in determining behavior. Affect will be a central concept in the theory and will be treated in two distinct ways. The theory deals with affect attached to present or past outcomes. It will also deal with affect attached to anticipated outcomes—those that have not yet occurred. In addition, the theory attempts to define that affective domain typically referred to in the organizational literature as job satisfaction.

Having listed these seven concerns, we must next examine each of them in a bit more detail.

Defining Behavior

In this and in the following chapters, the term *behavior* will have a very specific meaning. *Behavior* is defined here as an "ongoing act" or process. It is the "doing" of something by an individual and should actually be viewed more as the verb "behaving" than as the noun "behavior." The basic unit of behavior in the theory is called the *act*. An act has two defining characteristics or dimensions. They are (*a*) *amplitude,* which is the total commitment to an act as defined by the amount or quantity of individual resources (time and effort) allocated by the individual to the task of performing or doing that act (i.e., carrying out that process); and (*b*) *direction,* the specific kind of activity or process being carried out or performed. Note that the amplitude dimension does not refer to the amount of the act or to the behavior itself but to the amount of the individual's resources allocated to the act. This distinction may seem trivial since, in nearly every case, they are conceptually indistinguishable. That is, the amount of behavior is conceptually identical to the amount of the individual's resources allocated to the act. However, we prefer to use the individual resource allocation frame of reference in defining the amplitude of an act in order to make it clear that the amplitude of an act must be defined in terms of either time, effort, or some combination of these two variables since, and this is *extremely important,* time and effort are the primary resources available to an individual entering into an act. Time and effort are the two basic dimensions of commitment to an act. In performing any act, one can control the length and intensity of behavior in carrying out the act.

This can be stated another way. Ideally, when an individual decides to "do" something (i.e., decides to behave and therefore to perform some act), that individual must (a) first decide what act he or she is going to perform or attempt to perform (the direction dimension of an act); and then must further decide (b) how much of his or her resources (effort) are going to be "committed" to the performing of that act. Thus, one can view amplitude as a measure or dimension of *total effort* commitment on the part of the individual to the performing of an act. Commitment, in turn, can be expressed in terms of the two basic dimensions already mentioned, time and effort. If we define effort in terms of the amount of energy "spent" on the act per unit time, then time and energy can be combined into a composite measure of total effort expenditure upon the task on the part of the individual or $T \times E = C$.

Behavior, then, will be viewed as being a problem of resource allocation on the part of the individual in which he or she has a wide variety of options available at any moment with regard to possible acts that can be performed (have resources allocated to them) and the amount of resources, which may or should be allocated to each option or act. To illustrate by example, right at this moment, you, the reader, have decided to perform the act of reading this particular material. In so doing, you have chosen or specified the direction of your behavior (or a large part of your current behavior). The amount of time that you spend engaged in this act, and the intensity or energy you devote to the act (degree of concentration) per unit time are the two determinants of your total effort expended on this act. If while reading this passage you are simultaneously performing some other act (e.g., listening to the radio, talking to a friend, etc.), then you are "time sharing" and your behavior is multidirectional in that your total resources are being shared, or distributed, across more than one act.

Several points need to be made at this juncture. First, it is not necessary that an individual use all of his or her resources at any given time. We will assume that people operate at various levels of total activation from moment to moment, and that it is rare for any individual to put forth maximum effort for even very short time spans except in unusual, emergency situations. Second, we need to try to distinguish between relevant acts and trivial acts (this distinction is fuzzy, since the same act may in certain instances be considered trivial; in other situations, relevant). We all recognize that we rarely attend to or allocate resources completely to a single act to the exclusion of all other acts, no matter at what level of overall efficiency we happen to be operating. If an individual is using, for example, 80% of his or her resources at a given moment, it is unlikely that all of these resources are being devoted to a single act, *even if such is the desired intention of the individual.* As you are reading these words, you may desire to have all your concentration centered upon the act of reading, but you are probably doing many other things, of which you are only partly aware, at the same time (such as tapping your fingers, scratching your ear, doodling, daydreaming, or humming), as small or large fragments of your attention wander away from your chosen act from moment to moment. These are trivial acts—trivial in the sense that we do not really want to deal with them. We do not regard them as interesting, or important. Many of these trivial acts may be considered very nearly random behavior on the part of the individual (e.g., tapping fingers, cracking knuckles), while others are not at all random but are consciously motivated acts designed to result in a rewarding outcome for the individual (e.g., scratching an itch on one's ear). The random behaviors may be easily dismissed as trivial, since no theory, including ours, is particularly interested in dealing with random events. However, the theory *is* designed to deal with any form of conscious, motivated behavior—even the scratching of ears. However, we shall arbitrarily treat such acts as trivial, and will use the theory to deal with acts having relationships with outcomes of greater importance to the individual than the feeling of satisfaction or relief obtained from a well scratched ear.

The mechanism used to distinguish trivial behaviors from nontrivial behaviors is as follows: If a behavior produces or creates an observable entity or thing and if that thing that has been created by the behavior is viewed as being *important to some observer,* then the behavior is a relevant behavior to that observer. In the theory, we refer to those things that are created by performing an act as *products.* Those products which are said to be evaluated by either the individual performing the act (self-evaluation) or by some external observer (other-evaluation) are by definition relevant products. By extension, any behavior or act that can produce such products becomes a relevant behavior to the evaluator. This definition will be explained in greater detail in Chapters 2 and 5. At this point, we simply wish to establish that the theory does distinguish between relevant and trivial behaviors and that relevance is a flexible concept that depends upon who is observing the behavior. What is relevant to one observer may be trivial to another observer.

We can express these points as follows: Let

C_r = commitment to relevant acts
C_t = commitment to trivial acts
C_T = total commitment
C_M = maximum possible commitment

and thus

$$C_T = C_r + C_t$$

and we can define the ratios

C_T/C_M = general level of activation of the individual
C_r/C_T = level of efficiency of behavior

Behavior versus Products

The point made in the previous paragraph concerning products being those things produced by the process of an act is a critical aspect of the theory and needs elaboration. In the development of the theory, the act, which is recognized as being the basic unit of behavior, is not necessarily the most important unit. We will see that those things produced by acts, which are called products, are of equal importance. In fact, we take the point of view that the concept of a *perceived product* may be the most critical unit in the theory. The focus on products rather than on behavior in the theory is, we believe, an extremely important distinction from other theories. We have taken this approach because it is rare, in a phenomenological sense, that individuals either witness, observe, or evaluate actual acts (the time and effort spent doing something). As will be pointed out later, it is actually the *results* of acts that typically concern us, not the acts themselves. The results of the acts are called products in the theory. Therefore, although we have been talking about a theory of behavior, by the time we finish we may decide that we could refer to it just as easily as a theory of products, since products play such a critical part. The general form of the behavior to perceived products sequence as it relates to the theory is diagrammed in highly simplified form in Figure 1.1.

We start with the basic process, which is the act itself, or the basic unit of behavior over which the individual can exercise direct control in terms of amplitude and direction (direction, incidentally, being a special way of looking at amplitude, in that direction is specified by amplitudes greater than zero for any act). The act, or process, in turn, creates things or "products" as a result of carrying out the act. The act brings these products into existence as entities in the sense that the act of typing creates

FIGURE 1.1 *The behavior to products sequence.*

words on a page. Every act must have *some* result (product) even if it is only a simple change in the basic state or position of the individual performing the act. The products, or results of the acts, are then perceived either by the individual directly or by some other entity such as another person or an organization. These perceived products, which are the result of an individual's conscious behavior, are the essential units in the theory.

The Role of the Environment

The fact that the behavior of an individual may be influenced greatly by the environment or setting (both specific and general) in which the individual exists and behaves has been one of the major accepted truths in psychology. An organism does not exist in isolation. Indeed, the $S \overset{\leftarrow}{\to} O \to R$ system makes it clear that the stimulus world, which is defined by the physical and social environment of the individual, plays a major role in the determination of behavior (the response). Any theory of behavior, therefore, necessarily includes environmental or contextual factors as an integral part of its theoretical system. That is, the S term in the $S \overset{\leftarrow}{\to} O \to R$ pattern must be dealt with in substance.

In attempting to deal adequately with the very complex issue of environmental influence on individual behavior, we have found it necessary to make important distinctions concerning environmental characteristics as to (*a*) how they came into existence; and (*b*) the way in which they influence behavior. Both of these distinctions are important to the theory as it will be presented in the following chapters.

To put these distinctions in perspective, one must first recognize that when we are talking about the environment (or the S term in the $S \overset{\leftarrow}{\to} O \to R$ system), we are, of course, talking about a concept. This concept includes *all* the definable or specifiable characteristics of the stimulus world of the individual, including both the physical and the social characteristics. We are *not*, at this point, talking at all about how the individual perceives these characteristics. We are viewing the total environment of person *i* from the viewpoint of a detached, omniscient observer with the power to completely specify the true characteristics or dimensions of this environment *without* reference to individual *i*. This concept of an environment is an idealized one, which can only be approximated in everyday reality, since all systems for specifying environmental characteristics are man-made systems based upon arbitrary definitions of characteristics; not on factual systems based upon proven characteristics. Further, many systems for defining environment are based upon the way in which individuals respond to that environment rather than upon any characteristics of the environment itself. That is, in such systems the characteristics of the stimulus world are *not* independent of individual i in that the dimensions are established by observing and measuring the responses of people to their environments.

For example, consider the environmental dimension of stress. We have great difficulty in trying to define what is or what is not a stressful environment without reference to the individual and/or his or her responses to the environment. We cannot agree on the characteristics of a stressful environment in the absence of such behavioral referents, since the concept of stress itself is a behavioral concept. That is, we are using a system of classification of the environment based upon individual behavior referents rather than environmental characteristic referents. This is a circular and, therefore, potentially self-defeating approach, particularly when we know with certainty that different people react in quite different ways to the same environment. There are certainly people by environment interactions that prohibit circular systems from defining precisely the essential characteristics of the complex stimulus we would call the environment.

Yet the strategy remains a widely used and popular approach to the understanding of environments. For example, in the case of describing very simple environments, such as tasks, we often use such descriptive dimensions as task difficulty or task complexity. Such systems are used because we believe that these dimensions of the task can influence behavior, but our logic is based upon the vast amount of evidence that performance is different (poorer) on some tasks than it is on other tasks. We then label the poor performance tasks as difficult and the good performance tasks as easy. This system is circular in that the measure of the dimension is based upon behavior—since we have used a behavioral concept to define the task dimension. Thus, if we start by defining a task as difficult because individuals perform less well on that task then they do on another task, which is, therefore, easy, it is not particularly meaningful to conclude that people respond differently to more difficult tasks than they do to easy tasks.

There are many other examples of behaviorally based systems for classifying environments on either a micro or a macro level. Consider, for example, those task-description systems which are based entirely upon the ability or aptitude of the individual that is tapped by the task. Such systems have been developed in both the cognitive (e.g., Guilford, 1956, 1967) and the noncognitive, perceptual–motor domains (e.g., Fleishman, 1962, 1967), and in each instance elaborate taxonomies have been developed that are based entirely upon the way in which large numbers of individuals have responded to different tasks in terms of performance measures. These systems, if they reflect anything, reflect the characteristic ways in which people react to the environment. They are not characteristics of environments themselves. Further, as Tyron (1979) and others have argued compellingly, they may not reflect any basic characteristics of the population of individuals.

Not all task-description systems are based upon response referents. There are numerous instances in which nonbehavioral referent systems have been developed for tasks in attempts to provide classifications of task difficulty, task complexity, etc. Such examples typically use various structural properties of the stimulus and are often based upon systems taken from other disciplines (e.g., linguistics, mathematics). They are systems for describing things, not people. Although they are not always as successful as one would wish (e.g., information theory did not prove to be the ultimate answer), they do avoid the difficulties inherent in systems predicated upon responses measures.

The same issues arise when one considers those taxonomies of environments generated on a broader scale than that of task dimensions. Most notable in that context are the organizational theories that provide principles for the systematic structuring of work environments into types or groups. Such attempts have generally taken two major paths. First, there are classification attempts based primarily or exclusively upon organizational variables (i.e., characteristics of the environment itself). Typically two types of variables have been used to form such classification schemes—either separately or jointly. They are (a) organizational structure variables; and (b) organizational function variables. The second approach classifies organizational environments into clusters based upon measures taken upon the individuals existing within the organization. Again, these are response measures of individuals based upon the individual's reaction or response to his or her environment, as was the case with taxonomies of tasks. There is one major difference, however; the response dimension itself has changed. It is no longer a measure of performance. Instead, it is a measure of individual *affect* toward or of *belief* about the environment. Such measures are called different things by different people, but usually they are referred to as "morale" or average job satisfaction if the basic measure is an affect measure or as "climate" if the basic measure is a belief measure. A mixture of the two kinds of measures has sometimes been used to provide a classification scheme according to something called organizational "values."

Taxonomies dealing with environments larger than organizations are hard to find, although certain kinds of national descriptors or labels could be called taxonomies. We refer to nations as being industrialized or agrarian, and we refer to their governments as being conservative, liberal, democratic, socialistic, etc. Similarly we have the "old world" nations, the "new world" nations, and the "third world" nations. These are groupings of environments based on extremely broad dimensions.

We believe that trying to understand the influence of environment upon the behavior of the individual through the use of classifications that either specify parts or huge segments of the environment as "types" using *any* technique is not viable as methodology. In addition, we believe that techniques based wholly or in part upon the responses of individuals to the environment are particularly nonproductive and circular. However, all classification schemes are arbitrary creations. The nature and the complexity of such systems and also the number of different systems will be limited only by the ingenuity of the people desiring such taxonomies and by the number of different dimensions and measures they can create.

In summary, in our opinion, it is not wise to approach the environmental influence by the question "What are the critical or basic characteristics (or dimensions) of the environment?" We would argue that a richer and more productive perspective on environmental influence is provided by working within the context provided by the question "What are the critical or basic *processes* by which environmental characteristics influence individual behavior?" If a process orientation is adopted, one no longer needs to be concerned with systems of classification of environments based upon either behavioral or nonbehavioral referents.

At the beginning of this discussion, it was mentioned that the theory distinguishes among certain environmental characteristics. These distinctions are distinctions concerning processes, not distinctions of kind or of type. The theory identifies two critical processes—the process of how environmental characteristics come into existence, *attribute creation* and the process by which environmental characteristics influence behavior, *attribute influence.*

Attribute Creation

Some characteristics of the environment are subject to change as a function of the behavior of the individual. The environment that does not respond to the behavior of the individual in some systematic manner is rare. Therefore, an important aspect of any environment is its capacity to react to the output, or acts, of the individual in an analogous manner to the way in which the individual reacts to outputs of the environment. All those characteristics of the environment that are contingent upon the behavior of the individual will be referred to as *reactive characteristics* of the environment. In the theory, such characteristics are contingent upon the behavior of the individual through the way in which the environment (a) perceives the behavior of the individual (i.e., *measures* the behavior of the individual or the product created by the behavior of the individual); (b) the way in which the environment *evaluates* these perceptions of the basic behavior of the individual (most of which will be product evaluations rather than evaluations of actual behavior or acts); and (c) the way in which the evaluations of behavior are in turn converted into objective outcomes to the individual. These objective outcomes are the characteristics or attributes of the environment which are contingent upon the individual's behavior.

The second type of environmental characteristics are those that are not contingent upon the individual's behavior and thus are *nonreactive attributes*. They may be relatively permanent characteristics, or they may be highly variable or volatile characteristics in which the variability is either nonsystematic or, if systematic, is contingent upon things other than the behavior of the individual.

As an illustration of the distinction, consider the work environment of an individual having many characteristics or attributes including the two of salary and geographic location. Normally, the salary of an individual is a reactive characteristic—that is, it will be, to some degree contingent upon the behavior of the individual. The characteristic of geographic location would be a nonreactive environmental characteristic—in this case a very stable one.

Attributes are, therefore, of two classes—those whose magnitudes are to some degree a function of the behavior of the individual and those whose magnitudes are completely noncontingent upon behavior. Further, the process by which reactive-attributes magnitude is related to behavior is the three-stage sequential process outlined earlier.

Attribute Influences

Environmental attributes can influence individual behavior in two different ways. The first is what we call *influence through affect*. This is influence which occurs via the individual's motivational process. Certain characteristics of the environment are perceived by the individual as having reward properties, and because of these perceptions, the motivational state of the organism will be changed as a function of the organism's affective response to the characteristic. This change in the motivational, or temporary need, state will in turn influence the anticipated reward prospective of future environmental characteristics, and this can and will influence the behavior of individuals.

The second way environmental characteristics influence behavior is called *influence through constraint*. Many characteristics of the environment set limits on people's behavior. We see these constraining characteristics in nearly every environmental setting. A carpenter is constrained by the variety of tools he owns. A pole vaulter is constrained by the type and quality of his vaulting pole. A clerk is constrained by the model of type-writer he or she has been assigned.

Influence by constraint is a passive influence, whereas influence by affect is a dynamic process involving the individual. Both types of influence are important, and the theory includes both sources as important aspects of the explanatory process. A crucial point is that *any* given environmental characteristic can influence behavior by both processes—affect and constraint. For example, a new typewriter may significantly improve the output of a clerk by removing the constraints imposed by an outdated machine. In addition, the clerk may attach definitive reward properties in the form of a positive affective response to the new type-writer.

To summarize, environmental characteristics are either reactive or nonreactive, depending upon whether they vary as a function of the behavior of the individual. Further, environmental characteristics influence behavior either by affect, by constraint, or by some combination of both processes. Whereas most reactive characteristics are intended to influence behavior via affect, nonreactive characteristics can and often do exert affective influence.

Individual Differences

Within the context of the theory, individual difference variables play an important but static role in the determination of individual behavior. *Individual differences* (ID) are defined in the theory as the relatively stable, long-term characteristics or attributes of the individual, such as needs, aptitudes, personality variables, and abilities. Also included here are the shorter term, momentary motivational states of the individual, since they act upon, or influence, certain processes such as perception in the manner of the other ID variables already mentioned. However, these short-term motivational states are much more important as the basic mechanism of the motivational process to be discussed.

Although the importance of individual difference variables is large, the manner of influence on behavior in the theory is primarily through the process of *setting constraints* in the same way that certain environmental characteristics set constraints. Thus, ID variables may be thought of as moderating variables; placing certain limits upon the individual's repertoire of acts and on the way performing the act is transformed into a created product.

Individual differences enter into the determination of behavior in the theory in many different ways. Every process postulated within the theory is influenced by ID variables. Although pervasive, this influence is exclusively one of internal constraint.

The further development of the effect of individual differences within the theory seemed unnecessary and untractable. The grouping or classifying issue arises immediately if one tries to deal with ID variables in a more extensive fashion. As has been pointed out, our position is that grouping strategies, whether they are used to classify environments into types or to classify individuals into types, are not helpful. With people, such attempts typically rely upon classification systems based upon (a) abilities; (b) aptitudes; or (c) personalities. The issues here are the same as in the case of environments, except that the problem is reversed. In the case of environmental classification, systems were often developed by seeing if groups of individuals responded similarly to a subset of tasks or environments. If so, then that subset of tasks became a group or type. In the case of individual classification, typings generally are based upon the principle of grouping a subset of individuals based on a similar response to a composite of tasks or environments. We define a person's aptitude in terms of how he or she responds to a variety of environmental problems, tasks, or test items—the opposite process from defining the difficulty of the task from basically the same response. Further, we define personality in much the same way, although ID variables are generally valence or belief measures rather than performance measures as in the case of ability or aptitude.

Therefore, we have chosen to define individual differences within the theory in terms of gross, traditional categories of abilities, aptitudes, personality, and so on, not because we believe they are unimportant, but because we believe the conceptual problems involved in describing individual differences in a definitive way are extremely difficult (Tyron, 1979) and beyond the scope of the present theory. The role of individual differences in behavior may be understood without recourse to a more elegant system than is used in the current form of the theory.

The Perceptual Process

One needs to distinguish between perception as a process and perceptions, which are cognitive states of awareness or knowledge. The perceptual process is the way in which specific perceptions, or cognitions, are formed or created. Cognitions play a major role in the theory, since the theory is a cognitive theory which assumes rational, conscious behavior on the part of the individual. If behavior is conscious and rational, it is naturally based upon "cognitions" of many varieties. As we have said, a *cognition* is defined in the theory as a specific perception on the part of the individual. Cognitions may arise directly from the external world of the environment via our primary sensory processes, they may be based upon the perception of something retrieved from the individual's memory, or they may be formed internally within the individual by the processes of thinking or reasoning. Thus, perceptions can be either of external states (the environment) or of internal states (the self). Perceptions may be simple or basic cognitions, or they may be complex, derived cognitions formed through elaborate thought processes. They may be either of the states, or of the environment, or of the self, or, *and this is very important to the theory,* they may be perceptions of relationships between states (contingencies) as opposed to the perceptions of the states themselves.

We may thus define the following terms as they are used within the theory:

> *State:*   Any distinguishable characteristic of one's self or of the environment. These characteristics may be either physical or metaphysical, in the sense of being states of affect, such as a feeling or a belief.
>
> *Cognition:*   A perception (and therefore a conscious awareness) of a state of the environment or of one's self or of a relationship among states (contingencies).

Simple cognitions of states and of contingencies in the system are often built into complex cognitions on the part of the individual. For example, one such complex type of cognition is referred to in the theory as "perceived role." Perceived roles play a central part in the theory outlined in the following chapters. It will be proposed that role cognitions are critical in the determination of individual behavior. It will also be suggested that there are many, different kinds of roles that can be identified as influencing behavior—even the simplest types of behaviors.

The fact that the theory assumes that all behavior is predicated upon cognitions or perceptions reemphasizes the earlier stated importance of the environment. The question of how well the perceptions of the individual concerning the states of the environment and environmental contingencies correspond to actual environmental states and contingencies is always present.

The Motivational Process

The basic motivational mechanism employed by the theory is the mechanism of need and of need satisfaction. Whereas the needs of any individual are assumed to be permanent characteristics and can be viewed as ID variables, the temporary need state (the drive, arousal, or need satisfaction component of the theory) is the dynamic representation of the momentary motivational state. It is this temporary, fluctuating level of need deprivation that creates or provides the motivational force to the behavior—the impetus to perform some act at some overall level of commitment. It does this through (a) the mediating mechanism of attaching positive or negative valences to perceived potential outcomes, which, when combined with perceptions of contingencies between products and evaluations of products, and between evaluations of products and received outcomes, result in utilities for the basic behavioral unit of the theory (products); and (b) modification of its own momentary state or level as a function of the perceived outcomes, both extrinsic and intrinsic, being received. Thus the motivational process can be viewed as a "future oriented" dynamic system based upon anticipated need satisfaction.

The theory attempts to distinguish, on a conceptual level, between intrinsic and extrinsic outcomes (and thus also between intrinsic and extrinsic motivation). *Intrinsic outcomes* are defined as those outcomes that occur (are created by and are perceived by the individual) as a function of the individual's own measurement system and evaluation system. They may or may not be performance based—tied to one's level of performance on a task—in any direct sense. *Extrinsic outcomes* are all other perceived outcomes received by the individual that are attributed to the environment.

The Learning Process and the Role of Memory

The theory is one of choice behavior or of resource allocation, not a theory of response acquisition. It is an attempt to deal with an individual's reasons for performing certain acts with certain levels of commitment in preference to other acts or other levels of commitment. It is not an attempt to deal with how these acts are learned. One must, of course, recognize that learning is an essential aspect of any theory of behavior in that it is a major process or mechanism whereby the system may change or modify itself. Learning is one of the primary procedures of alteration in the theory. Learning mechanisms provide a means for the system to be dynamic, since learning permits the basic parameters of the system to change through experience. This applies to both individual parameters and to environmental parameters, since the environment, like the individual, certainly is capable of change. This is an important point which we should not let escape us quickly. We must not lose sight of the idea that the environment can change, or adapt, or be influenced by experience in the same manner as the individual, and that it is therefore meaningful to talk of learning from both the viewpoint of the individual and of the environment in a comprehensive explanation of behavior. The theory continually will emphasize the "organismic" aspects of the environment, and an adaptive environment is one such organismic property.

Learning occurs within the theory in three ways: first, through the process of each behavior or act having the potential for causing a change in certain of the ID components of the theory—most notably abilities (which, of course, include knowledge factors as well). It is recognized that repeated performance of an act by an individual will influence the level of ability of the individual to perform that act. Second, learning occurs through the process of the individual's perceptions of self and of the environment leading to a modification of his or her ID variables of need, personality, and/or ability (particularly the knowledge component of ability). The third way learning enters directly into the theory is through the perceived contingency cognitions of the theory. As we have seen, each act generally results in outcomes being received by the individual. These outcomes are either subjective (internal) outcomes or objective (external) outcomes. They provide the individual with an opportunity to reassess, modify, or alter his or her contingencies. There are three major kinds of contingencies that are central to the theory. They are:

$C_{A \to P}$: The contingency that a given act will result in a given product or a given amount of that product.

$C_{P \to E}$: The contingency that a given product, or amount of that product, will result in a given evaluation on the part of some evaluator.

$C_{E \to O}$: The contingency that a given evaluation will result in a given outcome (reward).

Further, one could argue that the $C_{P \to E}$ values are further reducible into two subcontingencies such that

$$C_{P \to E} = C_{P \to P'} + C_{P' \to E}$$

where

$C_{P \to P'}$: The contingency between the amount of an actual product created and the amount of that product that is perceived by the evaluator.

$C_{P'\to E}$: The contingency between the amount of the product perceived and the evaluation given by the evaluator.

Thus the theory, through these contingency mechanisms, rests heavily upon the notion that individual behavior involves the process of coping with uncertain relationships between events. Over time, learning permits the individual to modify his or her knowledge about these contingencies, and thus alter his or her behavior as a result of the change in knowledge.

It might be useful to represent these contingencies in pictorial fashion to provide a clearer picture of the role each plays and the influence that changes in their values are apt to have upon behavior (see Figure 1.2).

Finally, it should be pointed out that, although the theory deals with individual acts, we believe that individuals rarely behave (i.e., choose one act) in isolation. It is more likely that individuals behave according to a strategy having to do with "patterns" of acts—a global concept including a number of individual acts performed in some sequence and with some specified proportion of a person's total resources allocated to each act in the sequence. What is learned, therefore, are not individual contingencies but complicated patterns of multiple contingencies associated with strings of acts taking place over long periods of time. In addition, this learning occurs in the presence of slow and noisy feedback systems. The learning of these contingencies is a difficult and complex process under the best of conditions, and it is literally amazing that it occurs as well as it does under the conditions that actually exist.

In fact, as is explained in Chapters 4, 5, and 6 on role behavior, motivation, and decision making, it will be suggested that individuals behave on the basis of global patterns of expected products which are *initially* determined by the learning of contingencies, but which become fixed "template" strategies that are rarely updated or evaluated. Thus, it will be suggested that the learning of contingencies plays a less forceful role in individual behavior than the pure form of the theory might suggest.

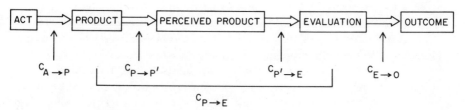

FIGURE 1.2 *The act-to-outcome sequence with transition contingencies.*

There is no memory mechanism explicit within the theory as presented. A memory process or mechanism is assumed to exist, but it did not seem necessary to make such a process a formal part of the theory. That is, cognitions can be and are stored by the individual for varying lengths of time and are then recalled or retrieved as needed—particularly cognitions related to contingencies. There are two ways of viewing this process within the current theory. The first is to view the abilities portion of the ID component as the memory location in the theory. This is compatible with the notion that knowledge factors make up a substantial portion of the abilities component and that knowledge is one way of defining stored cognitions. For example, a perceived contingency between an act and a product, $C_{A \rightarrow P}$, which is stored in memory is a component of the individual's knowledge at any moment. A second, less compelling view concerning memory is that the memory process is not represented in the theory but may be thought of as a "depth" dimension for each of the cognition types (i.e., storage occurs at each site in the theory).

Affect

Any cognitive theory of behavior must have affect as a central concept, since affect is necessary for a functioning motivational system. Affect is defined as a psychological state, or feeling—and therefore a cognition—of pleasure, happiness, well being, or satisfaction. Affect can be either positive or negative. In the theory, affect typically will be discussed in terms of specific outcomes associated either with the self or with the environment. Thus, a particular environmental characteristic, or outcome, is perceived by the individual as having caused certain affective reactions which can be either positive or negative. Since the theory distinguishes between intrinsic and extrinsic outcomes, it can distinguish logically between intrinsic and extrinsic affect. Further, actual affect associated with outcomes perceived as having occurred can be distinguished from anticipated affect, which is the expected feeling of pleasure or satisfaction associated with outcomes that might potentially be received. Anticipated affect is referred to as either a *valence* or *utility* in the theory.

Many theories of organizational behavior have labeled the present affective state with the label of "job satisfaction" or some similar title. A number of these theories have concerned themselves with explaining or at least dealing with the issue of relationships between affect and behavior. This has been a pervasive and dominant interest of psychologists interested in the behavior of individuals in the work environment for over half a century. The premise for such effort has been the assumption (one which has never been well supported by data) that (a) affect may be a cause of behavior; (b) behavior may be a cause of affect; or (c) both (a) and (b). The research literature is filled with attempts to demonstrate one or more of these assumptions with only modest success.

The theory presented in the following pages is quite concerned about affect. Indeed, it will be apparent once the theory is presented that affect, both present and future, plays a major role in the determination of individual behavior within the theory, and in our view, affect deserves and will receive considerable attention.

This chapter has provided a general context for the specifics of the theory to be presented in the following sections. The intent was to indicate the general position that has been taken with regard to a number of important issues in any theory of behavior. That is, we have tried to provide brief explanations for such questions as (a) "What are the roles of the basic processes of motivation, learning, and perception in the theory?" and (b) "What is the view of the theory toward the influence of the environment and of ID variables in the determination of the behavior of an individual?"

Following chapters present the theory in detail, and attempt to deal with a number of major issues or concepts of central interest to organizational theorists such as climate, leadership, job satisfaction, motivation, role theory, and decision making. These concepts or processes are defined in terms of the theory and related to prior conceptualizations of the same concepts.

2

The Theory

Chapter 1 presented a series of general issues involved in our theory of behavior in organizations. We attempted to clarify our assumptions about its major components and processes. With this general discussion in mind, we now turn to a description of the theory itself in three stages. First, the general structure of the theory; second, definition of the key variables; and, third, the interrelationships between the variables. Subsequent chapters will show how the theory deals specifically with such issues as roles, decision making, and motivation.

In its most basic form, the theory can be viewed as a stimulus–organism–response (S → O → R) paradigm. Figure 2.1 presents a complete graphic representation of the theory. Since the theory predicts *individual* behavior, it is obvious that the organism involved is the individual. The response is the person's behavior; and the stimuli are those environmental events that impinge upon the person. Thus, in simple terms, the theory deals with the way in which the person perceives some subset of the enormous variety of stimuli available in the person's environment, processes them, and finally produces behavior.

However, even at this very basic level of analysis, more is involved than a simple S → O → R pattern. In our view, the environment is a system that acts very much like an organism in its own right. That is, it is a system possessing the same primary mechanisms as the individual. Although we shall argue that the environment consists of more than just the organization to which the person belongs, let us assume for the present that the environment consists only of the organization. The theory suggests that the organization is also a responding entity. Stimuli impinge upon it; some of these stimuli are perceived, they are somehow

23

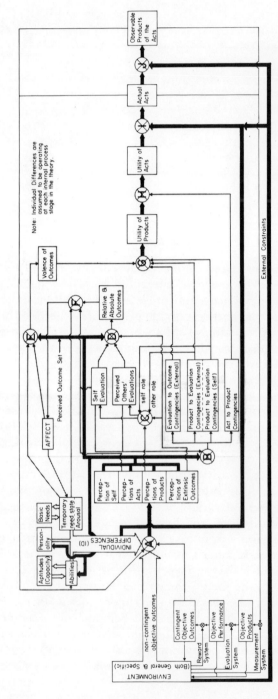

FIGURE 2.1 A schematic representation of the theory. Individual differences are assumed to be operating at each internal process stage in the theory.

24

processed, and the organization produces responses. This is a different view of the environment than that taken by some approaches to organizational behavior. Often, the environment or the organization is implicitly treated as a static entity emitting stimuli to the individual.

A critical point in the present theory is that these two entities, the individual and the organization, are interrelated. They are in a very real sense connected to each other; whereas both are active entities in their own rights, they dynamically influence each other. Both show the $S \rightarrow O \rightarrow R$ pattern, but *the responses of the environment are a major component of the stimuli of the individual, and the responses of the individual are a component of the stimuli of the organization.* This is not meant to suggest that the only source of stimuli to the organization is from the individual. Clearly, the organization receives stimuli in the form of economic conditions, government regulations, the actions of other organizations, and stimuli from other individuals in the organization. We treat this as a given, and do not specifically deal with it in the theory. Nor do we mean to imply that all the relevant stimuli the individual receives come from the organization. Some of these stimuli come from sources outside the organization, and even from the individual's own behavior.

This interaction between the individual and the organization can be further exemplified with systems concepts. Both are open systems. Both receive inputs in the form of energy, resources, information, etc. Both process these inputs, and both create outputs in the form of behavior. What we are pointing out is that one subset of the inputs to the organization is the outputs of the individual, and one subset of the inputs to the individual is the outputs of the organization.

This notion of two interacting systems, both operating in the same basic $S \rightarrow O \rightarrow R$ paradigm has a very important implication for the theory. It suggests that if both of these entities operate in an $S \rightarrow O \rightarrow R$ paradigm, they ought to have many similar characteristics. That is, there are many characteristics and processes which should be parallel in the two entities. As the theory was developed, this fact became more and more clear to us. There are many parallels in the functioning of the organization and the functioning of the individual, and this shall be brought out explicitly in later discussions.

Definitions of Symbols Used in Theory

Before we describe the theory in detail, definitions of the symbols used in Figure 2.1 are needed. There are three symbols used: boxes, arrows, and the symbol $\otimes$. A box is meant to represent some specifiable state, or construct. It reflects a permanent or temporary state of the organism or of the environment, which at least in theory, exists in a specific, measurable quantity at a given point in time. It admittedly would be quite difficult to measure accurately some of these states; either because of our lack of good instruments, or because of the highly changeable nature of the state. However, in principle, they exist in a specific amount at any point in time.

The arrows in the figures are meant to convey sources of influence. An arrow between two variables or states indicates that the specific value of the one has some impact or influence on the other. It is important to note that the placement of the arrows is crucial to the theory. We are arguing that *a given state (box) is determined by the prior states whose arrows lead to it, and the influence a given state has on any other state is determined by the arrows leading from it.*

The last symbol in the model is a *processing circle,* designated by the symbol ⊗. This symbol is meant to reflect the fact that aspects of two or more states or variables are combined in some definable way, resulting in a new state or variable. In the case of individuals, these process points may be viewed as the major cognitive processes necessary for the production of rational behavior. In the case of the organization, these process points have an analogous function; they are the mechanisms whereby the organization makes important judgments or decisions.

Key States and Variables in the Theory

Key variables and states in the theory can now be explained, after which the interrelationships among these key variables will be discussed.

Environment

In general, the *environment* is seen as the total set of external stimuli that are available to the person, a subset of which are ultimately perceived. Our focus tends to be primarily that of the work environment (i.e., the organization), but other aspects of the individual's environment such as his/her family and community, must be considered as part of the environment. If we assume that the theory will be used only to predict behavior in organizations, it could be argued that we need to consider only aspects of the organizational environment. This is simply not the case. The explanation of rational behavior is viewed as a resource-allocation process. That is, given the limited amount of an individual's two primary or basic resources—time and energy—the individual must allocate these resources to various acts or behavior categories; presumably in such a way as to maximize some sort of rewards. Therefore, as explained in Chapter 1, the amount of resources he or she allocates to behaviors relevant to the organization is not a fixed quantity. The quantity of resources devoted to the organization will be a function of the organizational rewards associated with behavior in the organization, but also will be a function of the rewards associated with competing behaviors by environmental sources outside the organization. As demands from family, social groups, community, etc. for the person's resources increase, the person must either increase the total expenditure of resources by putting in more time or exerting more energy; or redirect resources to these activities from other activities. Since the resources devoted to the organization are affected by those outside sources of influence, they are relevant to the organizational behavior. However, even though factors outside the organization have an effect on behavior in organizations, the environment of greatest concern to us is the organizational environment.

In the theory, we distinguish between general and specific environments. This is a somewhat arbitrary distinction. The specific environment can be thought of as typically representing the immediate environment with which the person interacts directly. That is, it is those people, things, and conditions with which the individual has direct face-to-face contact. In contrast, the general environment normally would consist of those aspects of the organization with which the person does not have direct, fact-to-face contact.

The general and the specific environments contain physical and social elements. They include objects and physical conditions as well as people and their interactions. More specifically, the general environment would include such things as the general physical or objective characteristics of the organization, the physical surroundings, the technology, the policies of the organization, and the organization's goals. The specific environment would include the individual's physical working conditions, the equipment used, the task, the work group, and the immediate supervisor.

Objective Products

This construct refers to the external environment's measured perceptions of the products produced by the individual. Recall from Chapter 1 that behavior consists of acts and that these acts are goal directed and result in the creation of products. The theory specifically deals with the products. The person creates or produces a large variety of products.

Many of these are never seen or perceived by anyone in the organization since they are produced in situations where they are not observed by anyone except the individual. Other products are emitted in situations where others are present, but are not perceived or not recorded. Finally, there are those products which are, at some point in time, perceived or recorded by someone in the organization. It is these last products that form the category of objective products.[1] Thus, the objective products are those products which, from the large number of products created by the person, are actually perceived (i.e., measured) by *someone* in the person's environment. In other words, they are products that enter the awareness of some viable other.

There are a large number of potential others in a person's environment (peers, subordinates, supervisors, etc.) who may be measuring or perceiving a given person's products. However, they do not all have the same measurement system. That is, certain products which are carefully and consistently measured by a peer may go totally unnoticed by a supervisor. Furthermore, the measurement systems of different people in the environment may measure products of quite different levels of molecularity. For example, a college professor's colleague may observe rough drafts of articles and the amount of time the professor spends doing research, while the dean only perceives or measures published papers. As we shall discuss in more detail in later chapters, these differences in product measurement systems are by no means random. They are ultimately tied to those products others see as important for the fulfillment of the target person's role.

Objective Performance

The *objective performance* variable reflects the fact that a subset of the products that are encoded or measured (objective products) are placed on an evaluative continuum. Once these products are so evaluated, they become objective performance. A person creates a large number of products. Some of these are encoded or measured by others (peers, supervisors, top management, etc.) in the person's environment. Of the products that are encoded, a subset is considered by the other as important enough to evaluate. Once this evaluation takes place, either formally or informally, the other has placed the measured product on a good–bad evaluative continuum. When this is done, we speak of objective perfor-

1. We use the term "objective" here and when we speak of "objective" performance to refer to judgments made about the person by people in the external environment. We do not mean to imply that they are somehow unbiased or repeatable, but that they are not made by the person himself or herself.

mance. Thus, in this theory, the term performance is used in a *very* specific way. It refers to products that actually have been located on some evaluative continuum. Until this evaluation is completed, we do not speak of performance—only of products.

This objective performance can be on a basic level such as whether the person is a contributing member of the organization, or whether or not he or she comes to work regularly. It can also include an assessment of overall performance. More typically, it is multidimensional, reflecting a number of factors upon which a given evaluator judges performance.

As is true of objective products, there are several objective performances, the number depending on the number of different evaluators. A given other member of the organization evaluates a certain set of products in forming an assessment of the individual's performance. Another member of the environment may use a completely different set of products in arriving at his or her evaluation of the same individual. We would expect, for example, that a supervisor might use a different evaluation system than would a peer. As will be seen in Chapter 5, on roles, the evaluation system used by a given evaluator is closely related to the role that evaluator feels the individual should be fulfilling.

This notion of evaluated products is extremely important to the theory. We are arguing that the person engages in a large number of acts. These acts in turn result in products. It is these products, not the acts, which are processed by both the organization and the individual. Furthermore, we define the material of interest to the theory as those products which are *evaluated* by some part of the environment or by the person himself (herself). In other words, products that are not evaluated by someone are defined as not being of interest, and the theory does not deal with them. If a person scratches his ear during a meeting, under most circumstances this product will not be noticed, much less evaluated. Thus, this behavior is irrelevant to the theory.

The use of this evaluated-product principle accomplishes three things for the theory. First, it allows us to dismiss the near infinite number of acts and products produced by a person that are not worth the effort of prediction. Second, it enables us to define that elusive concept, *organizational behavior*. We define organizational behavior as those products which are evaluated by someone in that organization or by the focal person. Thus, unless a product is first observed, then measured, and finally placed on some good–bad evaluative continuum by someone in the organization or by the individual, that product does not help to define the set of behaviors we call organizational behavior. In essence we are arguing that such nonevaluated products are not relevant in the organizational context.

The third implication of the evaluated-product principle is that it allows us to deal with the issue that all organizational behavior is not of the same level of molecularity. One could speak of a salesman contacting a customer, making a sale, or selling a certain amount of merchandise in a month. Each are products, but the former products are subproducts leading to the latter products. Given that products vary in molecularity, the problem becomes one of specifying exactly the products that should be investigated. Since the theory predicts products, these products must be specified. Most approaches to organizational behavior imply that some specific set of products are identifiable, and that members of the organization would agree on what they are. Our position is that the level of specificity or molecularity of these products is subject to large variation, and the characteristics of the evaluation system determine the degree of product specificity. More precisely, the products that are actually measured and evaluated are the products of relevance for that situation. This suggests that there is no one set of products that is of universal importance. If a set of products is actually evaluated by persons of interest to the researcher or practitioner, it is relevant for study. If the products are not evaluated, they are irrelevant. Therefore, to answer the question of which products should be investigated in a given situation, we need to ask which products are evaluated in the organizational entity that the researcher or practitioner wishes to study.

Study of those products that are evaluated in a given organizational unit is necessary for the understanding of influences on and consequences of behavior in that organizational unit. However, the particular set of products evaluated in a unit are not necessarily the best or most appropriate set of products. It may be that members of the organizational unit are evaluating products that by some criterion are not appropriate, or they are not evaluating products that are appropriate.

Contingent Objective Outcomes

Contingent objective outcomes are those things or events that the environment provides to the individual as a function of the evaluation system. They would include such things as merit pay raises, promotions, feedback, recognition, and many others. The critical point is that these outcomes are based on evaluated products (objective performance). That is, the amount of the outcome is based on the level of objective performance. The person receives many other outcomes from the environment that are not a function of his or her level of objective performance such as the retirement system, physical working conditions, and the geographic location of the organization. Since these outcomes are not a function of objective performance, they would be considered noncontingent outcomes. They enter into the person's perceptual system as shown by the heavy arrow going from the environment to the individual's perceptual system in Figure 2.1.

The contingent objective outcomes can be thought of as part of the formal reward system that is reactive to the individual's behavior. In Chapter 1 we distinguished between reactive and nonreactive environmental attributes or characteristics. Reactive characteristics are those which vary systematically as a function of an individual's objective performance (evaluated products), such as the outcomes of pay or job level. Nonreactive characteristics are stable environmental attributes that do not vary as a function of performance but only become accessible to the perceptual system of the individual through the process of affiliation with the environment in question (e.g., the organization).

It could be argued that all outcomes from the environment are in fact contingent. The individual must be associated with a member of the organization to obtain the outcomes. Thus, the outcomes associated with a health insurance plan can be obtained only if the individual is a member of the organization. This is certainly true from the individual's point of view. However, this is not the perspective that we use in making this distinction between contingent and noncontingent outcomes. The perspective used here is that of the organization. From the organization's viewpoint, the level of outcomes associated with hospitalization insurance does not vary as a function of performance on the job. People of different levels of performance on the same job receive the same medical benefits. Thus, whereas the organization may intend that some of these noncontingent outcomes should be rewards, such allocation is not a reaction to the individual's performance.

The advantage of the distinction between contingent and noncontingent outcomes is that it allows us to isolate and identify the process by which the environment deals uniquely with the individual. As we shall see, the processes involved in the environment's measurement, evaluation, and reward systems for a given individual become important influences on the behavior of that individual.

Individual Differences

We have defined the key variables making up the individual's external environment. Inside the individual, reflected in the shaded area of Figure 2.1, are those variables representing the organism in the individual's $S \rightarrow O \rightarrow R$ sequence.

The first cluster of variables in the organism are ID variables. We admit that ID variables are an important influence on behavior. Psychologists for years have tried to deal with individual differences, focusing efforts on their identification and measurement and attempting to clearly discriminate between different classes of such variables. Some of the problems inherent in this effort were discussed in Chapter 1. We are not proposing a fully developed conceptual system for distinguishing between the various classes of individual differences, but we do divide them into several classes. These distinctions are not always sharp, but they serve a heuristic value in that different classes of ID variables influence behavior in different ways. The first distinction is based on the type of variable. Three classes or types are discussed: (*a*) aptitudes–abilities; (*b*) personality; and (*c*) needs. The other distinction is on the basis of the relative permanence or stability of the given variable.

Aptitudes and Abilities

The first class consists of *aptitudes* and *abilities*. Both terms refer to the person's power to perform an act. When we speak of *aptitudes* we are referring to relatively permanent characteristics that reflect the individual's limitations or *potential capacity* to perform an act. The aptitudes reflect the maximum possible capacity to perform given acts. They are seen as upper limits which are not easily changeable, and that have a strong influence on the performance of an act as well as on the extent to which practice or training can modify the performance of that act.

In contrast, *ability* reflects the individual's currently developed power to perform an act. It is distinguished from aptitude in that the latter is a relatively permanent potential. Ability is changeable as a function of learning or experience. If we are concerned with how well a person can perform an act at a given point in time, we are dealing with ability. If we are concerned with the ultimate possible development of how well a person can perform an act, we are dealing with aptitude.

There are many kinds of abilities and aptitudes. We shall not attempt to develop a taxonomy of these variables, but there are many abilities–aptitudes that influence behavior. We conceptualize these as a profile; a profile of aptitudes for a given individual. Any person has different upper limits as capacities in different aptitude areas. At any time, there is a profile of abilities that reflects currently developed power to perform certain classes of acts.

Needs and Temporary Need State

The second class of individual differences variables is *needs–temporary need state*. The term *need* reflects a preference notion. A need implies that the person has a preference for certain kinds of outcomes over others (i.e., in receiving certain kinds of outcomes as opposed to not receiving them). When this relative preference shows high covariance over a given class of outcomes, we speak of a need for that class of outcomes. Needs are analogous to aptitudes in that they are fairly permanent characteristics of the individual. They are changeable, but this change is a slow process.

Needs can also be viewed in terms of a profile. A variety of needs exists with varying levels of strength or preference. This preference is independent of the current, temporary level of satisfaction of that need. The category of *temporary need state* is somewhat different. Here, we are referring to differences in preference at a specific point in time, when the preference level is partially a function of the amount of the need-satisfying outcome class the person has received in the recent past, or anticipates receiving in the near future. However, although needs and temporary need states can be conceptualized as profiles, it is not productive to attempt to generate an exhaustive list of what these needs are.

The temporary need state reflects the current level of satisfaction of the more permanent needs. It reflects the degree to which different needs are satisfied or are not satisfied at any given time. This level of need satisfaction is highly changeable as a function of the situation and the rewards received. The motivating force that produces behavior ultimately comes from the needs. Although we speak of a relative preference notion in the definition of needs, there is more involved than preference. As needs become less and less satisfied, force, in the form of arousal is developed within the person to satisfy the needs; and it is the presence or absence of preferred or desired outcomes that influences the degree to which needs are satisfied.

The picture that emerges is one of an individual behaving to satisfy his or her needs. This could lead to the implication that people are totally controlled by their needs, in turn resulting in a rather deterministic view of behavior. But, as the theory is developed, it should become clear that our view is not really deterministic. People are highly cognitive creatures, and the cognitive events occuring in their heads have a great deal to do with how they behave. It is this active cognitive processing that results in such things as perceptions of contingencies, evaluations, and outcomes. It is also this processing that results in the anticipated value of future outcomes. We shall be arguing that this anticipated value of outcomes, which is both future oriented and heavily based on elaborate cognitive processing, is a comparatively direct determinant of behavior. Although needs and need satisfaction influence the anticipated value of outcomes, needs are by no means the only influence on this anticipated value.

Needs are the source of the motivational force influencing behavior, but the force is modified and filtered through the elaborate cognitive processing of the individual.

However, let us return to the discussion of temporary need state. When we refer to need satisfaction, we are referring to the temporary state of fulfillment of specific needs. At a given time, one need may not be satisfied or fulfilled, while a different need may be completely satisfied. When a need is not satisfied, arousal is produced. Specifically, an unsatisfied need creates forces within the person that lead to satisfaction of that need. The more important the need and the stronger the deprivation, the stronger the force. This arousal or force is directed, however. It is need-specific. When a given need is not satisfied, the force or arousal that is created is directed at satisfying that specific need. This need-specific arousal ultimately has affects on the valence of outcomes.

In addition to this need-specific arousal, the temporary need state–arousal construct also includes the *general* state of arousal of the person at a given moment. Although it is not our purpose to state the precise determinants of this general arousal level, it is associated with the level of stimulation the person is experiencing. Part of the stimulation would come from the relative dissatisfaction of the person's needs, and another part would come from the degree of stimulation in the environment.

Personality

The last class of variables in the individual differences set is constituted of those variables we typically think of as *personality* characteristics. As a class, it can be distinguished from aptitudes because it does not directly reflect any concept of capability to perform an act. It is distinguished from needs in that it does not directly reflect a relative preference notion. It does reflect the fact that there are fairly permanent characteristics of a person that presumably affect behavior, but which could not be said to reflect a relative preference for classes of outcomes. For example, locus of control is a personality characteristic in that a person high in external locus of control does not prefer that the environment control his or her rewards, but instead simply perceives or has a belief state that the environment does in fact control those rewards. Personality is not seen as having a permanent and temporary aspect as are aptitudes and needs. Rather this class of variables is viewed as being fairly permanent in nature.

Personality variables as we have classified them may be described as consisting of two types of individual attributes. First, a personality characteristic may consist of a specific or generalized belief state about one's self or one's environment, which in turn may have a substantial and systematic influence upon behavior. These beliefs are somewhat different than the beliefs that constitute general knowledge and information possessed by the individual, which are located in the abilities box. Bias and prejudice belief states are examples of variables that are classified as personality variables within this system.

A second type of personality variable consists of specific and generalized patterns of behavior that the individual has developed as mechanisms to handle and to process input from the environment. Thus we speak of behavior patterns such as aggressiveness, irresponsibility, compulsivity, etc. as personality-type behavior patterns typifying individuals.

We assume that both learning and genetic factors are important in the establishment of personality characteristics and individual differences. However, it is not an objective of the theory to deal extensively with personality or any other individual difference characteristics except to acknowledge that they are powerful moderators of behavior at all levels of the theory.

Perceptions: Self, Acts, Products, and Extrinsic Outcomes

We turn next to the primary *perceptions* construct in Figure 2.1. Note that whereas the four classes of perceptions are in separate boxes in the graphic representation, they are all connected as subclasses of initial individual perceptions. This is meant to reflect the idea that all four classes are simply different types of primary perceptions formed by the individual in response to stimuli from the environment. The logic of distinguishing among them in the theory is that each of these classes has differential effects on other variables in the theory. Thus, for clarity of presentation, they are separated in the initial stages of the theory.

We have said that the perceptions in these boxes are basic perceptions in the sense that they are formed from stimuli coming from the environment and are a result of the initial sensory process. In essence they are perceptions that involve a measurement process or system of the individual applied to sensory input impinging on the individual at any given moment. These perceptions are the building blocks for later stages of information processing. Many other cognitive or perceptual states are included in the theory, such as valence of outcomes, which are also perceptions, but these perceptions are the result of specific and sometimes elaborate cognitive processing. That is, these basic perceptions are assumed to be combined with other variables. Other states may also be combined, judged, evaluated, and so on to form various new perceptual or cognitive states. This, however, should not be taken as an implication that these initial perceptions are uncomplicated either in process or result.

Perceptions of self include perceptions about the person's own characteristics and attributes. These tend to be relatively permanent characteristics such as perceptions of abilities, personality, physical characteristics, and so on. *Perceptions of acts* are the person's perceptions of his or her own behavior. They are the perceptions of the direction and amount of expended resources. *Perceptions of products* refer to the person's perceptions of his or her own products. Note that these perceptions of acts and products do not imply any evaluation of these acts or products. In essence, these two sets of perceptions reflect the person's own measurement system for his or her own activities. That is, the individual selectively attends to and encodes (measures) a subset of the acts and products he or she creates. This is an example of the analogy between the person's processing characteristics and those previously discussed in reference to the environment.

The final set of perceptions is *Perceptions of extrinsic outcomes*. We use the term extrinsic because the level of outcome is determined by the external environment. Later we shall argue that another class of outcomes, intrinsic outcomes, exist for which the amount of outcomes is determined by the person himself or herself.

We use the term *outcome* in a very general sense for this set of perceptions. Outcomes are any state, event, or condition that the person is presented with in the context of being in that environment. When we talk of perceived extrinsic outcomes, we refer to the subset of this totality of environmental stimuli that is actually perceived by the person. One could also think of outcomes as positive, neutral, or negative rewards. However, there is a distinction between outcomes and rewards. When a person perceives an outcome, he or she perceives *how much* of that outcome has been received. Once the person has perceived the quantity of the outcome, he or she attaches affect to that outcome. It is only after he or she has attached some degree of affect to that level of the outcome that we speak of a reward. For example, there is a difference between a person's perception that he or she has been given a 10% increase in salary and the attractiveness or unattractiveness of that 10%. Admittedly, the process of attaching affect to an outcome occurs very quickly in most cases. However, there is still a conceptual difference between the "how much" perception and the "how good" perception. The former is the result of a measurement process, the latter is the result of an evaluation process.

These outcomes, then, would include perceptions of organizational rewards, as well as other outcomes that the organization provides but which are not designed, per se, to be rewards to the individual. In addition, these perceptions would also include perceptions about the physical environment, such as working conditions, task characteristics, and physical and structural properties of the organization. Finally, they would include perceptions about that part of the environment composed of people. These people could be peers, a supervisor, the president of the company, a spouse, or people in a similar profession at some distant location who may not even be known to the person on a face-to-face basis. The perceptions could include inputs, abilities, rewards, perceived expectations others hold for the target person, attitudes, the degree to which they fulfill their own roles, among others. Thus, the perceptions of other people in the environment include not only perceptions about other people's behavior and personal characteristics, but also perceptions about how the target individual thinks others should behave, and how the target individual thinks others think he or she should behave.

Affect

As was mentioned in the introductory chapter, *affect* plays a central role in this theory. The affect variable in the schematic of the theory represents the pleasure or satisfaction experienced by the person at a given point in time. It is the current level of happiness or pleasure resulting from rewards already received. This is distinguished from anticipated affect, which is reflected in the valence of outcomes construct. This affect variable is meant to reflect reward-specific affect. In other words, we are not only postulating generalized levels of affect but are also stating that a person can have one level of affect associated with one reward or class of rewards and a quite different level of affect toward another reward or class of rewards. Certainly one can conceptualize some process by which outcome-specific affect is combined into a composite, or overall, affect measure.

This construct of affect as used in the theory is similar to the conceptualization of job satisfaction as it has been dealt with in the organizational psychology literature. When we ask how satisfied a person is with his or her pay, we are essentially trying to measure the level of affect associated with that outcome or reward. One could also ask the person to indicate in some overall way the general level of affect his or her job produces. Our position is that such an overall measure of job satisfaction is essentially asking the person to indicate some sort of average or composite of the reward-specific levels of affect he or she experiences with job-related rewards.

Affect is an immensely important variable in the theory. *However, we do not treat it in the way that job satisfaction has been traditionally treated.* As was mentioned in Chapter 1, we are not taking the position that job satisfaction, either as a composite or in the form of reward-specific affect, has any direct influence on behavior. The level of affect towards rewards received on a job exists at some level at any point in time, and can be measured. Such measurements can be useful in assessing how positively or negatively the individual evaluates the rewards he or she is receiving. We do not deny that such information may be of value for a variety of purposes. However, as will be seen in the motivation chapter, it should not be expected that these evaluations directly relate to behavior. Such a position completely ignores the complexity of processes influencing behavior.

It is also important to distinguish between *affect* and *arousal.* Arousal is need-specific, and provides the basic force for behavior. It is this force, channelized and filtered through a complex set of cognitive processes, which provides the basic motivation for behavior. The level of the temporary need state and the arousal that comes from the dissatisfaction of needs influences affect. That is, the level of affect generated by a given outcome will be influenced by the degree to which that outcome satisfies needs. The affect, however, is associated with outcomes. As a concept, it is associated with outcome, not needs. Finally, affect is an attractiveness-related variable which does not, in itself, have motivating properties. Anticipated affect, in the form of valence of outcomes, does carry with it motivating properties, but this motivating force comes from its connection with need satisfaction–arousal.

Contingencies

The next cluster of variables in the theory is that of contingencies. Figure 2.1 shows three major sets of contingencies involved in the theory. The first set relates acts to products, the second set relates products to evaluations, and the third set relates evaluations to outcomes. All are complex sets of perceptions (or cognitions or belief states) that are built from cognitive processing of the basic perceptions just discussed.

Act-to-product contingencies are the perceived contingencies between a person's own acts and the results of these acts. They are the first in the series of perceived contingencies that ultimately tie behavior to outcomes and rewards. The process is one in which acts are generated, products are thereby produced, a subset of these are perceived, the perceived products are evaluated, and outcomes are allocated. If affect is attached to these outcomes, they become rewards.

The act-to-product contingencies, then, compose a set of perceptions about the relationship the person sees between his or her acts and the resulting products. An act has two components, amplitude and direction. Products also have their complicating factors. There are a large number of potential products, varying in molecularity. Different evaluators in the person's environment measure not only different products produced by the person, but use different levels of molecularity of the same products in this measurement.

The perceived contingencies are therefore quite complex. We are not taking the point of view of most expectancy theories that there is some overall effort-to-performance contingency (expectancy) that is unidimensional. Rather, there are whole patterns of relationships between sets of acts and sets of products. How the person deals with this complex state of affairs represents a key aspect of our view of motivation, and will be presented in Chapter 6.

The second set of contingencies is that of *product-to-evaluation contingencies*. Here the contingency is between products produced by the person and the evaluation of his or her performance. As discussed previously, there are a number of different evaluators. Examples would include a supervisor, a subordinate, or the person himself or herself. We view the evaluation process as one in which a given evaluator measures specific products. These products are combined into an evaluation. The evaluation may be unidimensional, but more typically is multidimensional. To make the evaluation, the evaluator considers both the amount of the products produced and the importance or weight of those products. Thus, the head of an academic department might measure number of publications, quality of the journals published in, frequency of getting research grants, and research-related awards as products that he or she combines, undoubtedly with different weights, in evaluating performance in research. Teaching performance might be evaluated by measuring teacher ratings and number of graduate student committees.

A central tenet of this theory is that this evaluation system is intimately associated with the concept of roles. That is, *the evaluation system used by a given other (or the person himself or herself) is related to and indeed defines the role that other has for the individual.* This evaluation system defines the products the person is expected to produce, and also describes their relative importance through the use of a weight in combining the products into an evaluation.

Obviously, a given evaluator may not be able to articulate the products and weights he or she uses in the evaluation. Furthermore, even if the evaluator is able to articulate them, he or she may not communicate them. Finally, even if he or she does attempt to communicate them, they may not be perceived accurately by the person. Thus, it is not surprising that perceived product-to-evaluation contingencies may be quite different from the actual contingencies, allowing ample opportunity for differences in role perceptions to occur between the role the evaluator has for the individual and that individual's perception of the role that evaluator holds for him.

The person does have a more or less accurate perception of the way different evaluators evaluate his or her performance. These perceptions define the set of product-to-evaluation contingencies. Note that in the diagram of the theory, the product-to-evaluation contingencies are broken up into two components: contingencies related to the self and contingencies related to others. The first represents the way the person combines his or her own products into an evaluation of his or her own performance. This combination reflects both the products he or she measures and the means of weighting these products to form a self-evaluation of performance. The product-to-evaluation contingencies of others reflect how the focal person perceives others in the environment evaluate him or her. These sets of perceived contingencies will be different for different evaluators, since different evaluators measure different products and weight them differently. However, whether the evaluator is the person himself or herself or someone else in the environment, specifying these contingencies specifies the perceived evaluation system by indicating perceptions of (a) what products are measured; and (b) the relative importance of these products in the evaluation system of that evaluator.

The third set of contingencies is that of *evaluation-to-outcome contingencies.* This set of contingencies is composed of the person's perceptions of the way the evaluation he or she receives is translated into actual outcomes by others in his or her environment. There is a related process that occurs for his or her self-evaluation, but it operates differently, and will be discussed later. Here we are referring only to the external system.

These evaluation-to-outcome contingencies reflect the external reward system as perceived by the person. When the products a person creates are evaluated, they are placed on some good–bad continuum. When this process is completed, we speak of performance. The evaluation-to-outcome contingencies, then, are the person's perception of how his or her performance is reflected into outcomes from the environment. These contingencies indicate which dimensions of performance are being considered and the relative importance of each in determining the actual level of outcomes the person receives. Thus, these contingencies do represent the individual's perception of the reward system.

We have argued consistently that there are a number of evaluators, and thus a number of different reward systems. Therefore, there are different contingencies perceived for different evaluators. A variety of conflict situations in which one evaluator (and outcome provider) gives outcomes on the basis of very different products than another evaluator is thus possible.

These product-to-evaluation contingencies are intimately related to the concept of power. That is, to the extent that a given evaluator in the person's environment utilizes strong contingencies between the person's products and valued outcomes, that evaluator is said to have power over the person. This is an explicit conceptualization of power that permits a precise definition of the power construct. As we shall see in Chapter 5, on roles, it has interesting implications for the concepts of role conflict and the effects of role conflict.

While these three contingencies (act-to-product, product-to-evaluation, and evaluation-to-outcome) are distinct, they share a number of common features. They are all contingencies, but they are also *perceived* contingencies. Thus, they may not reflect the actual state of things. Accurate or not, they are assumed to form the basis of an individual's behavior. They are, in a very real sense, the building blocks for rational behavior. They are capable of change as the person gains more experience in the environment, as the environment itself changes, or through verbal mediation. The importance of these contingencies will be further stressed in Chapter 3 when the judgment process as it relates to the theory is examined.

Internal Evaluations: Self-Evaluation and Perceived Other's Evaluations

The next set of two variables deals with internal evaluations. The first is the *self-evaluation;* the person's evaluation of his or her own performance. Specifically, self-evaluation represents the placement of the person's own products on a good–bad continuum. It is his or her personal evaluation of his or her own products. It may be similar to and in part based on objective performance as evaluated by some external other, but not necessarily so. That is, the person's evaluation of his or her products may or may not agree with the environment's evaluation of those products. Its analogue in the environment is objective performance. For both states, products are measured and evaluated; a level of performance results. For objective performance this occurs in the environment; for self-evaluation, it occurs within the individual.

In addition to the person's evaluation of his or her own products, there are evaluations by a variety of others in the person's environment. The person has some perceptions of these evaluations, and these are located in the *perceived others' evaluations*. These perceptions represent the individual's impressions of the goodness or badness of the evaluation different others in the environment place on his or her products. There will, of course, be a number of these perceived other evaluations. Conceptually, there will be one for each evaluator the person perceives to be present in his or her environment. However, we are not implying that the individual carries a firm cognition of how everyone in the environment evaluates his or her products. Some evaluations will be more fully articulated and salient than others. The differential salience will be a function of the power of the evaluator to control valued outcomes for the person. The most salient evaluators exist where strong evaluation–to–outcome contingencies between products and the awarding of valued outcomes by the evaluator are perceived by the person.

Finally, the perceived other's evaluations are the individual's perceptions of how well he or she fulfills roles provided by others. This perception of role fulfillment may be quite different from the evaluator's perception of how well the individual is fulfilling the role the evaluator has for the individual. And, as we shall see in Chapter 5 on roles, this discrepancy has important implications.

Relative and Absolute Outcomes

This portion of the theory deals with the individual's perceptions of the *outcomes* he or she has received. It reflects perceptions of outcomes actually received and thus is not anticipatory in character. It includes both the outcomes generated by the environment (extrinsic outcomes), and those outcomes the person generates or administers to himself or herself (intrinsic outcomes).

When we speak of absolute outcomes, we are referring to a perception of how much of the outcome the person has received. A $100 per month raise, a promotion to a specific job, and a specific type of formal recognition are examples of outcomes that establish a perception of the absolute quantity of the outcome the person has received. As has been mentioned, affect is eventually attached to these outcomes and they become rewards. This absolute level of outcome is only one aspect that will determine the ultimate level of affect attached to the outcome. Another aspect is the relative amount of that outcome. For many kinds of outcomes, especially extrinsic outcomes, the person compares the absolute level received to both (a) his or her expectations of the level of that outcome that should be received; and (b) to the level of outcomes other people in that environment have received or will be receiving. Both types of comparisons will influence the ultimate level of affect associated with the outcome.

Thus, relative and absolute outcomes include perceptions of the absolute level of the outcomes received, as well as the level of outcomes relative to expectations and comparisons with others.

Valence of Outcomes

Valence of outcomes refers to the affect the individual anticipates he or she will experience when a given outcome is received. These valences can apply to outcomes received before (e.g., an annual pay raise), or to outcomes never experienced such as anticipated promotion to a new position that could be received at a future time.

Valences can be positive, neutral, or negative. The level of valence is a function of the level and direction of affect anticipated to result if the outcome is obtained. It is important to recognize that this affect may not match the actual affect the person will experience when the outcome is received. For example, the promotion may not produce as much positive affect as the person anticipated that it would.

Utility of Products

The utility of products is the anticipated value the individual perceives as being associated with the products he or she could generate. Since the utility of a given product is formed by a combination of product-to-evaluation contingencies, evaluation-to-outcome contingencies, and valence of outcomes, this utility can be conceptualized as the extent to which that product will lead to valued extrinsic and intrinsic outcomes. As with valence of outcomes, it is anticipatory in nature in that it reflects the utility of products that might be produced in the future.

The person has utilities for many different products. These will include products that have been generated in the past as well as products not yet been generated but that the person perceives could be generated in the future. Also, utility cognitions will be present for products at different levels of molecularity. A salesperson, for example, may have utility cognitions for contacting a customer, following up an order, and a specific dollar volume of sales, even though the first two products are seen as subproducts of the last. The person does not have a conscious cognition of the utility of every product he or she has and could produce; the person is more selective than that. The salience of products to the individual is a function of (a) whether these products are evaluated; and (b) the power of the evaluator to make valued rewards contingent on that evaluation.

Utility of Acts

The utility of acts represents the anticipated value the person perceives as being associated with different behaviors. It is formed from a combination of the utility of products and the act-to-product contingencies. Ultimately, it reflects the extent to which different acts are perceived as eventually resulting in valued outcomes. Recall that we view acts as the doing of a behavior, not the result of behavior; that is a product. Acts have both amplitude and direction. The direction component is the nature of the act, what is being done. The amplitude component consists of resources in terms of time and energy that the person commits to the act. The utility of a given act is seen as ultimate value or payoff that exists for expending time and energy resources in doing that act. It is the anticipated attractiveness associated with various amounts of commitment to the act.

This pattern of utilities associated with different acts is the result of the complex processing the person must perform in deciding how to behave. It represents the person's behavioral intentions as to how he or she will distribute resources to acts—in terms of both direction and amplitude. It is the person's conscious, cognitive intentions of how much time and energy will be expended and how he or she will expend it.

Actual Acts

With the consideration of *actual acts,* we move again outside of the organism in the S → O → R sequence. The actual acts are the responses in the sequence. This is reflected in Figure 2.1 by the fact that the shaded area ends before the actual acts box. It should be abundantly clear by this time that we view behavior as the result of stimuli from the environment and complex cognitive processing within the individual.

Actual acts are behaviors the person emits in terms of both amplitude and direction. They are the concrete manifestations of the utility of acts, but they will not match exactly the behavioral intentions. A number of factors intervene between the intentions and the actual acts. These factors include both ID variables, especially abilities, and a series of environmental constraints.

The actual acts are, in principle, observable and measurable. They could be measured in terms of (a) their direction (i.e., which acts are emitted); and (b) their amplitude (i.e., the time and energy devoted to them). However, although actual acts can be measured, in most cases they are not measured by people in the environment. That is, people typically measure the result of acts, the products.

Observable Products of the Acts

The last construct in the theory is *observable products of acts.* It reflects the consequences of the acts in terms of the things produced by the acts. As we have said, the act is the doing and the product is the result or consequence of that doing. It is these products, not the acts, that are typically observed and measured by the environment. This is not to say that all products are observed and measured. Many may never be observed by anyone outside the person, and the person will not consciously perceive many of them. Of products emitted in situations where they may be observable, not all will actually be observed, and of those observed, not all will be evaluated. They are part of the responses in the $S \rightarrow O \rightarrow R$ sequence, and they are fed back to the individual and the environment in the form of new stimuli.

Interrelationships between the Variables: The Causal Sources of Influence

We now turn to an examination of the interrelationships between the separate states or variables in the theory. Recall that these interrelationships expressed by the arrows in Figure 2.1 are statements about both the determinants and the consequences of variables. A given state or variable is accounted for by the indicated arrows of influence going to it, and the influence a given state or variable has on any other state is defined by the arrows of influence leading from it to these other states.

To describe these interrelationships, we will discuss the major clusters of variables in the graphic representation of the theory. Each of the arrows of influence going to the variables (i.e., the determinants of each variable), will be described, as will each of the arrows of influence coming from it (i.e., its consequences or effects).

The Environment

The first system of variables to be considered is that constituting the environment. There are two classes of inputs into the environmental system. The first class comes from the person, and the other class consists of inputs into the person's environment from sources outside that environment. This latter class is not shown formally in Figure 2.1 but is merely assumed to exist.[2] This is the multitude of influences outside the

2. To speak of something as coming from "outside" the environment presents certain obvious conceptual difficulties, since the environment can be defined, if one so wishes, to include nearly everything, including the focal person.

person's general and specific environment, including economic conditions, government regulations, characteristics of the community, and more. Clearly, these influence the environment, which ultimately effects the individual. However, these influences on the environment are not dealt with formally in the theory.

The second class of inputs into the environment is related to the behavior of the individual. One of the major processes occurring in this section of the theory consists of a series of smaller processes involving (a) the measurement; (b) the evaluation; and (c) the outcome-allocation systems that are applied by the environment to the individual's products. However, the person's products may also actually change the state of the environment. For example, if a nurse in a hospital suggests a change in procedures, the suggestion may be evaluated positively, and the nurse may even receive outcomes for his or her initiative. If the product (the suggestion) is implemented, the nature of the environment, in this case the task, will also be changed. This ability of the person to change the environment is represented by the three arrows going from (a) objective products to the environment; (b) objective performance to the environment; and (c) contingent objective outcomes to the environment.

Each of these three arrows allows for a different kind of influence on the environment. The first arrow deals with those instances in which the results of a person's behavior have impact, even though the products are not necessarily evaluated. For example, the social interaction of a person may change the social structure of his or her peer group, but this social interaction may not be evaluated by the supervisor. The second arrow represents probably the most common type of influence the person has on the environment; the level and type of evaluated products, or performances, has some impact on the environment. The nurse example mentioned above would be applicable here. Another example would be a situation in which an extremely high performer actually causes an evaluator in the environment to change the nature of the evaluation system. This might occur when the high level of performance causes the evaluator to redefine what constitutes truly excellent performance. The last of the three arrows indicates that the actual level of outcomes the person receives can influence the environment. At the most basic level, giving these outcomes depletes the resources of the environment, and thus influences the environment's ability to give outcomes in the future. In addition, the level of outcomes an individual receives at any time will influence the outcome he or she will receive in the future: A person who receives a large raise is not likely to receive another for some time.

In essence, these three arrows indicate that the person can have direct influence on his or her environment; the nature of it, including stimuli the person receives from it, as well as the nature of the measurement, evaluation, and reward system. This dynamic, interacting nature of the person–environment relationship is an important characteristic of the theory.

The environment has a number of effects in the theory. The first is described by the large arrow leading from environment to the processing circle A and then on to the perception boxes. This arrow represents the stimuli generated by the general and specific environment, including such things as the physical characteristics of the environment, task characteristics, leader characteristics, and so on. Recall that it does not include the outcomes given to the person by the environment that are reactive to his or her performance. These come from the objective outcomes. Taken together, these two arrows represent all the external stimuli impinging on the person. Whereas these two sources are the total set of stimuli, not all stimuli will be actually perceived by the person.

The next source of influence from the environment upon the individual is depicted by the arrow going from the environment to process point I between utility of acts and actual acts and the process point J between actual acts and observable products of acts. These two arrows reflect the moderating or constraining influence the environment has at these two process points. One could consider them as various types of environmental constraints beyond the direct control of the person. Examples could include quality of equipment, availability of resources, degree of cooperation of others on interactive tasks, and so on. The computer programmer who has every intention of working on a specific program, but who has not been supplied with the necessary information, may not be able to work on it. If the necessary information is available, the programmer may not be able to debug the program if the computer has not run the job. The first case would be an example of an influence occurring between utility of acts and actual acts. The latter case would be an influence occurring between actual acts and observable products.

Note that these constraints can operate without being perceived. The theory suggests that they operate directly from the environment. After or during their occurrence, the constraints may be perceived, but not always, and it is not necessary for them to enter the individual's awareness for their influence to manifest itself upon behavior. Finally, we do not mean to imply that these environmental influences always serve to decrease commitment to the act or the amount of the product generated. In some cases, they will increase them. For example, if the person assigned to a task is given superior equipment or receives unexpected help from a coworker, the product may be superior to what it would have been without these influences.

The last set of arrows coming from the environment reflects specific systems used by the environment to process information it receives from the individual and to respond to it. The systems considered are the *measurement system,* the *evaluation system,* and the *reward system.*

The measurement system is depicted in Figure 2.1 by the arrow from environment to the processing circle just before objective products. There are a large number of observable products of acts produced by the person. Only a subset of these products are perceived or encoded by the environment. The measurement system is the template or filter system used by the environment to select the products that it considers relevant. This filtering system is not random; as we shall see, it is associated with the role concept. It is a set of contingencies defining the importance of the individual's products to the organization.

There are, of course, a number of measurement systems, the number corresponding to the number of evaluators or role-senders in the environment. Thus, anyone in the environment who has some interest in the behavior of the individual has a measurement system for that person. The types of products that it measures will vary considerably, but a system exists and presumably could be identified empirically.[3]

An example that will be used throughout this section is the job of a college professor. The professor produces a variety of products such as lectures, tests, grades, drafts of papers, published papers, attends faculty meetings, and sits on committees. Evaluators could include students, colleagues, the department chairperson, and the dean. Each of these evaluators measure a different set of the professor's products. Students typically do not see drafts of papers, whereas some colleagues do; the dean does not attend faculty meetings, but the department chairperson does. Each of these evaluators makes some sort of judgment as to the quantity or nature of the professor's products that that evaluator observes. The judgment is the evaluator's perception of what that professor has done.

In essence, then, the measurement system reflects a judgment process whereby a given evaluator (*a*) selects a subset of products produced by the individual from all the products he or she produces; and (*b*) assesses how much or what type of product has been produced. This specification

3. The measurement system is a part of the environment. Although it can be changed, for significant periods of time, it is fairly fixed. This fairly fixed system that exists in the environment is represented by labeling the line from the environment box the measurement system. We will use this type of presentation several times in the theory. The notation reflects the idea that the fairly fixed measurement system of a given evaluator is *applied* to the changing products of an individual. The actual application of the system to the products of a given individual is a *process,* and is reflected by the processing circle symbol ⊗.

of products and their quantity or nature is then labeled objective products.

The next system is the evaluation system, reflected by the arrow from the environment to the processing circle between objective products and objective performance. This arrow reflects the system that an evaluator uses in translating a determination of how much of which products the individual has produced (objective products) into a determination of how good or bad the performance (objective performance) of that individual is. What we are talking about here is a set of contingencies between products and performance that are analogous to the product-to-evaluation contingencies that the individual uses. The evaluation system specifies the relationship between objective products and the favorableness of the evaluation on a good–bad continuum of performance. More precisely, the contingency may be thought of as a weight or slope concept that relates changes in the amount of the product to changes in the level of the evaluation. Different products vary in how much they influence the evaluation, that is, the contingencies differ for different products. This contingency or amount of influence characterizes the salience or importance of that product to the evaluator. A product that has associated with it a high product-to-evaluation contingency is one in which changes in the amount of that product result in large changes in the evaluation. Thus, it is an important product. For a product with a low contingency, changes in the amount of the product will have little effect on the evaluation and thus be less important.

This notion of the contingencies reflecting importance is critical to the theory. We have mentioned several times that the product-to-evaluation contingencies and their counterparts in the environment's evaluation system are intimately associated with the role concept. We can now explain this a bit further. Most approaches to the role concept deal with expected levels of behavior or expected tasks to be performed. Our approach is a significant departure from these conceptualizations. The role is defined here by the contingencies between products and the evaluation of these products. Once these contingencies have been identified, the role has been defined.

However, before expanding this point further, we need to deal with another issue that has implications both for the evaluation system and the role concept. This is the issue of the multidimensionality of performance. So far in the discussion we have implied that all objective products are combined by their contingencies into an overall evaluation of performance. Frequently, performance is evaluated along a series of dimensions. These dimensions reflect major classes of products in the mind of

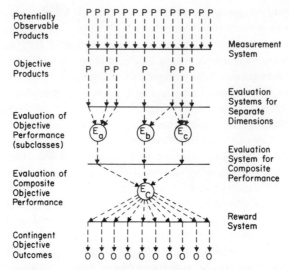

FIGURE 2.2 *The measurement, evaluation, and reward systems.*

the evaluator. For example, the dean may evaluate a professor in the areas of teaching, research, and service.

The conceptualization of the evaluation system deals with this issue by allowing for the fact that subdimensions of performance may be formally evaluated along with overall performance. This is shown in Figure 2.2. Here, we see that a subset of the observable products is measured, making them objective products. These products are then combined into three dimensions of objective performance evaluation (E_a, E_b, E_c). These could be teaching, research, and service, using our previous example. These three dimensions are then combined into overall composite performance (E_C), and outcomes based upon these evaluations are eventually given to the individual.

Thus, we can speak of contingencies between the products and the dimensions of performance evaluation, and contingencies between the dimensions and overall performance evaluation. These systems can be conceptualized as a series of prediction equations of the following form:

$$E_a = C_{P_1E_a}P_1 + C_{P_2E_a}P_2 + C_{P_3E_a}P_3 + \cdots + C_{P_kE_a}P_k \qquad (2.1)$$
$$E_b = C_{P_1E_b}P_1 + C_{P_2E_b}P_2 + C_{P_3E_b}P_3 + \cdots + C_{P_kE_b}P_k \qquad (2.2)$$
$$E_c = C_{P_1E_c}P_1 + C_{P_2E_c}P_2 + C_{P_3E_c}P_3 + \cdots + C_{P_kE_c}P_k \qquad (2.3)$$

and

$$E_C = C_{E_aE_C}E_a + C_{E_bE_C}E_b + C_{E_cE_C}E_c \qquad (2.4)$$

In these equations, the P_i values represent the measured products associated with the performance dimensions a, b, and c. The terms $C_{P_2E_i}$ are the product–to–evaluation contingencies. The E_a, E_b, and E_c terms are the levels of evaluated performance along those three evaluation dimensions. The last equation indicates contingencies between the individual dimensions of performance evaluation and overall performance evaluation.

In the example of the college professor, a large number of products are produced. Some are not observed by the evaluator (the dean) such as drafts of articles, how often the professor meets with students, and the nature of interactions with departmental colleagues. Many products are observed, that is, measured by the dean. These might include number of publications, grants, awards, teacher ratings, participation in university committees, and involvement in community service projects.

If we assume that, in the dean's evaluation system, there are three subsystems for evaluation of teaching, research, and service, the dean must take these measured products (objective products) and use them to arrive at an evaluation of the professor's performance along each of these three evaluation dimensions. To do this, the dean must weight the amount of each of the objective products by the contingency he or she sees between that product and the dimension in question. For the research dimension, for example, the products of number of publications, grants, and awards might be heavily weighted, while participation in community projects, how the professor dresses, and how he or she treats graduate students would have a zero contingency.

Although in many organizational settings performance is considered and evaluated as multidimensional, there is always a need for some overall evaluation of performance. When outcomes such as promotion and salary raises are considered, they typically are based on some overall evaluation of performance. Thus, in this example, the dean must combine the evaluations on the three dimensions into one evaluation of overall performance. Here again, contingencies come into play in that performance on each of the three dimensions is weighted to obtain overall performance. This contingency is analogous to the other contingencies in that it reflects the degree to which changes in the evaluation along that dimension are followed by changes in the overall evaluation. Thus, it reflects the importance of that dimension for overall performance.

It is frequently difficult to judge whether performance is assessed multidimensionally or on an overall basis in any given situation. However, this is not really a problem. A single set of weights could be developed for relating products to overall performance by algebraically combining the product to dimension contingencies with the dimension to overall evaluation contingencies. This process would be equivalent to combining the two stages of evaluation in Figure 2.2 into a single evaluation system that directly relates objective products to a composite evaluation.

In summary, the evaluation system does several things. First, it defines which products the evaluator will attend to. We argued previously that the evaluator chooses to measure only a small subset of a person's products, and the selection of this subset was not random. We are arguing that the choice of products to measure is based on the contingencies the evaluator has between the product and his or her evaluation. Those products with nonzero contingencies will be attended to. Those with zero or near-zero contingencies will be attended to much less, or ignored.

Second, the evaluation system defines how the evaluator combines objective products into classes. That is, it defines the dimensions of performance that the evaluator sees as relevant. Third, through the various contingencies, the evaluation system defines the relationships between products and evaluations. These contingencies specify the importance of products in determining performance. Finally, taken together, these characteristics of the evaluation system define the role the evaluator has for the person by defining the products that are important, the dimensions of performance that are relevant; and how, through the contingencies, these products and dimensions combine to result in overall performance.

The last of the three systems coming from the environment is the reward system. This reflects the set of rules that evaluators use in attaching outcomes to an individual's performance. The evaluation of the individual's performance has been made (objective performance) and the result of this evaluation is in the form of a good—bad judgment along a series of one or more dimensions. This specification of performance is then fed into the processing circle. The reward system is applied to this performance data, and contingent objective outcomes are generated.

The reward system also can be described as a series of contingencies. At the simplest level, these contingencies relate overall performance to a series of different outcomes. Figure 2.2 displays this graphically. These contingencies reflect the extent to which variations in the level of the evaluation result in changes in the level of the various outcomes. That is, where changes in the goodness or badness of the evaluation are followed by large changes in the level of the reward, a strong contingency exists. Where changes in the level of the evaluation are not followed by changes in the level of the outcome, the contingency is low.

This type of conceptualization works well for outcomes that are based on the overall evaluation. As we have said previously, many outcomes are of this type. However, in many situations, some outcomes are a function of the level of performance on performance dimensions more specific than overall performance. For example, the college professor who is evaluated highly on the dimension of research may be selected to be on promotion review committees, whereas another professor whose teaching is particularly good may be able to obtain special audio-visual equipment. Thus, even though both may have the same overall performance, different patterns of evaluation on the multiple dimensions may result in different outcomes.

Two other points about the reward system must be mentioned. First, recall from our discussion of the boxes that this reward system and the ensuing objective outcomes represent the *intended* reward system. Outcomes that are not part of the intended reward system go directly from the environment to the perceptual processing circle. Second, as in the case of measurement and evaluation, there are always a number of different reward systems operating. Supervisor, peers, and so on have and use quite different systems.

Individual Differences

The next section of the graphic representation of the theory is the individual differences section. It includes the variables aptitudes, abilities, personality, basic needs, and temporary need state (arousal). These variables taken together reflect the set of important individual differences that influence the person's behavior. As a group, they have four general ways of influencing behavior. The first is reflected by the large arrow leading to the perceptual processing circle (process point A). This indicates that individual differences affect the way in which the individual perceives the variety of stimuli that impinge upon him or her. The individual differences variables will influence the choice of stimuli attended to, and will also influence the manner in which or degree of accuracy with which they are perceived.

The second general influence of individual differences is to moderate or constrain the translation of utility of acts into actual acts. This source of influence is shown by the line going from the individual differences cluster to processing circle I between those two boxes in the diagram. The level of utility of a given act will not predict directly whether the person will emit that act. The person's individual characteristics, particularly his or her level of ability to perform that act, will influence whether the act is done, and how well or poorly it is done.

The third source of influence is in the attaching of affect to outcomes already received and the attaching of valence to future outcomes. The first is shown by the line from temporary need state to processing circle F, and the second by the line from the temporary need state to processing circle E. These sources of influence reflect the fact that the affect attached to an already received outcome is in part a function of the level of temporary deprivation of needs that that outcome satisfies. Likewise, this level of deprivation influences the anticipated affect (valence) associated with future outcomes.

The last general source of influence of this cluster of variables is not formally shown on the graphic representation. The theory we are presenting is basically a cognitive theory, one in which the individual's cognitive processing of complex stimuli form the bases for behavior. This cognitive processing occurs at many different places in the theory. Wherever such processing occurs within the individual, individual differences influence the way that processing is done. For example, a person's level of intelligence or cognitive complexity will influence his or her ability to deal with complex contingencies. Thus, whenever the theory indicates that the person must somehow process certain pieces of information, it is assumed that the individual differences variables influence this processing. Specifically, individual differences variables are assumed to have input at each of the major process points A through I that involve cognitive processing.

With these general points in mind, we shall now turn to the specific variables in this section. Recall from the previous discussion that the individual differences cluster is composed of relatively permanent characteristics (aptitudes, personality and basic needs) and more changeable characteristics (abilities, temporary need state).

In terms of the more permanent characteristics, whereas they tend to be fairly stable, it is probable that they will change slowly over time. This process is represented by the fact that each has an arrow or causal influence going to it. Aptitudes can be influenced over time by changing abilities. As a person acquires more and more skill (ability) in a certain area, it becomes easier for him or her to acquire even more skill in that area. Basic needs over time can be influenced by the temporary need state. If a need is consistently satisfied it may begin to decrease in importance. A basic need which is frequently not satisfied may increase in importance. Finally, personality can change over time, as a function of the person's behavior. There are probably other sources of influence that change personality, but we are not prepared to develop such mechanisms in this theory.

The first of the temporary individual differences variables is abilities. Clearly, abilities are influenced by aptitudes, but they are also influenced by practice and training. This type of influence is reflected in two ways in the diagram. The first is a direct link—acts and products to abilities. This represents the practice issue. When acts and products are produced, they have some impact on the person's subsequent ability to perform those acts and products. That is, there is some influence on the actual objective contingency between acts and products that is independent of any perceptions of these contingencies. The second source is shown by the heavy arrow from the perception boxes to abilities. This arrow reflects the cognitive or learning aspect of changing abilities. That is, changing abilities having a cognitive component must be accomplished by a change in perceptions about the self and the environment.

The last individual differences variable is the temporary need state. It is influenced by basic needs in the sense that a given level of deprivation of an important need will create more arousal than the same level of deprivation of a less important need. It is also influenced by the affect variable. If a level of reward that the person has received is perceived as high, positive affect results. If it is low, negative affect results. This level of affect will then influence the temporary need for that class of outcome.

Perceptions

The next section displayed in the graphic representation of the theory in Figure 2.1 is the set of perception variables. As the figure indicates, there are three major sources of stimuli forming these perceptions: noncontingent objective outcomes, contingent objective outcomes, and the individual's own acts and products. These stimuli comprise the totality of the stimuli processed by the individual. This processing includes a filtering process through which the person selectively perceives a subset of the total set of impinging stimuli. It also includes a perceptual distortion process whereby individual differences variables influence the nature of the process of encoding these stimuli into actual perceptions.

The total set of perceptions are broken down into four subsets: self, acts, products, and extrinsic outcomes. This categorization is used since some of these specific kinds of perceptions have effects in unique ways on other states or variables within the theory. However, the entire set of perceptions influence other parts of the theory. Thus, the dark arrow coming out of the perception boxes goes to several other places in the schematic, indicating that the entire set of perceptions is capable of exerting influence on those places in the theory.

The three types of perceived contingencies form the next set of variables. Specifically, we are dealing here with act-to-product contingencies, product-to-evaluation contingencies (both for self and for others), and evaluation-to-outcome contingencies. These contingencies are perceptions formed through cognitive processing of two classes of perceptions. The first class is the "building block" perception in the four perception sets. As Figure 2.1 indicates, the total set of perceptions feed into the processing circle B. The other class of perceptions that impact on the processing to form the contingencies is that consisting of the two types of internal performance evaluations: self-evaluation and perceived others' evaluations. This source of influence represents the fact that product-to-evaluation contingencies and evaluation-to-outcome contingencies require a perception of the nature of the evaluation for their formation.

The processing occurring here is essentially that of determining relationships between the elements. There are three ways these perceptions of relationships can be formed. The first is through direct pairings of events that impinge on the individual. That is, the person has perceptions of his or her own products and perceptions of his or her evaluations. With these two sets of perceptions, product-to-evaluation contingencies can be formed. A second way these contingencies can be formed is through verbal mediation. An evaluator in the environment can actually tell the person what these contingencies are. Before the products are produced, after they are produced but before an evaluation is made, or after the evaluation is made, the evaluator can provide information to the person about the contingencies. This can be done in a general way such as defining the major dimensions of performance, or specifically in terms of products to be measured, their importance, and the relative importance of each dimension of performance. The third way these perceived contingencies can be formed is through modeling. The person may observe the products of others and how they are evaluated and thus form contingency perceptions.

These contingencies have some particularly interesting characteristics. One issue is that they are analogous to the contingencies that exist in measurement, evaluation, and reward systems in the environment. That is, they reflect the person's perception of that external system. Furthermore, as in the case of the environment, there are multiple evaluators and thus multiple sets of product-to-evaluation contingency sets. The number of sets the person deals with cognitively is determined by the number of evaluators in the person's environment that control outcomes valued by that person. That is, the number of evaluators who have power over the person is that set of others who the person perceives as having strong evaluation-to-outcome contingencies between that evaluator's evaluation and outcomes of importance to the person.

Another aspect of the analog between the contingencies in the external environment's measurement, evaluation, and reward systems and the perceived contingencies is related to the role issue. These perceived contingencies, especially the product-to-evaluation and evaluation-to-outcome contingencies are essentially the person's role perceptions. That is, by defining these contingencies, we define how the person perceives which of his or her products are measured, how they are weighted, what dimensions of performance are used, and how these are weighted in determining evaluations and ultimately outcomes. A different set of role perceptions exist for different evaluators. How the person deals with these differences is discussed in Chapter 5, on roles, and is related to role conflict.

In addition, these role-related perceived contingencies include a set of role perceptions for which a parallel is not found in the environment. This is the self-role, and reflects the person's own perceptions of which products should be measured, how they should be weighted, and how they should be combined. As we shall see in Chapter 5, differences between this self-role and the roles perceived by the person to be held by others in the environment has interesting implications for understanding role conflict.

Perceived Evaluations

The next section of the theory deals with the person's evaluation of his or her own performance. This includes both the self-evaluation—how well the person perceives that he or she is fulfilling the role the person has for himself or herself; and perceived others' evaluations—how well the person perceives that he or she is fulfilling the roles others have for him or her. These evaluations are formed in processing circle C.

As can be seen in Figure 2.1, several types of perceptions serve as inputs to this process of forming perceived evaluations. One source is the person's perceptions of his or her own products, and is indicated by the arrow from perceptions of products to the processing circle. These perceptions form the basic set of personal outputs that are to be evaluated. However, information about one's own products and the evaluation of these products can also be obtained from outcomes provided by the environment in the form of feedback about products or about performance. This effect is indicated by the arrow from perceptions of extrinsic outcomes to the processing circle.

The other two sources of inputs into the formation of evaluation perceptions come from the product-to-evaluation contingencies. Recall that these contingencies are intimately related to the role concept in that these sets of contingencies specify which products are measured, how they are weighted, and the dimensions of performance that are used in the evaluation.

These sources of influence are combined in the processing circle. For the perceived other's evaluation, the process is analogous to the environment's evaluation system. That is, the process can be conceptualized as a set of linear equations similar to those described in the discussion of the environment's evaluation system. The result of the process is a determination of how well the person perceives himself or herself as fulfilling the role sent by an evaluator in the environment. More precisely, it reflects the person's perception of the placement of his performance on a good–bad continuum in the eyes of that evaluator. For example, let us take the external role that is sent to the individual by the supervisor. The person's perception of this role is located in the product-to-evaluation contingencies. It can be viewed as a set of equations, with each equation defining the product-to-evaluation contingencies relevant to one dimension of performance. The elements in each equation specify which of the products that the person perceives will be evaluated and the weight each has in this evaluation. These equations (i.e., the role perceived as being sent by the supervisor) may match the set actually used by the supervisor, or it may be quite different. That is, role perceptions may be accurate or not. In any event, it is the role the person *thinks* the supervisor is sending him that is being used by the person to form his or her perception of the supervisor's evaluation.

With this perceived sent role in the person's cognitive system, the process of estimating the perceived other evaluation that the supervisor has for the person is one of applying the perceptions of products to the equations and calculating the evaluation. A similar process would occur for other external roles sent from peers, subordinates, etc.

The same type of process operates for the self-role. Here, however, we are dealing with the person's own internal evaluation system. That is, the person has his or her own set of perceptions (i.e., contingencies) of what his or her role should be, and evaluates his or her performance in terms of that set of contingency equations. This self role may match the sent roles quite closely, or it may not. As we shall see, the determination of how well the person feels he or she is fulfilling the self-role, and the rewards he administers to himself based on this evaluation are closely associated with the notion of intrinsic motivation.

Outcomes and Affect

At this point in the theory, the person has perceptions of his or her behavior and extrinsic outcomes and has formed evaluations of his or her own performance, both in terms of the self-role and roles sent by others. The next part of the theory involves the process whereby a person evaluates the outcomes received and experiences affect based on these outcomes.

The first step in this process is the formation of perceptions of relative and absolute outcomes. These perceptions are formed in processing circle D. Examination of the sources of influence going to that processing circle shows how these perceptions are formed. The first input is the perceptions of extrinsic outcomes. This influence comes from the heavy arrow representing the entire perception set, but because of its special importance, a direct link is also shown between perceptions of extrinsic outcomes and the processing circle. This source of influence represents the raw, unprocessed perceptions of how much of different externally mediated outcomes the person perceives he or she was received.

Other sources of influence to the processing circle are represented by the heavy arrow from the major perception set, and the arrows coming from the self and other evaluations. These influences in combination provide the inputs for the person to develop what we have termed perceptions of relative outcomes. These perceptions of relative outcomes have a powerful effect on the affect associated with outcome. In many cases they will have more influence than the absolute, actual amount of the outcome.

Processing circle D deals primarily with the determination of the relative amount of outcomes. The perception of absolute amounts of outcome is fairly straightforward in that these perceptions flow from the perceptions of extrinsic outcomes box through processing circle D to perceptions of absolute outcome directly. The determination of relative outcomes is more complex.

The notion of relative outcomes includes two issues. The first is a comparison of the absolute outcome with the outcome the person perceives that others in his or her environment have received. Here we are dealing with an equity concept. That is, the person has perceptions about the level of outcomes that other people in the environment have received and has perceptions about what others' products and evaluations have been. These perceptions come through the heavy perceptions arrow. These perceptions are combined with perceptions of one's own self-evaluation and perceived evaluation of others to form a basis for comparing actual levels of outcomes to perceived equitable levels of outcomes. We are suggesting that an equity notion is operating whereby the person compares his or her inputs and outcomes to those of others to form some perceptions of the relative amount of outcome he or she has received.

In addition to an equity type comparison, we also suggest that comparisons with expectations of levels of outcomes also are made here.

That is, based on perceptions of the environment, past outcome allocation history, or knowledge of evaluation to outcome contingencies, a
person has certain expectations of levels of outcomes he or she will
receive. These expectation perceptions are involved in his or her assessment of the relative amount of outcome he or she has received.

This combination of equity and expectation comparisons can be
exemplified by considering the outcome of a pay raise. Assume that the
person has just received a 10% pay raise. This perception is processed
directly into a perception of an absolute outcome of a 10% raise. However, the person will also make a relative assessment of the magnitude of
that raise. Suppose he had the information that the supervisor was to get
6% of his salary budget for raises. The person expected to get somewhat
more than 6%, let us say 8%, since he felt that his performance was
somewhat above average. Thus, the raise he received was higher than
expected, and would be judged to be relatively high. But suppose that in
discussions with his peers he finds that others whose performance he felt
were equal to his got 12% raises. He would reevaluate the 10% raise, and
conclude that it was not as high as he previously thought. Thus, both
expectations and social comparison notions influence the judgment of
the relative amount of outcome.

Once this judgment is formed about the relative and absolute amount
of outcomes, the next step is to attach affect to these outcomes. Although
these two processes can be separated conceptually, they would occur
typically at essentially the same time. The attachment of affect occurs in
the processing circle F. Both relative and absolute outcomes are included
because they both may be involved in affect formation. For example, the
10% raise may be related to several different needs. The money itself
may enable the person to buy certain things that he values, thus, the
absolute level of the outcome is related to affect. However, the relative
amount may be related to need for recognition. In other words, a given
level of outcome may produce positive affect because the absolute level
satisfies certain needs, but negative affect because the relative level does
not satisfy different needs. Thus, the overall affect associated with the
outcome is an averaging of the positive and negative affect.

The basic affect-attaching process, then, is basically one of comparing
the level of outcome with the temporary need state. While this is rarely a
conscious cognitive process, we suggest that the more dissatisfied a given
need is, the greater the affect generated by outcomes related to it. Perceiving high levels of an outcome that satisfies a currently dissatisfied
need will produce more positive affect than high levels of an outcome
that satisfies a need that is not as strong. Likewise, low levels of outcome

for a highly unsatisfied need will create more negative affect than low
levels of outcomes for a largely satisfied need.

Thus far in our discussion of outcomes and affect we have been focusing on extrinsic outcomes. However, there is another class of outcomes
that are internally mediated, and are termed intrinsic outcomes.

When we speak of intrinsic outcomes, we are referring to outcomes
which are not controlled directly by the external environment, but are
mediated by the person. There are two different types of intrinsic outcomes. The first is associated with those kinds of tasks where actually
performing the act leads directly to affect. For example, lying in a hot
tub after a 10 mile hike or reading a good novel are pleasurable acts. In
more general terms, we are referring to acts or tasks that are in and of
themselves fun, exciting, or pleasurable. There is no evaluation of relative or absolute levels of the outcomes from this kind of act. Their influence is shown by the arrow going from perceptions of acts to processing
circle F. This is meant to reflect the direct link between doing this type of
act and the affect associated with it. As in the case of the outcomes, the
level of affect actually experienced will be influenced by the temporary
need state. For example, a person who has spent all day reading work-
related material may experience less positive affect at reading a novel in
the evening than he would if he had been involved in physical activity all
day.

The second class of intrinsic outcomes operate differently from those
leading directly to affect. This is the class of outcomes that are a function
of the person's own level of performance. There is a class of internally
mediated outcomes (e.g., a perception of accomplishment or achievement) that is contingent on how well the person feels he or she has
fulfilled his or her self-role. The process involved is one in which, as a
result of the self-evaluation, the person in essence administers outcomes
to himself or herself directly as a function of the self-evaluation. For
example, the person who feels he or she has performed very well in
relation to his or her own self-role will experience positive affect related
to needs for achievement or accomplishment. This rather direct attachment of affect to the self-evaluation is shown by the arrow going directly
from the self-evaluation processing circle F.

Thus, we speak of three different types of outcomes that influence
affect in different ways. The first is externally controlled outcomes that
are processed to yield perceptions of both absolute and comparative
levels of outcome before affect is attached. The second type of outcomes
comes directly from performing the act and is inherently pleasureable,
fun, painful, etc. The third type is also intrinsic in nature, but is based on

the self-evaluation. However, all three are influenced by the temporary need state in that the level of dissatisfaction of the needs satisfied by the outcomes will influence the level of affect produced by the outcome.

Valence of Outcomes

The next section of the theory deals with the formation of valence of outcomes. Recall that we are talking here about the affect the person anticipates experiencing when the outcome is actually received. For example, the person has some anticipated affect for a future promotion, a pay raise, or some form of formal recognition. These outcomes are also anticipatory in the sense that some of them may never have been received before, such as promotion to a new position.

These valences form one of the principal building blocks of the motivation process in the theory. They are formed in processing circle E in the graphic representation. Examination of the sources of influence leading to this processing circle explains how these valences are formed. The first source of influence is represented by the heavy arrow labeled perceived outcome set. This arrow is essentially the combined set of basic perceptions. It contains not only perceptions of outcomes that have already been received, but also other outcomes which could possibly be received. However, there is no affect or desirability component associated with these outcomes as they enter this processing circle. This attachment of desirability or anticipated affect is accomplished in the processing circle E, where the other two sources of influence—affect and temporary need state—come into play.

Specifically, affect represents the positive or negative feelings associated with levels and types of rewards that have already been received. Thus, the affect resulting from a 10% raise that has been received will have some effect on the anticipated desirability of a future 10% pay raise. Likewise, the temporary need state will influence the attractiveness of a given outcome, since the temporary level of satisfaction of needs satisfied by the outcome will influence its anticipated affect.

Utility of Products and Acts, and Actual Acts

Once valence of outcomes have been established, the next step is the determination of utility of products. From this point to the actual acts is a central part of the motivation process in the theory. This section becomes rather complex, and a detailed treatment will be discussed in Chapter 6. However, a general overview can be presented here.

The utility of products is a complex set of perceptions formed from three basic sources: valence of outcomes, evaluation-to-outcome contingencies, and product-to-evaluation contingencies. The problem faced by the individual is complicated; namely, how valuable are the various products that could be generated. This set of judgments is formed on the basis of the anticipated affect (valence) that will accrue from these products. However, in order to maximize valence, the person must consider the way both he or she, and external sources in his or her environment, evaluate outcomes and the way outcomes are allocated on the basis of these evaluations.

This process is complicated by a number of factors. First, there are many different evaluators and outcome allocators. Supervisors, peers, the person himself or herself, and so on all influence the utility of products for the person. Somehow the person must combine and reconcile these frequently competing forces. Second, the products measured and evaluated by different people in the environment vary in their level of molecularity. For example, the supervisor probably evaluates more molar products than a subordinate, or the person himself or herself. Thus, the person must deal with these qualitatively different measurement-evaluation-reward systems. Third, some of the contingencies are nonlinear. For example, the degree to which one socializes with peers may have an inverted U-shaped contingency in the supervisor's evaluation system. Too much or too little socializing may be viewed as negative, while some intermediate level is seen as positive. Finally, the person does not consider the utility of a product in isolation. A given product will have a different utility depending on the pattern of other products being produced. The utility of a given product will go down if the person has not generated or is behind on the generation of other products that are seen as highly important.

With all these complexities, which we shall treat in detail in Chapter 6, it may seem impossible for the person to actually behave—one pictures the individual standing in the halls of the organization, lost in thought; weighing and balancing complex contingencies, utilities, and evaluations. One of the central aspects of our treatment of the motivation issue is that a person rarely does deal with all this complexity. The person simplifies the process in specific ways. Most importantly, once the utility of products is formed at any time, it guides the person's behavior from that point on. That is, in the person's day-to-day activities, the utility of products is considered, but all the other processes which lead to these perceptions are not generally considered.

The perceptions of utility of products are next combined with act-to-product contingencies to form the utility of acts. In somewhat simplified form, this process is one of determining the value of a set of acts based on the degree to which these acts will lead to valued products. That is, those acts which are seen as leading to valued products will have a higher utility than those acts which do not lead as readily to valued products.

This set of perceptions about the utility of acts forms the behavioral intentions of the person. However, before these intentions are translated into actual acts, two sets of factors come into operation. The first is the individual differences characteristics of the person, particularly his or her abilities. The person may see a given act as high in utility and thus intend to emit that act, but the quality or type of act that is actually emitted will be modified by the level of ability to perform that act. The other factor influencing this process comes from the external constraints operating in the environment. Here again, the translation of intentions into actual acts may be hindered or facilitated by aspects of the environment.

Observable Products of Acts

Finally, we have the observable products of the acts. These products are formed by the acts, but again, external constraints in the environment can facilitate or hinder the process, and thus influence the nature of the product.

Concluding Remarks

In the beginning of the chapter, we pointed out that the basic nature of the theory is two organisms interacting. We characterized this interaction as follows as shown in Figure 2.3. Thus, each organism follows the $S \rightarrow O \rightarrow R$ paradigm with its own feedback loop, and the responses of one organism form part of the stimuli for the other.

It should be clear now, however, that we are not suggesting that the environment is actually one organism. We have repeatedly stressed that the organism is composed of a number of people who evaluate the individual's products and who give that individual outcomes. It is important to note that the environment is composed of people, and it is these people that measure and evaluate products and give outcomes.

Another salient aspect of this parallel structure of the individual and the environment is that there are a number of processes that occur in both. The outcomes from the environment are analogous to the prod-

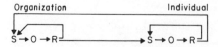

FIGURE 2.3 *The organization–person interaction.*

ucts of the individual. Both have a process for encoding outcomes. For the individual it is the perceptual filter; for the environment, it is the measurement system. Finally, both the individual and the environment have evaluation systems. For the environment, it is the actual evaluation system. For the individual, an analogous process occurs when affect is attached to outcomes. In both cases, the outputs (products or outcomes) are evaluated on a good–bad continuum. The process is more complex for the individual, but its effects are similar.

This chapter described the general framework, including variables, cognitive states, sequential relationships, and processing stages of the theory. In the chapters that follow, we discuss more content-related areas and show specifically how the theory deals with the topics of decision making, motivation, roles, and group processes.

3

Judgment

This chapter, as well as Chapter 4, is devoted to an examination of the judgment process. The theory, as it has been outlined, is a theory of choice behavior. However, the basic process that is operating at the critical process points within the theory is the process of judgment. Therefore, for a full understanding of the basic process stages, we must fully understand the judgment process; the explanation will be accomplished in two steps. Chapter 3 develops a taxonomic system that can be a helpful aid in understanding judgment. In Chapter 4, each of the individual process points within the theory will be examined, showing how the judgment process is a critical ingredient for the process involved. A word of caution with regard to Chapter 4 is probably appropriate. There must be a distinction between the theory, which is an exposition and development of the rational cognitive stages needed by man if he is to behave in the rational fashion postulated by the theory, and the way man actually behaves. The theory maintains that every stage, or process, is a necessary step in the achievement of rational behavior. It does not say that every time man performs a rational individual act, all processes are carried out. Behavior is a most complex phenomenon and man develops numerous mechanisms, or strategies, to simplify the overall behavior, or choice, process. These simplifying mechanisms are called *heuristics* and are individual coping techniques (shortcuts that developed to eliminate some of the individual process stages typically required for individual choice. This matter is further discussed in Chapter 4, where many of the heuristics employed by individuals are examined since they are important and relevant to an understanding of behavior. Heuristics do not provide a theory for explaining behavior; in fact, they may be described as action choices within the processes of the theory itself, but we will defer that point until later.

Before developing the taxonomy of judgment types, a vocabulary for the various terms used throughout this and other chapters can be outlined. The terms decision and choice will be used as synonyms to represent the end result of those broad classes of behavior involving the following three components:

1. *Information acquisition and storage*—through the mechanisms of perception, memory, and learning.
2. *Judgments*—including one or more of several different types of judgment (the more complex the decision process, the more types of judgment are involved)—in which stimulus objects are assigned locations on measurement and/or evaluation continua.
3. *Acts*—the actual commitment of basic resources of time and effort to alternative behaviors.

When we speak of the decision process or the choice process, we are referring to the entire sequence of cognitive events linking the three listed components into a process resulting in a decision or choice as manifested by some degree of commitment of time and effort to an observable act. We therefore conceive of a choice or decision as a result of the choice or decision process. The entire process is cognitive, and the end result of that cognitive process is an observable entity (behavior) called a choice or a decision. These entities (behaviors) are observable as what we have called products in the theory. We have distinguished previously, in Chapters 1 and 2, between the concept of an act, which is a process, and final end result of that act, which is a product. Thus, if a person says "I favor alternative A" or "Let's go for a drive," that person has made a judgment that is the result of his or her judgment process. These completed statements are themselves products. They were created by the act or process of decision making. The distinction, subtle but appropriate, is between the process and the result of that process, and is an important distinction to maintain.

The decision process as we defined it is the essence of cognitive behavior; thus the complete theory is a theory of the decision process. In Chapter 1, we pointed out that our theory might well be called a theory of decision or choice behavior (see page 3). We will systematically explore the extent of that proposition in Chapter 4.

A few additional comments are necessary regarding the three components of the decision or choice process. The information acquisition component will be considered here as a component that is basically perception and/or memory. We need to distinguish the processes by which one can acquire relevant information in a decision making situation. These two processes are what Björkman (1973) has called *feedforward* and *feedback*. Feedforward is information given to a person concerning the relevant characteristics of the task situation and/or the appropriate or correct contingencies involved in performing the task. Fishbein would define this as the a priori belief system of the individual (Fishbein & Ajzen, 1975). A decision maker can be advised by others, or he can read and absorb information relevant to the situation, or he can recall information from his own memory—all of these constitute forms of feedforward information in that they involve information acquired or brought into the cognitive system prior to engaging in the next stage—that of judgment. In contrast, feedback information is information acquired during or following the judgment process, and its source defines what we will refer to as a criterion system. Feedback always involves a criterion system. This criterion system is used to evaluate judgments already made, but once the information from the evaluation is obtained or acquired by the person, it becomes available as a source of information relevant to future judgments, and is therefore feedforward information for judgments as yet unmade.

A brief illustration may be helpful. Suppose an individual is performing a task and a second person is providing the individual with periodic summaries of the individual's performance. Imagine a student taking a piano lesson: The comments of the piano teacher about how well he or she is performing constitute feedback information to the student. The teacher also represents a criterion *system* that generates feedback (criterion information) to the student.

The information acquisition stage of decision making involves the accumulation of all information, from any and all sources, including memory, deemed to be pertinent to the subsequent stage of judgment. It thus consists of all feedforward information, even though some of that information may have been actually acquired via feedback from one or more criterion systems during the process of making previous judgments.

The judgment process is the second distinct component of the decision making process. It is the core or central process of the entire decision or choice sequence (i.e., the complete theory) since it is the major cognitive process involved in the complete theory. In fact, it is a fundamental, or micro, version of the entire theory. For this reason much of this chapter will be devoted to an examination of the judgment process since an understanding of this process is the essential ingredient to the understanding of all decision making or choice behavior.

The third and final stage of decision making is the action stage in which judgments are turned into actual goal-directed behavior via the individual's commitment of the basic resources of time and energy to the implementation of one or more alternative courses of action (choices). The theory is predicated upon the premise that human beings are rational, and that their rationality involves the notion of attempting to maximize anticipated positive affect (valence) by deciding upon or choosing those options that they expect to result in the greatest positive, or least negative, affect. This assumption about man's rationality is formulated through the subjective expected utility notion (SEU) which has been the basic premise for most decision theories since the early 1950s (e.g., see Edwards, 1961; Slovic & Lichtenstein, 1971). While this premise is clearly hedonistic in that the assumption is that individuals attempt to maximize anticipated satisfaction (or pleasure) associated with a choice alternative; it is a hedonism that permits self denial, self-sacrifice, and so on, as rational acts that can have very high valence under certain conditions. That is, as is pointed out in Chapter 6 in more detail, the prime type of reward is a perceived outcome having some degree of affect. The affect is itself defined as a subjective cognitive awareness of a state of happiness or pleasure that is associated with the perceived received outcome.

The Judgmental Process

We mentioned that the judgment stage is the key cognitive process in decision making. The process of human judgment is basic to an understanding of the choice act and indeed the entire decision process. Thus the judgment process is a very critical aspect of the complete theory and must be explored in considerable detail. After a careful definition of the judgment process, we will show how the process repeatedly manifests itself in key places within the theory.

The formal definition of the term judgment is as follows:

Judgment: The determination of the amount of a given variable Y that is associated with a given stimulus object, where that stimulus object is either an alternative course of action or an otherwise definable entity— either imaginary or real, that is, mental or physical.

To understand exactly how individuals "judge" stimulus objects, it will be helpful to adopt a particular viewpoint, or conceptual model, for the judgment process. The conceptual model which we will employ is the lens model paradigm of Brunswik (1956). This model is particularly useful in illustrating the three important elements of the judgment pro-

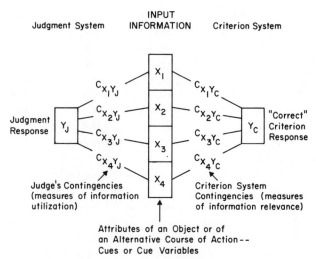

INPUT

Judgment System   INFORMATION   Criterion System

FIGURE 3.1 *A simplified schematic of the lens model paradigm for describing the human judgment process.*

cess, which are (*a*) the judgment system; (*b*) the criterion system; and (*c*) the input information.

We can begin by looking at a modified version of the original lens model, presented in Figure 3.1.[1]

The lens model in Figure 3.1 illustrates the three major constituents of the judgmental process. Consider an individual faced with the problem of evaluating (a term we will explain more accurately in a moment) a given "something." This something may be either an object (real or imaginary) or it may be a possible course of action. For example, a theater critic attending the opening night of a Broadway play must evaluate, or judge, the "object" that is the play. This object is an exceptionally complex stimulus that includes all the dimensions that make up the total play; the dialogue, acting, scenery, and so on. An example of the process of evaluating a course of action is provided by the illustration of a college freshman trying to decide whether to declare a particular major, such as chemistry or mathematics, as a commitment for his or her academic program of study.

1. The discussion of the lens model as treated here will be primarily conceptual. For more detail on the formal aspects of the lens model and its associated statistical characteristics the reader is referred to such sources as Hursch, Hammond and Hursch (1964); Hammond, Hursch, and Todd (1964); Naylor and Schenck (1966); Tucker (1964); Castellan (1973); Beach (1967); Einhorn (1972); Nystedt (1972); and Dudycha, Dudycha, and Schmitt (1974).

The thing being evaluated, whether it is an object or a course of action, will be referred to as the stimulus object. Every such stimulus object possesses one or more distinct attributes, which are in theory, potentially relevant characteristics or dimensions to the evaluator, or judge. They are relevant in the sense that they may be important to the judge in making a judgment. They may be useful pieces of information upon which the judge can base his or her judgment. These different attributes constitute the core of information available to the judge about that particular stimulus object. The attribute characteristics define the object and provide the basic information for the judgment made by the judge. This core of information constitutes the first major element of the judgment process. In Figure 3.1, this core of information is represented by the center part of the lens, where each X_i is a different attribute, or cue characteristic, of the stimulus object.[2]

The task of any judge is to examine, weigh, evaluate, and combine the information present in the various attributes (cues) of the stimulus object and arrive at a judgment concerning the location of the stimulus object on a judgment dimension that we will call the Y_J dimension. This judgment response is the second major element in the judgment process. The Y_J dimension may be either a unidimensional construct (e.g., number of red blood cells in a blood sample), or it may be a very complex, multidimensional construct such as the example of the overall quality of the new Broadway play mentioned previously. Furthermore, Y_J may represent either a psychological dimension such as the beauty of a piece of art or it may be a physical dimension such as the amount of anticipated sales for a new product.

The third major element in the judgment process is the criterion, shown on the right of Figure 3.1. The criterion is the "correct" amount of the attribute dimension being judged that is actually possessed by the stimulus object. Suppose the judgment task involved predicting the future success of job applicants in a sales job. An appropriate criterion might be average dollar sales per week for the year following initial employment. The criterion in a judgment task is the standard against which one can measure the accuracy and/or validity (Naylor, 1967) of the

---

2. In our discussion of stimulus attributes, or cues, we have treated them as being the actual attributes of the stimulus objects. Nystedt (1972) has pointed out that this is an incomplete and dangerous view of the lens model and does not take into account the way the individual judge actually perceives each attribute. Thus the perceived characteristics may or may not match the actual characteristics of the stimulus object. This distinction, and its importance to a cognitive theory such as this, will be made more explicit in Chapter 4 where one process point in the theory involves the process by which actual stimulus object characteristics are "converted" into perceived stimulus object characteristics.

judge's response and determine how correctly the judge located the stimulus object on the Y continuum.

Criteria for evaluating the judgment response are available in all judgment situations. Indeed, it is probably the rule that most judgment situations have many different criterion systems operating simultaneously—a fact that complicates the judgment process considerably. In such judgment settings, there will be a wide variety of different "correct" values for any judgment, where each different criterion value is generated by a different criterion system.

Judgment Systems

The cognitive process through which the judge arrives at a judgment as to the amount of Y possessed by the stimulus object is presented in the left-hand side of Figure 3.1. The connecting lines between Y_J and the various attributes of the stimulus object illustrate that the judgmental process assumes a rational world in which there are contingencies (systematic relationships) between information contained in the stimulus object and the response judgment made by the judge. That is, we would expect the judge to locate precisely the stimulus object on the Y continuum according to his or her perception of the defining attribute characteristics of the object being judged. The system used by the judge to do this is called the "judgment system" or "policy system" of the judge (Naylor & Wherry, 1964). The size of the contingency is a measure of the degree to which the judge "utilizes" that particular attribute.

Formal expressions of the lens model have represented contingency relationships between cues (attributes) and responses and between cues and criterion values in terms of (*a*) correlation coefficients; (*b*) regression weights; or (*c*) probabilities. We will use the general term contingency to refer to the degree to which stimulus attributes have some sort of systematic relationship to either the response of a judge or to the values generated by a particular criterion system.

Types of Judgment Systems

It is possible to distinguish between two classes of judgment systems as a function of the kind of response (*Y* dimension) required of the judge. These two kinds of judgment are *descriptive judgment* and *evaluative* (preference) *judgment*. A major point in Chapters 1 and 2 was the distinction between the process converting acts into products, called the measurement process, and the process converting products into affective measures of good versus bad, or like versus dislike, called the evaluation process. That distinction is precisely the same as the one used here to distinguish descriptive judgment from evaluative judgment.

Descriptive Judgment

Judgmental tasks that involve ordering or locating stimuli on an affect-free continuum will be referred to as descriptive-judgment tasks. In such tasks the judge is required to estimate, or to describe, as accurately as possible, the amount of Y possessed by the stimulus object. The judgment of Y is assumed to take place without any affective component, and the judge's actual response is a reflection only of the judge's ability and/or knowledge. Examples of such tasks would be most pure diagnostic judgment situations, such as medical diagnosis and insurance underwriting, and also would include various types of prediction tasks such as those performed by stockbrokers and weathermen.

In terms of the theory, making a descriptive judgment is a measurement process, not an evaluation process. Indeed, descriptive judgment is precisely the perceptual process around which Egon Brunswik developed his theory of probabilistic functionalism (Brunswik, 1943; Hammond, 1966). Brunswik was concerned with how man measured, or formed, impressions (judgments) about perceptual characteristics of objects such as size, distance, and motion. This process can be explained best by referring to Figure 3.2. We see from the figure that the judgmental process in descriptive judgment involves first perceiving the observable characteristics of the stimulus object and then forming a judgment

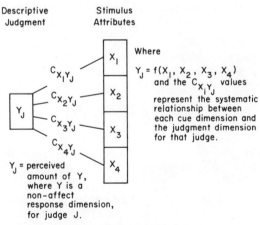

FIGURE 3.2 *Descriptive judgment.*

about the amount of some other perceived characteristic, namely, the amount of Y associated with the object.

As an illustration of a measurement judgment, consider the task of a man guessing people's ages in a carnival. You pay him \$1; if he guesses your age within ±2 years he wins and keeps all your money, but if he misses your age by more than 2 years, you win (and probably get a prize worth 25¢). The judgment response is on an age dimension and is, for all practical purposes, purely descriptive and free of affect. The stimulus characteristics in this task are numerous. He will use such cues as the kind of clothes you wear, the style of your hair, your facial appearance, the way you talk and behave, the age of the person(s) you are with, and many other attributes, both obvious and subtle, in arriving at his judgment. The way in which he uses and combines the information available in arriving at his judgment defines the characteristics of his judgment system. If we adopt a linear (additive) model as an appropriate model for describing this judgmental process, we can formally describe the judgment process as follows:

$$Y_J = C_{X_1Y_J} + C_{X_2Y_J} + C_{X_3Y_J} + \cdots + C_{X_nY_J} = \Sigma C_{X_1Y_J} \qquad (3.1)$$

Evaluative Judgment

Evaluative judgment involves an indication of preference by the judge regarding the stimulus object. It is an affective response to the stimulus as contrasted to the purely cognitive response involved in descriptive judgment. Evaluative judgment requires that some form of descriptive judgment precedes it. The location of a stimulus object on an affective continuum logically necessitates measurement (i.e., "description") of the object to oneself in terms of the stimulus dimensions that are likely to be affect-producing.[3]

In evaluative judgment, the Y continuum is always an affect continuum in the sense of representing the amount of positive affect (liking) or negative affect (disliking) that the judge has for the stimulus object. Therefore, the response is in terms of perception of the amount of goodness or badness or liking and disliking of the stimulus object as viewed by the judge. The response represents the preference of the judge for that stimulus object in the sense that if stimulus object A is given a value of Y_A from the judge, and if object B is given a value of Y_B from the same judge, and if $Y_A > Y_B$, one would expect that object A

3. The one instance in which it would not be necessary for descriptive judgment to precede evaluative judgment would be where the judge is provided with all pertinent characteristics of the stimulus object from either outside (instructional) sources or internal storage (memory) sources.

would be preferred by the judge over object B in any paired choice situation, since it elicits a larger positive affective response on the part of the judge. Actually, the underlying continuum in all evaluative judgment is probably a like–dislike continuum rather than a good–bad continuum, since the latter does not have to involve affect—although it will in most instances. Examples of evaluative judgment include judgment tasks such as that of the movie critic or of an olympic gymnastics judge. In each instance, the judge is asked to locate the stimulus object on a preference continuum that expresses the judge's degree of liking for that object.

Figure 3.2, which was used to illustrate the process of descriptive judgment, also can be used to illustrate the process of evaluative judgment. The only substantive difference is that with evaluative judgment:

Y_J = Perceived amount of Y, when the Y continuum represents the amount of liking, or preference for, the stimulus object.

The Role of Time in Judgment Systems

Before leaving our discussion of judgment systems, it is necessary to examine carefully the role of time in the making of judgments. Time can be a confusing variable, and an improper understanding of the time dimension in judgment can lead to unnecessary difficulties. All judgments are time specific. That is, every judgment has a time base in the sense that the judgment is intended to represent the amount of Y possessed by the stimulus object at some specific point in time or during some specific interval of time. If the judgment is the determination of the amount of Y currently possessed by the stimulus object, it is a judgment as to the present state of the object and is called a *concurrent judgment*. If it is a judgment concerning the amount of Y expected to be possessed by the stimulus object at some future time, it is a judgment of the future state of the object and is called a *predictive judgment*. Predictive judgments may be either point judgments (i.e., they are for a very specific and narrow time period), or they may be interval judgments (i.e., the time frame may be wide).

To illustrate, the following kinds of judgments are given as examples of immediate concurrent judgment:

1. Carnival weight guesser
2. Olympic diving judge
3. Photo interpreter
4. Aircraft identification spotter

Examples of judgments which are clearly predictive are tasks such as:

1. Weather predicting
2. Horse race betting
3. Employment interviewing
4. Insurance underwriting
5. Stockbroker recommendations

In some of the predictive tasks there is considerable variability in the length of the interval between the time the judgment is made and the time at which the judgment is to apply. The predictive judgments of a weatherman for tomorrow's weather obviously involves a time interval of about 12 to 24 hours, depending upon the time of day the prediction is made. Thus a prediction made at 6:00 in the evening has a time lag of 6 hours before the interval of 24 hours specifying "tomorrow" begins. Usually the predictive judgment is intended to apply for any or all of that 24-hour interval.

A predictive judgment about a horse race has a lag equal to the length of time between the time the prediction is made and the end of the race. The interval is easy to specify in this instance. In some kinds of predictive judgment, the exact interval is much harder to define. Consider the case of the insurance underwriter. An underwriter is required to make a judgment as to insurability of all new applicants for insurance. One time interval here is the interval between the time the judgment is made and the time the insurance actually goes into effect, but when the underwriter is trying to "place" the applicant on a potential risk continuum, the time interval becomes ambiguous. It is probably an interval consisting of the entire period the person would be insured (i.e., the applicant's entire ensured lifetime beginning the moment the person becomes insured and ending when the policy terminates). Thus predictive judgments often involve time lags and criterion intervals that are difficult to specify accurately.

Criterion Systems

Focus now shifts from the response side of the lens model to the criterion side so that criterion systems operating in various types of judgment situations can be examined. These systems are an important part of the judgment process; the critical role they play must be fully appreciated.

Criterion systems, like judgment systems, may be grouped into two

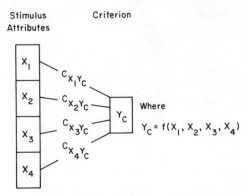

FIGURE 3.3 *The criterion system in judgment.*

major classes—*external criterion systems* and *internal criterion systems*. External systems may be further subdivided into two types, *objective* and *subjective* systems.

Before looking at these in more detail, a few additional comments are necessary concerning criterion systems in general. We have already stated that every judgment task has at least one criterion system operating, and in most tasks the actual number may be far more than one—particularly in more complex kinds of preference judgment tasks. Figure 3.3 presents a diagram of the basic criterion system (i.e., the right hand side of the lens model).

As the term criterion implies, we are talking about standards against which the actual judgment can be compared. A criterion value can be thought of as a measure of the true amount of the Y attribute possessed by the stimulus object. The issue of a true measure of Y is a very complicated question in most nontrivial judgment settings. There are a variety of ways of defining the true amount of Y possessed by the stimulus object. Each separate way of defining Y is a distinct and separate criterion system. These separate measures of specifying the true value of Y may all be operating at the same time in a single judgment task.

Now if these separate criterion systems all agreed with each other, multiple measures of the true amount of Y possessed by each stimulus object would be an advantage to the judge. However, if there is substantive disagreement among the criterion measures, serious problems can arise for the judge. He or she is faced with a conflict situation as to which criterion system should be used, or trusted, above the others. This decision among criterion itself then becomes a preference judgment, showing how convoluted the choice process can become.

External Criterion Systems

Those criterion systems that exist outside of the individual judge are the kinds of traditional criteria normally thought of as relevant to the judgment process. These systems involve standards, or measures of the true value of Y, that are obtained from, or generated by, some external source. They are of two general types; objective measures of Y, or subjective measures of Y.

Objective Criteria

Objective measures of the true amount of Y associated with a given stimulus object are frequently available. Many types of judgment tasks possess criterion systems with objective measures. We discussed the judgment task faced by a carnival performer specializing in judging the ages of individuals. Each stimulus object (person) whose age is guessed by our carnival man possessed a true value (actual age) on the Y dimension. This criterion information becomes immediately available to the judge following the actual judgment (guess). In this instance the criterion date is precise and exact—that is, assuming no lying or falsification on the part of the stimulus person, true information is provided to the judge concerning the value of Y (age) possessed by the person serving as the stimulus object immediately following the actual judgment.

Objective criterion measures are not always so precise. Suppose the task of the judge was to estimate a more complex kind of personal attribute. For example, suppose the judge is an employment interviewer making preference judgments of job applicants. The task of the interviewer is to select those candidates who are apt to be most successful as employees of the company. The actual Y dimension for the judge is one of preference for the stimulus object (the applicant), with the corollary that anyone who is "preferred" to a certain degree or higher will be hired.

What objective criteria exist for a judgment such as this? Depending upon the job in question, there are apt to be numerous measures used as a means of objectively defining the "true" success of the employee once the individual is hired. Number of units produced or number of dollars worth of merchandise sold are two examples. The number of days absent from, or tardy to, work are other measures which have been employed as objective measures of job behavior (measures of the goodness or badness of an employee) relevant to the success of employees.

Such measures even though they are objective, are not exact measures of the true value of Y possessed by the object, as was the case with the age of the customer example. These objective measures are situational in that they are a function of a particular situation. They are operational definitions of the Y construct. Each measure, number of units produced, days absent, and so on, represents a different way of defining job success. In such instances, the process of determining the quality of the judgments becomes complicated, since the answer depends upon which individual criterion, or which group of criteria, is used as a basis for assessing the quality of the judge's performance. Further, it is not known whether the criteria of job success used to assess the quality of a judge's decisions are the same criteria as those the judge had in mind when making the judgments about whether to hire the employees.

Subjective Criteria

Often, in judgment situations, an important standard of evaluation or comparison used as a measure of the true amount of Y possessed by the stimulus object consists of the judgment(s) of another person or group of persons. Thus one judgment or set of judgments becomes the standard by which the accuracy or correctness of another judgment is to be evaluated.

Subjective criteria are most important when there is a total lack of objective criteria or when more objective criteria have a substantial lag time before becoming available. Subjective criteria are actually present in every judgment situation and often exert a powerful influence upon judgment, even when objective criteria are readily available to the decision-maker. In certain judgment tasks, the decision-maker may perceive that it is to his or her advantage to be more attentive to subjective criteria than to objective criteria, for reasons which will be examined in more detail shortly. An example would be a situation in which the peer group defines the optimum judgment differently than does the organization.

Much of what we call social learning can be described as a process of acquiring human judgment skills in which another person's judgment serves as the criterion. All "tutorial" situations are examples of this kind of learning. Hammond, Stewart, Brehmer, and Steinman (1975) referred to this type of judgment situation as an "interpersonal learning" paradigm, in which one judge (the apprentice or learner) is faced with the task of learning the judgment system (criterion system) of another individual (the tutor, teacher, or expert), as shown in Figure 3.4.

We earlier used the example of a carnival age guesser as an example of a descriptive judgment task with an objective criterion. Suppose we change the situation to one in which the age guesser is trying to train his son for the task of age guessing. To do this, he strolls each day through the carnival grounds with his son. From time to time, he points out

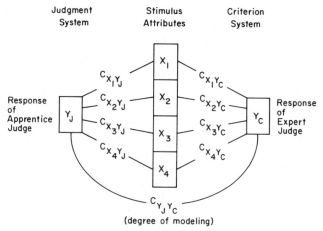

FIGURE 3.4 *An interpersonal learning, or role modeling judgment paradigm.*

different individuals and asks his son to judge the age of that person. Then he gives his son his own, expert prediction as to the age of the same individual (with an explanation of the method used to arrive at that expert judgment from the stimulus characteristics of the target person). The father's judgment is the criterion used by both father and son to judge the accuracy of the son's judgment system.

Perhaps a more reasonable apprenticeship might be to have the son sit beside his father as the father actually predicts ages, writing down his own predictions, and checking them against the true ages of people as well as against his father's predictions. If a true objective criterion can be made available, why not take advantage of it? In this example, it would indeed be preferable to judge the accuracy of the son's judgment against the true ages of people rather than against the prediction of the true ages made by his father—at least if he eventually wants to earn his own living at this work! But, as was mentioned earlier, accurate objective criteria often have a time lag associated with them or, in some settings, may not be available at all.

To further illustrate judgment situations that involve subjective criterion systems, we list tasks such as

1. Judging diving competition
2. Learning to bid a new system in bridge
3. Critiquing a new play

In each of these tasks, one standard for evaluating the adequacy (or "accuracy") of the judgment is the judgment of someone else. Most of us have witnessed the judging of a diving competition in which each judge gives each diver a score following each dive. This score represents the judge's assessment of how well the diver performed that particular dive. Since no truly objective criterion for measuring the goodness or poorness of a dive exists, it is difficult to determine accurately if a particular judge is doing a good job of judging. The only available criterion is the judgments of the other judges as a basis of evaluation, on the assumption that if our judge agrees with the other judges, he or she is doing well; if he or she disagrees with the other judges, he or she is not doing a good job.

The judgments of a drama critic provide an equally good example. What means do we have for evaluating the accuracy of a critic's judgment other than comparing it to the judgments of other experts in the same profession? Since no adequate objective criteria exist, the only recourse is to use the subjective criteria provided by the judgments of other critics.

Internal Criterion Systems

There is a third type of criterion system which plays so important a role in judgment that it is hard to understand why it has not been given more emphasis. Perhaps, since it is an obvious criterion system, it is taken for granted. Another, and more likely, explanation is that most people fail to distinguish between the "policy" of a judge and the actual judgments made by that judge—a subtle but very important distinction.

The easiest way to distinguish between what a judge actually does (i.e., the choices he makes) and his policy is to examine the linear model equations (3.2) and (3.3) below:

$$Y_J = C_1X_2 + C_2S_2 + \cdots + C_nX_n + CX_e \qquad (3.2)$$
$$Y_J{}^* = C_1X_1 + C_2X_2 + \cdots + C_nX_n \qquad (3.3)$$

Equation (3.2) postulates a model for describing, in formal terms, the actual judgments of our judge. In this linear model these judgments are assumed to be an additive combination of the values of the stimulus object cues multiplied by their respective contingencies (weights) *plus some error component.* In this model the nonerror portion of the equation is intended to represent the actual belief system or actual policy of the judge. This portion is shown separately in Eq. (3.3). It is this portion of the person's judgment system that represents the internal criterion system in the lens model sense (Figure 3.5). In other words, no matter how firm or committed a judge is—no matter how well defined his or her belief system might be regarding the way in which the cues are related to the judgment dimension—his manifest judgments are not going to be a

Judgment System   Stimulus   Internal Criterion System
(manifested policy)   Attributes   (error-free policy)

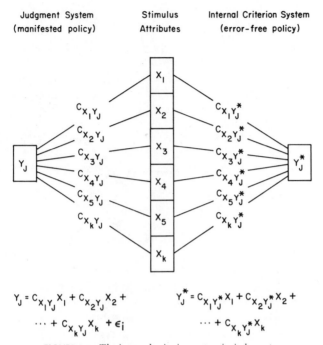

$$Y_J = c_{X_1 Y_J} X_1 + c_{X_2 Y_J} X_2 +$$
$$\cdots + c_{X_k Y_J} X_k + \epsilon_i$$

$$Y_J^* = c_{X_1 Y_J^*} X_1 + c_{X_2 Y_J^*} X_2 +$$
$$\cdots + c_{X_k Y_J^*} X_k$$

FIGURE 3.5 *The internal criterion system in judgment.*

perfect reflection of that person's actual belief system. No matter how
hard we might strive for consistency in our judgments, the facts are that
perfect consistency, (i.e., the exact implementation or use of a policy), is
almost never found in human judgment (except in extremely simple
kinds of judgment tasks).

The actual (true) policy of the judge [Eq. (3.2)] may, therefore, be
viewed as an internal criterion system that is always operating in every
judgment situation. Assuming a stable belief system (i.e., fixed contingencies) then the value Y_J^* is the judgment which the judge *wishes* to
emit or make to stimulus object i—it is the value on the response continuum that he really feels, according to his beliefs, to be the most appropriate value or location for describing the stimulus object. However,
Y_{J_i}, which is the judge's actual observed response to that stimulus object,
is usually not equal to Y_J^* as indicated in Figure 3.6.

Figure 3.6 shows the underlying processes that are involved in internal
criterion systems. Continuum I represents the basic true belief system of
the individual. This system is *never* directly accessible–it is a construct that
exists only by logical inference. We can make inferences about it from
data obtained either from continuum II (self-report data concerning

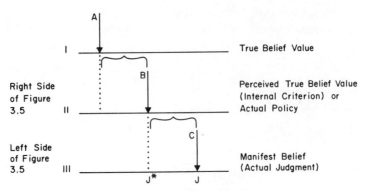

FIGURE 3.6 *The three separate belief continua involved in judgment.*

personal beliefs) or from continuum III (response data concerning actual judgments). Continuum dimension II is the internal criterion system. It is the true belief system which the individual *perceives himself as
having*. It may or may not be an accurate reflection of the person's true
belief system. To the extent that the two systems differ, there is a degree
of *unconscious* error or bias operating in the cognitions of the individual.
It is unconscious bias because it is not perceived by the judge, since by
definition continuum II represents what the judge believes his own belief
system to be and, therefore, for him, it is without error or bias. It, to him,
is truth. Thus, when we speak of Y_J* as being error free, we are doing so
only in terms of the self-perceptions of the judge—his own belief system
is to him without error, and thus always an acceptable internal criterion,
even though his perceived true belief system may not be an accurate
representation of his basic true belief values (continuum I). To illustrate
further the distinction between continua I and II, it is often found that
people who are prejudiced strongly against minority groups see themselves as not at all prejudicial. Their perceptions of their belief systems
are sharply at variance with their true belief systems (as represented by
the judgments of others or by observed behavioral measures, external
criteria).

This brings us to continuum III, which is the actual judgment continuum, Y_J, which is the manifest belief system of the judge. As Figure
3.7 shows, it will not always be the case that $Y_J = Y_J*$ because of the error
or bias factors influencing the judgments Y_J away from the perceived
true belief system value Y_J*.

The reader may find it puzzling that Y_J* will not always equal Y_J, but
$Y_J* \neq Y_J$ will be the rule rather than the exception. There are two major
causes for the error component present in the equation representing the

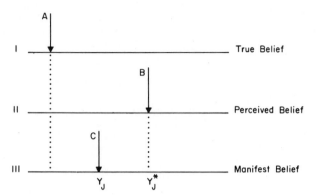

FIGURE 3.7 *An instance in which the manifest belief, or actual judgment Y_J, of an individual is closer to the true belief of the person than is the self-perceived belief.*

manifest behavior of the judge; systematic error sources and random error sources. Consider a judge who is judging the performance of gymnasts in an important international meet. Suppose this judge has a belief system, or policy, that is well established in terms of what kinds of observable behaviors of competitors will result in high scores from that judge. That is, this judge clearly understands what he or she is looking for in the performance of competitors and is capable of acting upon these beliefs. But further suppose that once the judging starts, the judge finds that he or she is not in agreement with the other judges. Thus perfect conformity to one's own internal criterion system results in disagreement with the external subjective criterion based upon the judgment of other judges. If our judge is a typical human being, this conflict between criterion systems will cause some confusion in future judgments—the external criterion system information will exert social pressures upon the judge to make judgments that do not exactly conform to the judgment generated by the person's true belief system. This is a bias type error that is a systematic source of distortion, and it may actually be viewed as a specific type of "cue" that is related to the actual judgment—and is therefore part of the true policy—but which is not included in the equation—it has been overlooked. The error portion of a policy is often large because cues have been excluded from the policy that should have been included.

Random error is a different matter. It occurs in the judge's equation for countless reasons. For example, to make error-free judgments about the quality of a gymnast's performance on the uneven bars, the judge must have a firm, fixed policy and adhere to it without fail; but it is also necessary to assume that the judge is capable of accurately perceiving all the relevant behaviors of the contestant. Thus a momentary lapse of attention on the part of the judge may cause the judge to miss a critical behavior on the part of the contestant. Thus the score of the contestant would be noticeably influenced by this perceptual error factor that has nothing at all to do with the policy of the judge. The input values for the X's would be simply inaccurate.

Finally, it is worth noting the possibility that, in some situations, a person's actual judgments, or Y_J values, may represent more closely the true beliefs of that individual than do his Y_J^*, or self-perceived belief value judgments (see Figure 3.7). In such cases, the person's actual behavior is a more accurate reflection of true belief than self-reports of belief by the individual.

The Problem of Multiple Criterion Systems

It should now be apparent that many different criterion systems exist in any judgment situation. In even the most rudimentary forms of judgment, there will always be an internal criterion system and probably one or more external systems—either objective or subjective. Any time we receive feedback from another person concerning their agreement or disagreement with our judgments, we are dealing with an external, subjective criterion system. For example, when a basketball referee calls a foul on a home-town player, and 15,000 angry fans rise in unison to protest that call, a clear-cut conflict is created between the internal criterion system of the judge (assuming he feels he indeed made the correct call) and the 15,000 external subjective criterion systems who obviously disagree with his judgment.

Since every criterion system present in a judgment situation can potentially influence the judgmental behavior of the judge, the greater the number of such systems present, the greater the cognitive complexity of the judgmental task. To which criterion system or systems should the judge attend (and thereby be influenced)? The rational answer is that the judge should, according to the theory, attend to that criterion system (or systems), which, when matched by the actual responses of the judge, are expected to result in receiving the outcomes (either internal or external) that are in turn associated with the greatest positive anticipated affect, or valence, on the part of the judge. The influence of criterion systems will always be influenced by the degree to which these criterion systems are related to outcomes possessing anticipated positive affect. This point will be discussed further in Chapter 4. However, we cannot overemphasize the importance of always recognizing the fact that multiple criterion systems are influencing judgments of individuals and that this is one reason why the human judgment process is such a complicated affair.

The Role of Time in Criterion Systems

Earlier we discussed the importance of the time dimension in judgmental response systems. Time is an equally important dimension of criterion systems, since there will often be time lags between the time at which the judgment is to apply and the time at which the criterion information about the adequacy of that judgment becomes available. This lag is shown in Figure 3.8.

When dealing with response systems, we distinguished between concurrent and predictive judgments on the basis of whether the judgment was applicable to a present state of the stimulus object or to some future state. That is, we distinguished between the time at which a judgment is made and the time-point at which the judgment is meant to apply. When the second point differs from the first, a case of predictive judgment exists. If the two time-points are the same, concurrent judgment occurs (Figure 3.8 shows a case of predictive judgment).

Ideally, we would like to confirm the accuracy of a judgment as soon as possible. Rapid feedback or knowledge of results is generally accepted as highly desirable from both an informational and a motivational point of view. Therefore, the question of how early, following the actual making of a judgment, is it possible to receive feedback from a criterion system about the accuracy of that judgment. The amount of time between the making of a judgment and receiving such feedback will be referred to hereafter as criterion lag. The amount of criterion lag is related to the kind of criterion system. Objective, subjective, and internal criterion systems have different lags, or will operate within different limiting values in terms of their potential for lag. Internal criterion systems have no lags at all. They are basically feedback systems which operate

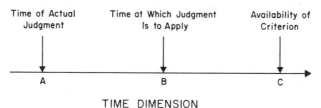

FIGURE 3.8 *An illustration of the time lag in criterion systems, where the distance $A \rightarrow C$ represents the lag between the time at which a judgment is made and the time at which a particular criterion measure becomes known or available to the judge.*

instantaneously—assuming that the individual is able to conceptualize them. Internal awareness states, or cognitions, are not subject to lags of any great magnitude since they are part of the state of conscious awareness of the individual.

Subjective criterion systems may have lags ranging from near zero values to of exceedingly long duration. Thus feedback from other individuals concerning the accuracy of one's judgments may be forthcoming at any time (see Figure 3.9). Objective criteria, however, cannot logically exist until one reaches the time-point at which the judgment is intended to apply. Thus no objective measure of job success at the end of two years' employment (promotion, salary, people supervised, etc.) can actually exist until the end of the two-year period. Any measure taken before then will be incomplete or insufficient. Therefore, when predictive judgments are made, only internal and subjective criterion systems can operate with time lags shorter than the time period between the judgment and its application. Objective criterion measures must wait until the end of the predictive interval before they can be available.

As the distance in time increases between the judgment and the criterion, there is a corresponding increase in the danger that the criterion system may undergo a change during the interval. This is true of both objective and subjective criterion systems. Criterion systems can and do change over time. Since society and societal values are constantly undergoing change, it is inevitable that the criterion systems (representing values of various aspects of society) will also change. The result is that predictive judgments are always at risk, since the criterion system characteristics assumed to be applicable at the time of the judgment may be totally changed by the time the judgment becomes operative.

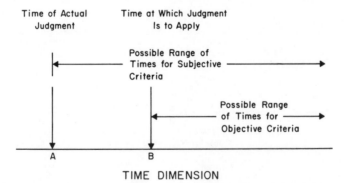

TIME DIMENSION

FIGURE 3.9 *The range of time lag values for subjective criteria and objective criteria.*

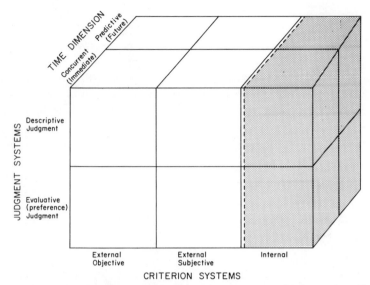

FIGURE 3.10 *A partitioning of the judgment spaces into distinct types of judgment depending upon the type of response continuum and the type of criterion system.*

The final point is that the internal criterion system is typically more important than is recognized. Further, a very strong argument could be made for the position that its importance increases with the amount of lag between the actual judgment and any valued external criterion. Internal criterion systems are also subject to change, although, in most cases, they probably are resistant to change or change slowly.

The Judgment Space

Figure 3.10 summarizes the previously outlined taxonomy of human judgment. This judgment space is partitioned into a total of 12 cells or types depending upon the dimensions of (*a*) type of judgment system (descriptive or evaluative); (*b*) type of criterion system (external objective, external subjective, or internal); and (*c*) time (immediate or future).

Any judgment task typically will fit only one combination of the time and judgment system dimensions. That is, any task usually can be classified as either descriptive or evaluative and as either concurrent or predictive. The criterion categories should not be considered mutually exclusive in that any task may have one, two, or all three types of criterion systems operating—often with different time lags.

Summary

The importance of the judgment process to an understanding of rational choice behavior has led to the inclusion of the material contained in this chapter. In the following chapters, the way in which the judgment process operates in such apparently diverse areas as motivation, leadership, roles, and climate will be outlined. In Chapter 4, the theory itself will be examined explicitly. How judgment operates at the critical process points in the theory will be discussed.

4

The Role of Judgment within the Theory

In the preceding chapter we discussed general issues related to the judgment process. We now turn to an examination of the various places within the theory where judgment is a central mechanism. Referring to the shaded portion of the complete diagram of the theory presented on page 24 in Figure 2.1 we see that major cognitive process points within the theory are indicated by the symbol ⊗. This indicates that certain mental acts, or cognitive processes, are carried out at these junction points creating new cognitions or cognitive states from prior cognitions or cognitive states according to some lawful and rational fundamental cognitive process. In most of these instances, the primary lawful and rational cognitive process involved is a judgment process—either descriptive or evaluative—belonging somewhere in the judgment space described in the previous chapter. Each of these process points will be examined in detail in this section, emphasizing the importance of the judgment process in each stage of cognitive processing. Each different process point in Figure 2.1 is identified by a different capital letter, A through J.

Once again we want to distinguish between the theoretical explanation of behavior developed within the following section and more practical behavior mechanisms for behaving which are degraded or simplified techniques developed by people for avoiding the complexities of carrying out all of the individual processes to be discussed in order to perform each individual act. Each of the processes is a complex mechanism in the overall sequential pattern of process mechanisms necessary for explaining with rational behavior. Each process mechanism is needed to provide a satisfactory explanation for rational behavior. However, it is *not* necessary to assume that each process stage must always operate to accomplish the performance of any specific act.

Most, if not all, behavior is accomplished through the use of heuristic techniques on the part of people. These heuristics are procedures, strategies, or approaches to behavior that are designed to simplify one's existence and to help one avoid the complexities of having to perform each of the to-be-discussed processes in every behavioral act. These heuristics are then degraded versions of the theory and are worth discussion in their own right. The last section of this chapter is devoted to a discussion of some heuristics that people use as a method of dealing with the complexities of behavior.

Initial Perceptions

The initial process point in the theory is point A in Figure 4.1. This is the process point at which the individual forms his or her initial perceptions of the entire stimulus world, as was pointed out in the original discussion of the theory in Chapter 2. This perceptual process consists of the process of descriptive judgment. Basic perceptions (cognitions) about the environment are the result of an internal measurement system within the individual, analogous to the measurement system operating in the environment. This internal measurement system responds to the stimuli impinging on our senses and quantifies them into definable, understandable cognitive states or events. This measurement can either be rudimentary (stimulus present or stimulus absent) or sophisticated, but in either case the process of measurement is judgmental, in which the individual assesses the incoming stimulus characteristics and uses them to locate the stimulus on a descriptive continuum.

This exact processing stage provided the context for Egon Brunswik's (1943) original work on probabalistic functionalism and the lens model paradigm as a descriptive model for the perceptual process. Although it is not our purpose to review extensively the empirical evidence underlying the appropriateness or utility of the descriptive judgmental process as a model for the main cognitive mechanism operating at this stage, it is nevertheless strongly substantiated by the work on person perception by Hammond *et al.* (1975), Brehmer (1970), Nystedt (1974), and others, as well as by the considerable work in the general area of what Naylor and Wherry (1964) have referred to as "policy capturing" (e.g., see the work of Goldberg, 1970). Further illustrations of the use of descriptive judgment systems to model the basic perceptual process within the framework of Brunswik may be found in the studies of Slovic (1969), Brehmer

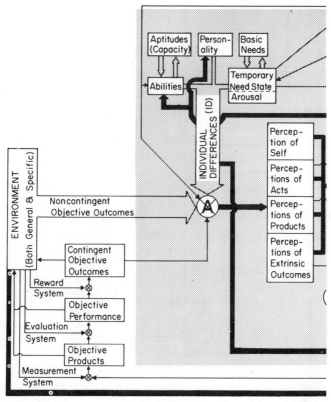

FIGURE 4.1 *Process point A in which initial basic perceptions concerning one's self and environment are formed.*

(1976), and many others. For an excellent summary of this research the reader is referred to Brehmer (1977).

The initial perception process is descriptive as opposed to evaluative, since it is assumed to consist of a measurement mechanism in which stimuli are converted into meaningful cognitions or perceptual events by the observer. This measurement process may proceed at various levels of sophistication; the levels closely corresponding to the traditional views concerning levels of measurement. The most rudimentary form of perception is simply an absolute threshold notion—the principle of *awareness*. The measurement principle here is a simple yes–no classification as to the presence or absence of a stimulus event. Thus it can be diagrammed as shown in Figure 4.2 in which Y_J represents a dichotomous variable with two states, awareness or unawareness of the stimulus, and

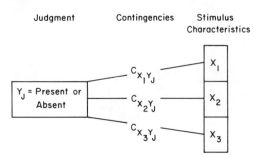

FIGURE 4.2 *Judgment of awareness of stimulus object.*

the C_{iY_J}'s represent contingency relationships between the several characteristics of the stimulus object and the Judgment dimension.[1]

The next level of perception (Figure 4.3) is the notion of identity or class membership. This corresponds to a nominal measurement system in which the observer classifies stimuli into their appropriate categories. This is the process by which an observer looks at an object and classifies it according to some meaningful classification system. The perceptual input is converted into either a simple or complex type of cognitive event. Thus you see an object and you recognize or identify the object as belonging to a class or category of objects labeled as chair, desk, or some other learned class concept.

The C_{iY_J}'s represent a set of acquired or learned contingencies between the amount of certain stimulus characteristics processed by the stimulus and the likelihood of that stimulus belonging to a given category, or having a certain identity or label. These contingencies may be viewed as the basis of a "cognitive template" which the observer uses to establish the identity of stimuli.

The third type of measurement that takes place in initial perception is magnitude judgment, in which the observer estimates the magnitude of a particular specific or composite attribute of the stimulus object (Figure 4.4). This magnitude estimation can be ordinal, interval, or ratio in terms of its scale properties depending upon the particular type of judgment made by the observer.

---

1. Parenthetically, we should point out that this is an instance in which one can get involved in an infinite regress problem in judgments of awareness. That is, if perception of awareness of the stimulus is predicated upon the awareness of the stimulus attributes (Xs) which determine awareness, then isn't there a preceding judgment needed concerning each X? And isn't that judgment in turn predicated upon even more basic Xs? To avoid this problem, we shall assume certain basic dimensions to any awareness–nonawareness judgment, which are primarily intensity dimensions.

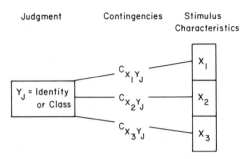

FIGURE 4.3 *Judgment of identity.*

The Perception of Acts and Products

It is extremely important that we distinguish between the perception of an act and the perception of the product of an act. In Chapter 1, it was pointed out that an act was a process, whereas a product was the result of that process—something which had been caused by, or which came into existence because of, the acts being performed. Further, we said that these products entered the awareness of an individual (i.e., became cognitions), through a measurement process. This measurement process is the type of descriptive judgmental process we have discussed in the previous section, in which the various characteristics of the stimulus object or event are used to arrive at a judgment about existence, class membership, or amount of some attribute.

The perception of an act is also a measurement process, but the kinds of measures involved are now very specific. As in the case of measurement of products, the measurement of acts can take place at various levels, the most basic of which is simply a recognition, or cognitive awareness, that the individual is actually engaging in a given act. However, it was pointed out in Chapter 1 that the primary dimension (mea-

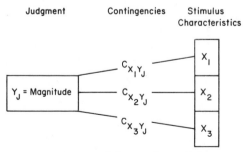

FIGURE 4.4 *Judgment of magnitude.*

surement concept) associated with acts as basic units of behavior was the dimension of amplitude, or degree of commitment of basic resources toward the carrying out of that act. Commitment, in turn, was said to consist of two separate behavioral dimensions, time and effort. Thus the relationship $C = T \times E$ was postulated as a means of expressing the measurement dimensions of behavior within the context of the theory.

Using these notions we can now express the measurement of acts within the judgment paradigm as a sort of hierarchical process of judgment. The first stages involve separate judgments concerning the primary behavior dimension of time and effort as shown in Figure 4.5.

These judgments, or measures, as to the degree or amount of time (Y_{J_T}) and effort (Y_{J_E}) then are used as cues to form a second level judgment, or cognition, as to the amount of commitment to the act as shown in Figure 4.6.

The question arises at this point as to how these judgments of time, effort, and subsequently of commitment are different from the judgments or products. The conceptual distinction between judgments (mea-

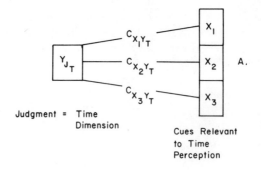

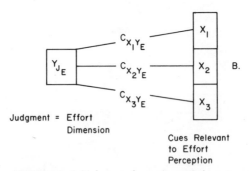

FIGURE 4.5 *Initial stage of commitment judgment.*

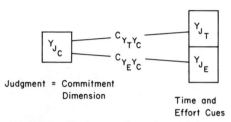

Judgment = Commitment
Dimension

Time and
Effort Cues

FIGURE 4.6 *Final stages of commitment judgment.*

surements) of acts and judgments (measurements) of products is that products are things created by the act, whereas time, effort, and commitment are things put into the act. For example, fatigue would be a product; effort is a behavioral dimension of an act which may have a contingency relationship with the product fatigue.

It is true that under certain conditions we may use the measures associated with acts as if they were products. Thus the perceived amount of time we put in on a given task may be treated by an individual as an end product deserving intrinsic and/or extrinsic outcomes. However, for our purposes, it seems best to maintain a clear distinction between the perception of acts as such and the perception of products that arise from the conduct of those acts. The necessity for this distinction will become apparent in the next section.

One additional comment is necessary concerning the notion of a hierarchy in the judgment process as it applies to the perception of products. We pointed out that the basic paradigm is one in which the judgment about the product is based upon a set of contingencies between cues and the judgment (C_{ij} values). But such a process assumes that the observer has previously perceived the cues—that is, the cues have entered the person's cognitive system. Thus this theory requires that a judgment process has taken place with respect to each cue prior to the judgment process that uses the cues. This implies that each cue must have cues of its own (second order cues) which in turn must have cues (third order cues) and so on, leading to a never-ending series of judgmental processes, as shown in Figure 4.7.

In fact, such a never-limiting series is not a conceptually or psychologically valid premise. There must be a termination point consisting of a set of basic perceptual cues, which by their presence, absence, or amount, determine all higher order perceptions or judgments. Researchers in tl e field of perception have devoted much of their energies in the past 40 years to research designed to establish what these basic perceptual cues are in each of the various sense modalties. It is not our intent to concern ourselves further with this issue, since, for the theory, we only need to

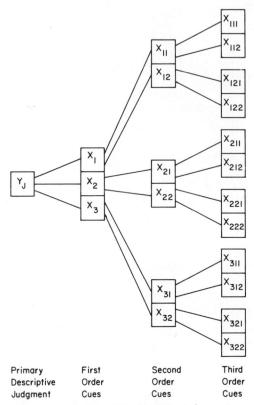

Primary Descriptive Judgment	First Order Cues	Second Order Cues	Third Order Cues

FIGURE 4.7 *The hierarchical structure of the descriptive judgment process in perception.*

consider the results of this initial process, particularly as it manifests itself in judgments of acts and products (also see footnote 1, page 94).

Contingency Perceptions

The second major process point in the theory is point B in Figure 4.8. The process of forming contingency relationships among various kinds of cognitions is assumed to occur here. It is here that the individual acquires a sense of the probabalistic nature of the world in which he or she exists. It is here that the basic contingency relationships among cognitions that form the basic foundations for all rational behavior are acquired.

The theory specifically deals with three kinds of contingencies. They are:

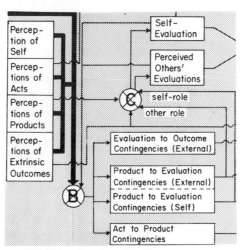

FIGURE 4.8 *Process points B and C in which the contingency cognitions (process point B) and the evaluation cognitions (process point C) are formed.*

1. Act → Product
2. Product → Evaluation
3. Evaluation → Outcome

The formation of these different types of contingency relationships is most accurately described as a process of descriptive judgment involving simple probability learning. We can diagram this process as shown in Figure 4.9.

In the application of this paradigm, it is assumed that the observer (a) observes the existence of some act; (b) makes a judgment (inference or prediction) about the corresponding existence of some product; and then (c) observes whether that product exists—for the moment we will keep the level of measurement of the act, product, and judgment variables as 0 or 1 (i.e., existence versus nonexistence). Many repetitions of this sequence result in the observer learning the correct environmental contingency ($C_{X_1Y_C}$) by comparing his own judgments about the product to the criterion values the actual product on trial after trial. The $C_{X_1Y_J}$ values represent the perceived contingency (probabalistic relationship) between the act and the product by the observer, and it is these contingencies that assume importance in subsequent judgment stages in the theory.

An important point is one concerning the degree to which it is necessary to assume that an actual response, or judgment, be made by the observer for the observer to develop a learned contingency $C_{X_1Y_J}$ that

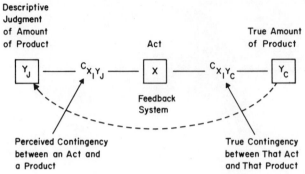

Descriptive
Judgment
of Amount
of Product   Act   True Amount
                                                             of Product

Perceived Contingency   True Contingency
between an Act and   between That Act
a Product   and That Product

FIGURE 4.9 *A simple lens diagram of the way in which simple contingency relationships are learned.*

represents the observer's beliefs about the true contingency $C_{X_1Y_C}$. This is an issue for which learning theorists have as yet been unable to provide definitive answers. Certainly we recognize that an individual can and will learn contingency relationships between events in the absence of any overt, observable response. In such instances, we might diagram the process as shown in Figure 4.10.

However, it is not clear whether or not a covert cognitive response is present. We shall assume that a covert, unobservable judgment response does exist and that it is a necessary component to the learning of contingency relationships, as shown in Figure 4.10. Indeed, it seems logically inescapable that Y_J must exist in a covert sense for the C_{XY_J} linkage to be formed on the basis of observed events. The C_{XY_C} contingency can, of course, also be acquired (learned) by the process of simply informing the judge of the correct contingency. This is the feedforward notion of Bjorkman (1973). Even in feedforward learning, one could argue that the judge makes a judgment or series of judgments in which both X and Y_J are covert. That is, a sort of mental rehearsal or exercising of the implications of the received rule (C_{XY_C} can be viewed as a rule) in all

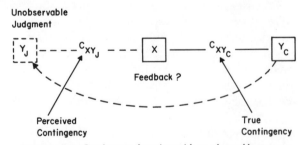

Unobservable
Judgment

Feedback ?

Perceived   True
Contingency   Contingency

FIGURE 4.10 *Contingency learning with no observable response.*

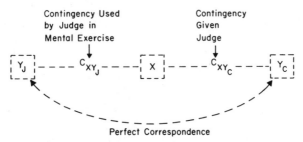

FIGURE 4.11 *The contingency learning paradigm where the true contingency is given the judge via feedforward procedures.*

likelihood still takes place. Thus we could diagram the feedforward situation as shown in Figure 4.11, where C_{XY_C} represents the feedforward information given to the Judge.

Each of the three different types of contingencies that are learned at the B process stage of the theory plays an important function at a subsequent process point, as will be pointed out in later sections. The evaluation-to-outcome contingencies are an essential ingredient to the determination of the utility of products (process point G). The internal and external product-to-evaluation contingencies constitute the basis of what are called "roles," which are treated at considerable length in Chapter 5, on role behavior. Finally, the act-to-product contingencies have their major influence upon behavior at process point H, at which the utilities of products are converted to the utilities of acts. Thus it should be apparent that the contingencies formed at this early process stage are a critical set of cognitions within the theory.

It was stated earlier that the type of judgment involved in learning these contingencies was descriptive judgment. Depending upon the circumstances, any or all of the various types of criterion systems may be present during the process of learning these contingencies. Similarly, the criterion systems may involve any of a variety of time lags. That is, the time lag for each individual contingency has the potential for varying across an immense range of values. Thus the individual is perpetually involved in the formation of these three kinds of probabalistic relationships, and the actual number of such relationships that exist is so large as to be almost beyond comprehension. For example, even if the contingencies are limited to simple relationships between two variables, such as the relationship between a single act and a single product, the expected number of such relationships is the number of acts in the person's behavior repertory multiplied by the average number of products potentially linked to each of the n_a acts. It does not take much imagination to quickly perceive that the learning of these contingency relationships is not a process to be viewed lightly.

Further, the assumption that the contingencies learned are limited to simple one–to–one relationships is, without question, unrealistic. In assessing, or learning, a relationship between event A and event B (e.g., where event A is an act and event B is a product), the learning inevitably takes place in the context of other relationships such as the relationship of A with other B's and the relationship of B with other A's. Thus, the judge considers not only the relationship between a given act and a given product in isolation, but in combination with other acts. That is, he or she often develops multiple contingency relationships in which a number of individual contingencies are combined into a larger, composite contingency.

The point is that the contingencies we learn are most likely to be complex sequential and/or conditional contingencies; not simple contingencies. We do not learn $A \rightarrow B$ relationships as much as we learn $A \rightarrow B/C$ relationships. We rapidly recognize, for example, that the contingency between engaging in certain acts and observing the result of a certain amount of a given product often depends upon what other acts are entered into by the individual. Few products are the result of individual acts. Rather they are the result of a sequence or a patterning of a number of basic behaviors. This issue will be discussed further on when we examine the possible discrepancies between the theory of rational behavior and how people actually behave. The complexity of the decision process in terms of a myriad of a conditional, sequential, and multiple contingencies that must be computed and processed by the individual forces the individual into processing-strategy heuristics that simplify his or her task. Small wonder, for example, that studies attempting to use reported subjective expectancies (a measure of contingency) typically fail to predict actual behavior with any degree of success, since such contingencies are gross estimates made concerning the relationship between, for example, the creation of a particular product and receiving a certain outcome. Such estimates ignore the importance of the act-to-product contingency completely, degrading the utility of the estimate. They also typically ignore the conditional or moderating aspects of other products, present or absent.

To illustrate the point with a brief example, consider the following two sets of contingencies that may be part of the belief or cognition system of a particular individual in a work situation.

Assume the individual is faced with trying to decide between two behavior options as to where to commit the basic resources of time and energy. The first option involves engaging in an act that has a contingency of .50 with the desired product, namely a successful repair job of the broken machine. The second act has a contingency of 1.00 with the second desired product, namely a clean work station. Each product in turn is related to an evaluation of the part of some criterion system (probably that of the foreman) through a contingency. This contingency expresses the likelihood that the desired product will result in specific evaluation on the part of the supervisor. Finally, each evaluation is in turn related to a valued outcome (one with positive valence) via a contingency of some perceived magnitude. (Remember all these contingencies exist as cognitions in the cognitive structure of the worker.)

Option A: Attempting to Fix Broken Machine
Act → product contingency = .50
Product → evaluation contingency = 1.00
Evaluation → outcome contingency = 1.00

Option B: Cleaning Up Work Station
Act → product contingency = 1.00
Product → evaluation contingency = .50
Evaluation → outcome contingency = 1.00

Assuming a multiplicative model, both sequences of contingencies result in the same overall contingency between act and outcome (i.e., .50). But the individual contingencies in each sequence are somewhat different. Asking the individual to tell you his contingency between a given product and the outcome would result in a multiple contingency of 1.00 for option A but only .50 for option B. Thus to see these contingencies as input into a predictive model would give a false impression of the true composite contingencies between acts and outcome since they fail to include the act-to-product contingencies.

Note also that if the individual is able to produce the product in option A, then everything is fine and he is assured of the outcome. Thus he need not concern himself with any other products. But the reverse is not true. Even if he successfully produces product B, he is far from assured of the desired outcome, so it may be in his best interests to try to produce product A as a backup strategy if he has sufficient time and energy.

The process by which we acquire knowledge or belief states (cognitions) about the three types of contingencies involved in this stage of the theory is complicated, as was pointed out previously. But the important notion is that the basic judgment process involved in contingency formation is one of descriptive judgment. This is true for each of the different types of contingencies, including the product-to-evaluation contingencies, even though one of the variables in these relationships is an evaluation response. The learning of the evaluation contingencies does not require the judge to make an evaluation judgment, only a descriptive judgment about the magnitude of an evaluation associated with a given magnitude of a product made by some other evaluation system than his own.

It is not our purpose here to examine the extensive body of research that has accumulated in recent years concerning the ability of people to learn contingencies of the type and complexity involved at this stage of the theory. This would require a lengthy digression into the fields of probability learning, Bayesian inference, multiple-cue probability learning and the entire concept-formation literature. There are a number of excellent summaries of this literature. The interested reader should examine some of the references such as Ebert and Mitchell (1975).

Evaluation Perceptions

The third major process point in the theory occurs at point C in Figure 4.8. At this stage in the overall cognitive sequence, the important process of evaluation takes place. This process involves the use of the contingencies formed in the previous section—process point B. Evaluations, you will recall, are the attaching of affect to products and, in the theory, this process is dealt with in detail through the utilization of role models. That is, the contingencies formed at process point A become the formal definition of roles expected of an individual—either by himself (self-role) or by others (external roles).

The way in which the role is carried (acted) out becomes the basis for evaluation of the behavior of that individual. Thus the individual's perceived products are transformed into perceptions or cognitions of units of goodness or badness by the observer via the mediating contingencies existing between products and evaluations. The mediating contingencies are the formal definition of roles, and thus roles and criterion systems are, in most cases, conceptually identical. This complex and important process is described briefly in Chapter 2 and in Chapter 5 in considerable detail, so we will not deal with it further except to point out that the process point involves both evaluative and descriptive forms of judgment.

This may at first appear incongruous. Would not one expect that the formation of cognitive states concerning levels of goodness and badness associated with products must, by definition, always involve evaluation judgment? The answer to this is yes if, and only if, we are concerned with the *self-evaluation* process. In self-evaluation, the judge is required to make an evaluative judgment about the location of products on a goodness–badness continuum as per the belief system of the individual. The response represents the individual's own affective reactions to the products in question and is, therefore, truly an evaluative judgment.

The case of judging the evaluations of others is more complicated. What the individual is required to judge in this instance is his own perception, or belief, concerning how some "other" will locate the individual's own products on the affective continuum. Thus the judge is being asked to estimate the affective response of some other to the judge's own products. This affective response of the other is actually a product, and in being asked to estimate its magnitude, the judge is making a descriptive judgment, not an evaluative one. These judgments are, at this stage totally affect free and thus are considered as perceived outcomes in the terminology of the theory. They, along with other perceptions of direct extrinsic outcomes, feed into process point D. In contrast, the self-evaluations are immediate affect cognitions, since self-evaluation cannot be viewed as being separable from the immediate affective response associated with it. Thus self-evaluations contribute directly to the affect state of the individual.

The Comparison Process

Process point D (Figure 4.12) is once again a descriptive judgment process, albeit one of a particular type—namely comparative descriptive judgment. Here judgments concerning the absolute magnitude of out-

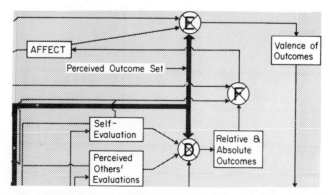

FIGURE 4.12 *Process point D, which involves comparative judgments, E, and F, which involve the attaching of affect to received outcomes (process point F) and future outcome (process point E).*

comes are converted into relative magnitudes based upon comparison with various reference outcomes associated with the population of reference others for that particular judge or individual.

The comparison process involves the use of expectancies by the individual as standards against which one's perceived outcome can be compared in order to make relative judgments based upon the size of the discrepancy between perceived actual outcomes and expected outcomes. Both one's self-expectancies and one's perceived expectancies of others are used as reference values in the comparison judgments. That is, they are the expectancies that form the basis for all judgments of relative outcome magnitude.

A given absolute outcome value can thus result in, or be converted to, any number of individual relative outcomes depending upon the number of reference expectancies operating in that particular instance. Thus an outcome of a $2000 per year pay raise (an absolute outcome value) for foremen making $18,000 per year can be converted into a series of relative value pay raises using such expectancies as (a) pay raise expected for all individuals having this base pay; (b) the pay raise expected for all individuals in the same type of work; (c) the pay raise expected for all workers in the same union; and (d) the pay raise expected for the foremen in an adjacent department. Each such discrepancy, whether it be positive or negative, becomes a relative outcome that can have affect attached to it.

Affective Cognitions

Process points E and F (see Figure 4.12) deal with the process of attaching affect to perceived outcomes. In the case of process point F, the process is one of attaching affect to perceived outcomes already received (both absolute and relative). In the case of process point E, we have the process of attaching an anticipated affect (called a valence in the theory) to an anticipated outcome. Both processes are evaluative in that they involve affective responses on the part of the individual. Whether or not both processes are judgmental is another matter. Process E, the attachment of anticipated affect to an anticipated or potential outcome, is a definite instance of evaluative judgment. It is also predictive judgment in that the time frame has become future oriented. This is the first time in the theory that we have encountered predictive judgments.

To call process F a judgment process is more difficult. In fact, whether or not this is a true cognitive process is difficult to say, since the attachment of affect to a received outcome can be an instantaneous affair.

These two process points, E and F, form the core of the basic motivational system within this theory and they are dealt with in greater detail in Chapter 6.

Utility of Products

In process point E, we encountered our first case of predictive judgment. Until this point, all the judgment processes examined, descriptive or evaluative, had been concurrent judgment rather than predictive judgment. In other words, the time frame was oriented for a now or present immediate tense in its application.

At process point G, we encounter predictive judgment for the second time in the judgment sequence. Here the judgments are future oriented, aimed at some time beyond that of the present and immediate (see Figure 4.13). We call these future-oriented judgments "anticipations" in the theory, since they represent anticipated states, or more accurately, perceptions or cognitions of anticipated states at some time in the future. All these anticipated states are affect-related. That is, they are anticipa-

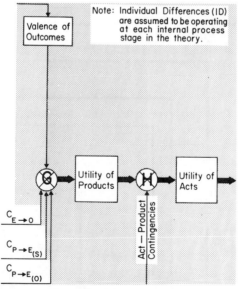

FIGURE 4.13 *Process point G, where utility of product cognitions are formed, and process point H, where utility of act cognitions are formed. Individual differences are assumed to be operating at each internal process stage in the theory.*

tions of the amount of affect likely to be associated with certain definable entities where the entities are either outcomes, products, or acts.

The future-oriented judgment at process point G is a judgment concerning the utility of various products. This utility represents the perceived values of individual products in terms of their capability of producing, various outcomes, that in turn have certain amounts of affect associated with them.

Since the future-oriented judgments have perceived values to individuals making the judgments, they are evaluative judgments. The products are being located on an affective, or evaluative, continuum that is basically one of anticipated affect. This process of evaluative judgment is theoretically a complicated judgment process. The overall utility of a product is the summation across countless evaluation systems and countless outcomes. Further, at least two separate types of contingencies (beliefs) are involved in forming these utility judgments—the product-to-evaluation contingencies and the evaluation-to-outcome contingencies. The theory keeps these two contingencies separate, but an interesting empirical question remains as to whether individuals are able to do so or whether they tend to behave more on the basis of a composite, or overall, contingency.

Utility of Acts

Once the overall utility of a product has been established, the theory proposes that this utility is converted, by anticipatory judgment, into the overall utility commitment to an act. This process occurs at process point H in Figure 4.13. The act-to-product contingency beliefs formed earlier play a central role in this process. The process is treated in greater detail in Chapter 6. The point here is that this process is another of the series of judgment processes in the model. It is evaluative judgment in that it involves the location of acts on a continuum of personal affect—that is, the favorability of the act to the decision maker or judge as a person. Further, it is predictive judgment in that we are dealing with anticipation of yet-to-be-experienced events.

In this chapter, we have been attempting to apply the taxonomy of judgment behavior developed in the previous chapter to key process points in the theory. We have pointed out how most of the cognitive process points in the theory may be viewed as processes involving judgment, and that the judgment process may be considered the central process for the entire theory, since it occurs in so many different places and is critical to so many process stages.

Let us now proceed to the second major section of the chapter, in which we will attempt to generalize observations concerning our knowledge about the processes of human judgment and how this knowledge has either direct or tangential implications for the way in which we should view judgment within the context of the theory itself.

Some Commentary on Judgment and the Behavior of Individuals

The present theory is based upon the assumption that man's judgmental behavior is probabalistic, and that much of man's behavior therefore depends upon his ability to process probabalistic information—that is, (a) learn probabalistic relationships; (b) store and recall them; and (c) use them effectively in a systematic manner. Examination of summaries of research dealing with man's ability to deal with probabalistic information provides evidence that man is indeed a rather effective processor of such information, although clearly his ability is influenced by many internal and external parameters (Slovic, Fishoff & Lichtenstein, 1977; Slovic & Lichtenstein, 1971). A further and recognizable assumption of the present theory as regards judgment is that it assumes that man is interested in maximizing the expected utility associated with any choice, or judgment, having affect associated with it. That is, the final process point in the theory, point J in Figure 2.1, represents the actual acts, or behaviors, selected or entered into by the individual. The theory assumes that man will enter into those acts (or combination of acts) that will maximize the anticipated affect or minimize the anticipated negative affect associated with those outcomes which, in turn, are associated with products produced by the acts.

Therefore, to avoid confusion, we point out that the theory does not rest upon any new fundamental promise of choice behavior. Our view is a traditional view. What is new is that we have attempted to clearly distinguish the numerous types and kinds of judgments that occur in the overall cognitive process of deciding which behaviors to engage in. Furthermore, we have attempted to impress upon the reader how important the judgment process is in the theory.

Real versus Theoretical Judgment Processes—The Degraded System

So far we have focused on an explanation of how the judgment process operates within the theory. As was pointed out, the theory, like all theories of behavior, represents an idealized viewpoint or explanation of the processes involved in deciding which acts or series of acts the individual will perform. The theory should be viewed as an explanation of behavior of the most idealized kind. It represents our view of how man ought to perform if man is truly rational, if the assumptions of the theory are valid, and if conditions are optimal for performing in the manner specified by the theory.

Unfortunately, there is an increasing body of evidence indicating that people do not utilize the cognitive system in its pure, or theoretically most effective, sense. They tend instead, for one reason or another, to use degraded versions of the system. These degraded judgmental strategies are often simpler ways of dealing with the making of judgments, and are based upon rules, or principles, of simplification that may be intuitively appealing or "logical" to the individual but which may or may not be effective substitution strategies for the entire "pure" process.

Thus it appears that although the theory proposes that the fundamental process involves constantly updating one's contingencies on the basis of new information and reviving and updating the utilities of acts and/or products to use these contingencies and utilities in a rational and systematic way, it often is not so. Judgments often appear to be more influenced by or explainable in terms of degraded decision tactics, which have been referred to as heuristic rather than representative of any true process.

Types of Heuristics

Heuristics may be classified into two types of behavioral strategies. We will refer to these types as *involitional* and *volitional heuristics.*

Involitional Heuristics

The distinguishing characteristic of involitional heuristics is their involuntary nature. They are simplifying strategies that are attributed to organismic characteristics, states, or tendencies of a nonmotivational or nonintentional kind. These strategies are not deliberately selected by an individual. They occur because of system characteristics of the organism. In terms of the theory, they are represented as internal constraints upon the complete process that have their influence at various critical process points.

Kahneman and Tversky, in a series of extremely important papers (Kahneman & Tversky, 1972; Tversky & Kahneman, 1971, 1973, 1974) have proposed at least three major involitional heuristic strategies or principles found to influence the behavior of individuals in judgment tasks. These are referred to as *judgment by representativeness, judgment by availability,* and *judgment by adjustment.*

Judgment by Representativeness

As proposed by Tversky and Kehneman (1971; Kahneman & Tversky, 1972) the perceived probability of an event or outcome is a function of the degree to which that event or outcome is judged representative of (or similar to) the population to which it belongs or to the process that created or generated it. For example, when judges were asked to evaluate the likelihood that an individual would engage in a particular occupation, the judgments were influenced by the degree to which the judge perceived the individual as representing the stereotype of individuals in that occupation, whereas rate factors (the total number of individuals in an occupation) were almost totally ignored.

Representativeness then is viewed as a process of comparing features of an event to those of the orginating structure and that probabilities (or contingency relationships) are determined by assessing similarity or what might be called "connotive" distance between cognitions.

Judgment by Availability

A second heuristic proposed by Tversky and Kahneman (1973) is that of "availability." A person may be said to be using the heuristic of availability whenever probability or contingency estimates are determined on the basis of the ease with which instances or examples of that association may be brought to mind or retrieved from memory. The availability notion is actually a reversal of the age-old notion that association bonds are made stronger through repetition or through increases in frequency since it says that judgments or relative frequency hinge or are based upon the strength of the association (Tversky & Kahneman, 1973).

Judgment by Anchoring

The third heuristic strategy proposed is referred to as an anchoring process involving the use of a natural starting point, or "anchor," as a first judgment; this value is adjusted in subsequent judgments to produce closer and closer approximations to the true value. The anchoring heuristic is similar to classical notions of adaptation theory since if one accepts the role of natural starting points, or anchors, in a judgment task, one must subsequently deal with the question of how these anchoring points are initially established.

Volitional Heuristics

Heuristics that occur as the direct result of conscious choice on the part of the individual are volitional heuristics. They are voluntary strategies selected, or adopted, according to the basic principles of rational choice. In the theory, volitional heuristics are viewed as individual acts that possess separate utilities and compete with all other acts for commitment on the part of the individual according to motivational principles that will be explained in Chapter 6. Volitional heuristics have not received as much attention as have involitional heuristics although they are probably the more important type of simplifying strategy.

Montgomery and Svenson (1976), in an interesting and provocative article, propose a principle of "minimizing cognitive effort" that is a compelling rationale for the existence of volitional heuristics. It may seem intuitively obvious that an individual wishes to minimize effort, yet we live in a society that tends to label such behavior as unworthy (lazy); in contrast, the traditional work ethic says that maximizing effort is good for one and for all. If one accepts Montgomery and Svenson's notion, the development of volitional heuristics to deal with cognitively complex problems is an inescapable result. Some possible volitional heuristics follow.

Judgment by Habit

A heuristic that plays a very large role in judgment behavior is that of habit. We tend to make judgments similar to those we have made in the past unless we have "sufficient" reason or justification to modify a behavior. We avoid having to process and evaluate information by using this heuristic, and it is therefore appealing and compelling as a strategy to adopt in situations where (a) the relative outcomes are not noticeably affected by increased accuracy of judgment; or (b) where large amounts of commitment (i.e., time and effort) are required to evaluate and process the information necessary to arrive at an updated set of utility values for various acts.

Judgment by Template Matching

Another type of heuristic postulated is that of template matching. Judges adopt a set of boundary conditions concerning the input information—cue values, which they perceive. These boundary values form a behavioral template for the judge. As long as the perceived cue values fall within these bounds, and thus match the template, the judge will respond in a standard, or habitual, fashion. Only when the cue values fall outside the limits set by the template will the judge attempt to process systematically the information and update his contingencies (beliefs) and utilities. This heuristic is basically a habit strategy having certain specified tolerance limits.

Judgment by Rules

Another type of behavioral strategy important in our lives is what we will call the heuristic of "judgment by rules." We make judgments according to certain sets of instructions or rules that have been given to us by others, such as our parents, friends, or social groups. Often we never evaluate the efficacy of these rules—we use them without hesitation or question time after time until for some reason they are shown to be totally inappropriate. For example, one overhears grandfather explaining to a child that in a tornado one should go to the northwest corner of the basement. Years later, in a tornado alert, the child automatically goes to the northwest corner.

There undoubtedly will be other heuristics proposed as mechanisms for coping with the human judgment process in addition to those mentioned. There remains small question that heuristics are an important behavioral strategy that becomes superimposed upon the underlying judgment mechanism. As was pointed out earlier, Montgomery and Svenson (1976) have made an excellent case for what they call the principle of "minimizing cognitive effort" in judgment. Crudely put, their position is that man is inherently lazy. In more sophisticated language, they have made the important point that there will always be a nonzero negative utility for the acts of computing contingencies, valences, and utilities. Thus other heuristics do and will exist for cognitive processing.

There is danger, however, in dealing with man's judgmental behavior in terms of the heuristic notion. Indeed, there is danger in dealing with any behavior in terms of heuristics. Heuristic strategies are just that—strategies—and as such represent individual difference characteristics of people as they perform as judges or information processors. The application of individual difference concepts to explain behavior has never been a particularly successful explanatory strategy and should not be counted upon here as being likely to achieve any more success in explaining judgment behavior than it has been in explaining perceptual–motor behavior, learning behavior, or forms of social behavior. While we can recognize—as indeed we should—that individual differences are important in judgment, it is the basic process that should be our primary focus.

The point to be understood is that heuristics, particularly volitional heuristics, are not basic or underlying behavior processes. They are

mechanisms superimposed over basic processes for purposes of simplification, and they can never be as effective as the underlying process itself
since they are always degraded versions of that process.

Probably the most important issue regarding heuristics based upon
motivated behavior is not one concerned with specific types of strategies
people develop but with why and when they modify these strategies. If
simplifying volitional heuristics are prevalent (and they unquestionably
are), then what kinds of events must occur (i.e., how badly must people
perform) before they are abandoned or revised? Indeed, how often are
such strategies ever examined critically by the individual?

In summary, we see the issue of how and when the individual updates
his or her volitional "strategies for living" by using the underlying fundamental behavior systems to update and modify the simplifying strategy as an important issue in understanding the complex behavior of
individuals. Further, we see the boundary conditions for such updating
as a question of extreme importance.

Concluding Comments

This chapter has provided an overview of the important role of the
judgment process throughout the basic theory, showing how we see it to
be involved in each of the major process points. In the subsequent chapters on motivation, roles, leadership, and climate this point of view will
emerge again and again as a theme.

5

Roles and Role Behaviors

Organizations require stable patterns of interdependent behavior from the individuals who populate them. These patterns of behavior often are described by a set of concepts called *roles*. Despite the frequent use of role concepts to characterize situations involving prescribed patterns of behaviors, the results of this approach are not as impressive as one might hope. For example, Biddle and Thomas' (1966) excellent collection of readings on role theory described the state of the art as both incomplete and lacking in denotative clarity. A more recent review (Roos & Starke, 1980) found that very little had changed and concluded that a good deal of uncertainty and confusion still existed in the role literature.

As has been implied earlier in this book, it is our position that role concepts are critical for the understanding of human behavior in organizations. Later in the chapter we shall explicitly define and describe the role process within the theory. Ways in which individuals learn roles will be dissussed, as well as broad issues concerning roles such as interrole conflict. Before developing our view of roles, we shall consider some generally accepted role concepts from the role theory literature.

First, role theory focuses on the behavior patterns of individuals or sets of individuals rather than upon single behaviors or acts. Role theory is unique in this sense since its concern is with complex groupings of behaviors as opposed to individual behaviors in isolation.

Second, a prerequisite for role theory is the assumption that during any given time period, an individual "displays" or enters into a set of observable and identifiable behaviors. This in turn requires some clear definition of behavior as an integral part of any role theory. Such a definition often has been lacking.

A third prerequisite is the existence of a system for determining what types, or classes, of individual behaviors will be included or excluded from the overall pattern or role. Without such a system roles become limitless and therefore meaningless from both practical and theoretical points of view.

Because of the large number of behaviors displayed by the individual, the problem of which behaviors should be included in the pattern of behaviors constituting the role becomes an extremely complicated issue. For example, most would agree that adjusting the tension on a machine's belt would belong in the set of behaviors relevant to the role of a machine operator; however, would talking with a coworker at the drinking fountain also be part of that role? Any theory of role behavior must provide a means of determining which behaviors are role relevant and which are not. In the theory proposed here, the answer to this question will depend upon the relevance of the behavior in the sense that "relevance of behavior" was defined in Chapter 1. We shall see also that the relevance of any particular behavior may vary considerably as a function of the frame of reference within which the role is being discussed. For now, we will accept the fact that a theory of role behavior requires the existence of a set of definable, observable, and relevant behaviors and that that existence provides the basic behavioral pattern constituting the foundation for role theory.

Role Types

There are different roles and role constructs which must be distinguished conceptually from each other. In talking about roles, it is convenient to remember that we are primarily interested in *patterns of individual behavior*. These patterns of behavior are associated with an individual or group of individuals. We will refer to the individual of interest as the *focal person*. This is consistent with the terminology of Kahn and his colleagues (Kahn, Wolf, Quinn, & Rosenthal, 1964; Katz & Kahn, 1978). Roles associated with anyone except the focal person will be referred to as roles associated with some "other." The other can be either an individual and/or a group of individuals representing the organization.

Role concepts employ behaviors that are referenced to the focal person but exist only in the cognitive belief structure of the individual(s) who has (have) some interest in the behavior of the focal person. These are *expected* or *prescribed* behaviors rather than actual or manifest behaviors. To the person who holds beliefs concerning the expected set of behaviors, the expected behaviors represent those that the person believes should be displayed by the focal person.

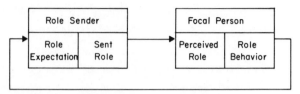

FIGURE 5.1 *The role episode (Adapted from Katz, D., and Kahn, R. L.* The Social Psychology of Organizations. *New York: Wiley, 1978).*

A single person who possesses a set of expected behaviors for the focal person is usually termed a *role sender,* and all role senders who hold such expectations for the focal person make up the focal person's *role set* (Katz & Kahn, 1978). It should be noted that although all role senders constitute the role set, they usually do not hold identical expected behaviors for the person. In fact, different members of the role set may expect discrepant behaviors from the focal person. For example, both superiors and subordinates are members of a first-line supervisor's role set despite the fact that they may expect very different, and often contradictory, behaviors from the supervisor.

Given the existence of the focal person's actual behaviors and the set of expected behaviors from the role senders, the final common theme running through most role theories is a process by which these two sets are communicated and compared. As was just mentioned, Katz and Kahn labeled the set of expected behaviors held by role senders as the *sent role.* The label connotes the fact that role senders must somehow communicate the behaviors they expect from the focal person to that person. The focal person must then form a perception of the sent role. In other words, the sent role must be *received* by the focal person. Once received, the focal person can react to it and display some behavior. This behavior then acts as an input into the perceptions of the role sender who usually evaluates it. The evaluation, in turn, acts as an internal input for the role sender and influences the nature of the role sent to the focal person in the future. One cycle of the whole role process, or *role episode* (Katz & Kahn, 1978), includes the sent role from the role senders, the focal person's behavior, and a feedback loop from the behavior back to the role senders. Figure 5.1 depicts the role episode in its simplest form.

Actual versus Expected Behaviors

The issue of making the important distinction between actual behavior and expected behavior often has complicated the role literature. Considerable confusion in defining a role precisely has arisen, in part, from the failure to distinguish clearly between the two. For example, in their review of the role literature Roos and Starke (1980) found the following three definitions of roles:

1. A general pattern of behavior accepted by a large number of persons in a culture or subculture.
2. Sets of expected behavior patterns held by those who interact with the individual occupying a position.
3. The actual behaviors of occupants of a given position within an organization or society.

Note that the first two definitions emphasize prescribed or expected behaviors, whereas the third deals with actual behaviors. Furthermore, the first definition reflects the group-oriented sociological view, whereas the second focuses on the individual. The third not only shifts from expected to actual behaviors, but refers either to specific individuals or to groups or classes of individuals. Obviously, our own preference will be for the individual orientation as reflected in the second and third definitions, since our theory is a theory of individual behavior.

In spite of the inconsistencies in the definition, it is evident that any complete treatment of roles must cope with both expected and actual behaviors. However, it is not necessary that both be incorporated into the definition. Which is considered the role per se is an arbitrary choice. We prefer to accentuate the expected or preferred attribute for two reasons. First, the expected behavior emphasis tends to be used more frequently in the psychological literature. Second, and more importantly, our emphasis all along has been upon the cognitive precursors of individual acts. Referring back to Figure 5.1, we see that expected behaviors are present in two concepts preceding the actual behavior. In one case, the expected behaviors are those held by the role senders for the focal person (the sent role) and in the other case they are the focal person's perception of what others expect him or her to do (the received role). The latter is the most immediate antecedent of behavior according to the model outlined in the figure. Therefore, our construct of a role will be based upon the cognitions or set of beliefs about the behaviors appropriate for the focal person rather than upon the actual or observed behaviors themselves.

A Problem in Using Behaviors to Define Roles

One final issue must be resolved before a precise definition of role can be offered. A closer look must be taken at the nature of the behaviors that constitute the expected behavior set (or, using the terminology of

Figure 5.1, the sent roles and the received roles). Behaviors, as role theories have traditionally defined them, vary on both a qualitative and a quantitative dimension. That they differ qualitatively is obvious (e.g., walking to deliver mail is qualitatively different from dictating a letter). They also differ quantitatively within any given type of behavior. Dictating one letter is different from dictating twenty letters and, likewise, the amount of time spent walking in a given day can vary considerably.

The typical development of the sent role or received role as found in most role-theory writings has assumed that the behaviors included in the role were described both qualitatively and quantitatively. Most descriptions of role behaviors in the literature imply not only what must be done but how much of each activity must be accomplished. However, a closer look at how roles are supposed to function shows that the quantitative nature of the behavior is ambiguous. Although it is not uncommon to specify the minimum amount of a specific behavior required, the upper limit of the amount is rarely stated. In most cases, it is assumed that the greater the amount of the behavior exhibited by the focal person, the better. When upper limits are imposed, such as in the case of roles sent to individuals by co-workers to restrict outputs, these limits usually are considerably above the minimum, leaving a wide band of acceptable levels of the behavior. However, the upper limits on the amounts of the behaviors generally are imposed by the focal person's ability to perform many behaviors. If all behaviors can be met at the minimum level and he or she can exceed these minimum levels, the focal person is evaluated more positively by the role sender.

The lack of specificity on the quantitative dimension presents a dilemma for the description of roles as sets of expected behaviors. The expected behavior set implies a clear specification of both the qualitative and quantitative nature of each behavior. In actuality, the amounts of the behavior required rarely are specified clearly for many of the behavior dimensions. The result is that the description of roles as expected sets of behaviors does not reflect what is actually expected by role senders because the expectations themselves are for open-ended classes of behaviors rather than for specific, well defined, behaviors.

A Definition of Roles

Following a general examination and overview of roles and the role concepts necessary in a theory of roles, role theory development within the theoretical framework of the previous chapters can be discussed. The remainder of this chapter will develop the importance of roles within the larger theory of behavior. We must establish precisely, within the specific context of the theory, what is meant by a role. The two terms subsequently needed to define a role are *role behavior* and *relevance;* they can be defined as follows.

Role Behavior Redefined as Products

We pointed out in Chapter 1 that the term behavior was to have a very explicit meaning. It refers to an ongoing process of committing an act. This process involves the individual committing the basic resources of time and effort to the "doing" of something. The particular something defines the direction of behavior, whereas the time and effort put into the act defines the degree of amplitude or commitment to the act. Further, we observed in both Chapters 1 and 2 that acts, which are the basic behavior processes, can be measured only in terms of the two commitment dimensions of time and effort and that these are often not easily observable or measurable.

This difficulty was resolved by introducing products, which were defined as those things that are created by engaging in a particular act or behavioral process. We pointed out that phenomenologically, people usually measure behavior in terms of the things created by their behavior (i.e., what was produced by the process). Thus, when we talk about a behavior such as typing, typing is viewed as an act; it is an ongoing behavioral process. We can then talk about one's commitment to that particular act in terms of the amount of time and effort put into the act. But when we measure the behavior, we typically do so in terms of such measures as number of words or pages. These measures are what we have called products in the theory. They are things created by the behavior.

In our treatment of roles, we will use products as the basic units of measured behavior. Therefore, roles will involve patterns of products as opposed to patterns of behaviors or acts.

Relevance of Products Defined as a Contingency

Earlier we pointed out that any theory of roles must define what it means by behavior as well as provide a rational system for determining what behaviors (in our case, products) are to be considered relevant to the role, since some behaviors are obviously important but should be excluded from the role.

Our treatment of roles will define the relevance of a product for a

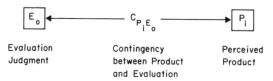

FIGURE 5.2   *The evaluation process.*

particular role as follows: *If the product of a focal person is evaluated by either the focal person or some specified other, that product is relevant to either the self-role or the role held for that focal person by the specified other.* Relevance is defined explicitly in terms of the evaluation process as considered in Chapters 2, 3, and 4. If a given product results in an evaluation judgment by an observer of that product (the observer can be either self or other), then the product is relevant to that observer and is part of the role for the focal person held by that observer.

In Chapter 4, the evaluation process was defined as a judgment of some product on a goodness–badness continuum. It can be diagrammed as shown in Figure 5.2. The figure shows that the relevance of a product can be defined precisely in terms of the contingency relationship existing between the particular product, P_i, and the evaluation judgment made by the observer. Clearly, if the contingency is zero, or nonexistent, the observer does not consider the product worthy of evaluation and the product should not be included in the role for the focal person held by that observer. On the other hand, if $C_{P_iE_o} > 0$, then there is some type of systematic relationship existing between the perceived product and the evaluation judgment, which means that that particular product is relevant to the person and thus belongs in the role that person holds for the focal individual.

The product-to-evaluation contingency represents the degree of association between amounts of a product and judgments about the value of that product as perceived by the evaluator. In role terms, we are proposing that the observer associates amounts of products with evaluations about the adequacy of the focal person's performance.

Role Defined as a Pattern of Contingencies

We are now able to provide an explicit definition of roles to be used within the theory. We have said that (*a*) a role is a pattern of relevant behaviors; (*b*) behavior can be viewed in terms of products; and (*c*) the relevance of products is reflected in a nonzero contingency between a product and an evaluation. Given these three conditions, a role is defined as: *a pattern or set of nonzero contingencies between a perceived set of products for*

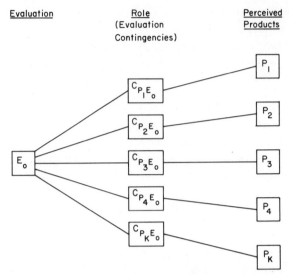

FIGURE 5.3 *The role defined as a set of product → evaluation contingencies for observer O.*

the focal person and the evaluation of those products on the part of some person (either self or other).

This can be diagrammed as shown in Figure 5.3. The set of contingencies in Figure 5.3 defines the observer's role for the focal person. Thus, the role is the set of nonzero contingencies, or

$$R_{CI} = \text{Role held by Observer O for Focal Individual I}$$
$$= C_{P_1E_0}, C_{P_2E_0}, C_{P_3E_0}, C_{P_4E_0}, \cdots C_{P_KE_0}$$

Further, these role contingencies may be viewed appropriately as *weights* that are somehow indicative of the *degree of relevance* or importance of the individual products related to the evaluation judgment of the observer. This characteristic of the contingencies is important, since any formal definition of a role should provide a sensible system for indicating the relative importance of the role elements.

Finally, given the definition of a role as the set of $C_{P_1E_0}$ nonzero contingency values, one can postulate different formal models for role implementation. For example, one might adopt a simple linear model for role implementation on the part of an observer. This model could be expressed as one for which the composite evaluation judgment of the observer, E_0, is an additive combination of the products of the contingencies times the amount of the products (that is, $E_0 = C_{P_1E_0}P_1 + C_{P_2E_0}P_2 + C_{P_3E_0}P_3 + C_{P_4E_0}P_4 + \cdots + C_{P_KE_0}P_K$). Obviously, there are many other possible models that might be postulated to represent the manner in which individuals implement role contingencies. However, the simple linear model proposed here has certain intuitive appeal, both because of its simplicity and because of considerable evidence indicating that such models are extremely powerful in terms of ability to explain large proportions of the explainable variance in information processing and judgment tasks.

Defining roles as perceived contingencies solves the problem mentioned earlier that upper limits on the amounts of products usually are not specified in roles. A contingency provides recognition of the fact that increasing amounts of a product may lead to higher evaluations. Furthermore, by not specifying the shape of the relationship between products and evaluations, the contingency notion can handle those cases in which the relationship in nonlinear. For example, co-workers' perception of the contingency between the number of units produced and their evaluation of the focal person may be one that involves a belief that the co-workers will hold more and more positive evaluations as more units are produced by the focal person up to a given point, after which additional products will result in negative evaluations. As long as the focal person holds some perception of the nature of the product's relationship to the evaluation across a range of possible quantities for a product, the role with regard to that product is defined for that individual.

Definition of Role Senders

The discussion of the set of role senders earlier in the chapter did not address the issue of the composition of this set. Who are the role senders for organizational members? A complete description of this set is not easy; in fact, it may be impossible. However, some consideration must be given to the way in which the set is conceived in our treatment of roles.

All would agree that those supervisors, co-workers and subordinates of the focal persons who have an interest in their behavior are members of the set of role senders. These individuals have specific expectations about how the focal person should behave, and they communicate these expectations to the focal individual in various ways. As one moves farther from the primary work group, it becomes less clear who should or should not be included in the role set. At first glance, it would seem appropriate to limit the role set to those who are members of the organization. Yet, such a limitation would exclude customers, union officials, spouses, and professional colleagues in similar positions with other institutions. At one time or another any of these individuals may have an interest in the way the focal person behaves and may communicate their expectations about role behaviors to the focal person. As Adams and his colleagues have demonstrated (Adams, 1976), the behaviors of crucial organization members in boundary positions requiring them to interact frequently with nonmembers of the organization (e.g., salesmen or lobbyists) are very much influenced by the roles sent to them by those outside the organization.

Just as the distinction as to who is a member of the role set as one moves farther from the primary work group members is not clear, neither is it clear when one remains close to the individual. From a functional standpoint, any individual or homogeneous set of individuals can provide a frame of reference for role behavior. In fact, focal persons can serve the same function for themselves. Past experience in the role, formal training, job knowledge, and so on, all contribute to expectations about contingencies operating in a role. In an analogous fashion to the role set member(s), the focal persons send themselves a set of role contingencies. Granted, their own sent role may be strongly influenced by other members of their role set; but it may be unique when contrasted to the role sent them by other individuals.

McGrath's (1976) conceptual framework for human behavior in organizations is useful for the delineation of role-set boundaries. He considers behavior in organizations as that subset of human behavior resulting from the interaction of the following three conceptually independent subsystems.

1. The physical and technical environment in which the behavior takes place
2. The social medium, or patterns of interpersonal relations in which behavior occurs
3. The "person system" or "self-system" of the focal person whose behavior is considered

From the focal person's standpoint, each of these three subsystems has a distinct set of contingencies between products and evaluations. Although there is no intention to anthropomorphize by ascribing "expected behaviors" to the physical and technical environment, from the perspective of the focal persons, the technical requirements of the task represent a set of contingencies that is no less of a sent role than the contingencies that come from others in the social environment. In fact, in highly technical environments, the restrictions of the equipment may demand greater conformity than any of the desires of other individuals with whom the focal persons work. Nevertheless, roles typically have excluded inanimate objects; we shall do the same.

The self-system is a different matter. The person system or self-system has certain contingencies between perceived self-products and self-evaluation. The self-system contingencies constitute a sent role that is an essential part of the role set. Later, we will show that the process by which the individual's self-role impacts on his or her eventual behavior is analogous to that of the sent role of any other role sender. Both provide a pattern of contingencies. Once the focal person behaves, the resulting product is evaluated by each role system. The only difference between the two roles is that, for the individual, the evaluation of products goes on within the focal person. That is, the evaluation is an internal one as opposed to an external evaluation imposed on the individual by others. Rather than place limits on the size of the role set prematurely, we will not attempt to say who does or does not send organizational roles to the role incumbent. We shall only categorize role senders in one of two mutually exclusive sets—the individual and others outside the individual.

In summary, the position taken here is that a role is a vector of perceived product-to-evaluation contingencies. This vector applies to the products to be produced by a focal person. Others beside the individual may hold role expectations, but to influence the focal person's behavior, this person must form a perception of the other's role for him or her. Typically, the focal person's perception of another's product-to-evaluation vector is termed the received role (see Figure 5.1). Finally, the total set of individuals who constitute the set of role senders cannot be specified without some knowledge of the particular situation. However, regardless of the actual members, it can be said that the set contains two subsets—focal person and other. The number and types of others depends upon the degree of heterogeneity among the role senders and upon the setting.

A Classification of Roles

We have mentioned that roles originate from two categories—the focal persons themselves and others in their environment—and that both the perceived roles and the actual behaviors or acts emitted by the focal persons play an important part in the behavior of organizational members. Figure 5.1 presented a simple model of the role process as it relates focal persons to others in their environment. However, the simplicity of the process is deceiving. Complications arise because of a heavy dependence upon focal persons' interpretations of others' wishes as well as upon other individuals' ability to observer and interpret the behaviors of the focal persons. As a result, several sets of roles can be enumerated in any given setting that are important for the effective functioning of the role system. Table 5.1 lists several such roles.

TABLE 5.1
A Classification of Different Types of Roles

Roles	Source	Perceiver
1. Role of other	Other	Other
2. Self role	Focal	Focal
3. Role from other (received role)	Other	Focal
4. Focal role behavior	Focal	Focal and other
5. Observed role behavior —Other	Focal	Other
6. Observed role behavior —Self	Focal	Focal
7. Focal perception of other's observed role behavior	Focal	Focal

The first role of Table 5.1, the role of other, is almost synonymous with
what we have previously described as the sent role. The only difference is
that the role of other makes explicit the fact that another may possess a
vector of contingencies that is the other's perception of the focal person's
role without communicating that role to the focal individual as is implied
from the "sent" notion of the sent role. Obviously, if the role is not sent it
has little chance of influencing the focal person; thus role of other and
sent role of other often are used interchangeably. Nevertheless, since
discrepancies between what the focal person believes others want him or
her to do and what they actually want done may be due to the way in
which the role is sent, there are times one may want to consider the role
itself independent of the sending process.

The second role in the table recognizes the fact that focal persons hold
a role for their own behavior. In an analogous fashion to persons in the
focal person's environment, they evaluate their own products using their
self role and judge their role behavior. Presumably, the self-evaluation
leads to some affective state. The notion of intrinsic motivation is closely
associated with the idea of self-rewarded behavior based upon some
self-evaluation such as this.

The role from other is exactly the same as Katz and Kahn's (1978)
received role. The two terms will be used interchangeably. The important fact to keep in mind about this role is that it exists only within the
perceptual framework of the focal person. In most cases, it will bear a
close correspondence to the role of other but, obviously, it does not have
to be similar. Typical role issues and problems such as the accuracy of the
received role are associated with the degree of similarity between what

others expect of focal persons and what the focal persons believe that others expect. These topics will be addressed later in this chapter.

Focal role behavior represents a qualitative shift from the first three roles discussed. In fact, as was pointed out, it is not a role for it is a set of acts rather than a set of product-to-evaluation contingencies. Nevertheless, it is extremely important, for it represents the inputs to the focal person's and the other's measurement system which leads, in turn, to judgments about the role products that were produced. The products are a necessary input into evaluations of role behavior both by self and by others.

Items 5 and 6 of Table 5.1 recognize that others observe the behavior of the focal persons and, in an analogous fashion, the focal individuals observe their own behavior. Observed role behaviors for others are represented by the feedback loop in Figure 5.1. For individuals, the observed behavior provides some internal feedback.

Item 7 of Table 5.1 is rarely discussed by role theorists, but we believe it is important if roles are to be understood from the focal person's point of view. It represents the focal person's beliefs about what others observed. After the focal person has behaved, the others may respond in a way that the focal person can infer an evaluation. To decide what that evaluation means in terms of behaviors expected by others, the focal person must make some judgment about the behaviors the others observed. These behaviors may or may not be the same ones the focal individual believes he or she emitted, but they are the essential ones for the evaluation to influence the focal person's behavior. Frequently, individuals realize that the others attribute a set of behaviors to them that are different from the ones that they exhibited. Yet, if such persons are to be able to interpret future evaluations and sent roles from these individuals, the focal persons must have ideas about what others believed were their products. The seventh role concept was added to Table 5.1 in recognition of this fact.

We have illustrated a few of the possible combinations that could be generated recognizing the distinction between senders, sources, actual behaviors, and perceived behaviors as well as perceived expectations. Although not complete, the list is sufficient to handle most of the major issues in role behaviors. Later treatment of role concepts will recognize and address the distinctions outlined here.

The Role Process in the Theory

The theory outlined in Chapters 2 and 3 focused upon the individual's choice of an act or a set of acts. How the role is learned by the focal person from members of the role set and how this learned role influences the focal person's choice of acts can now be described. Following the discussion of the learning of roles from others, the self-role and its influence on acts will be discussed.

Development of a Role from Others

Learning Product-to-Evaluation Contingencies

For focal persons to learn the set of product–to–evaluation contingencies others hold for them, some combination of three processes is hypothesized. The simplest of these is *direct communication.* Members of the role set may tell focal persons what it is they are supposed to do. This can be a face to face communication or a standardized job description provided by the others and administered to all focal persons who hold a given role. Open and direct communication of role demands enjoy almost universal acceptance as desirable states of affairs. Unfortunately, such concrete information is provided too infrequently.

In the absence of specific role descriptions from others, focal persons must infer the role they believe others expect of them. This inference takes one of two forms. First, roles may be inferred from observing other persons performing a role. Observations of others' products and the outcomes these others receive allows the focal persons to infer what must be the appropriate behaviors for themselves. This process is termed *modeling* and is a frequent way in which new employees learn their roles (Weiss, 1977). New employees watch others in positions similar to their own. They may make some preliminary judgment of those employees who seem to be doing well, then imitate their behavior. In this way, the role is formed from what they see others doing in the others' own role. The process is indirect because the communication of the role is not directed from the role senders to the focal persons. The role is indirectly communicated through a third party, and focal persons must first judge that the model is an appropriate source of information about what is expected of themselves.

Although roles are learned indirectly through modeling, the process need not be haphazard. Opportunities to model the behavior of others in order to learn a role often are planned carefully. For hundreds of years the skills of craftsmen and artisans were passed on from generation to generation by means of apprenticeships which strongly emphasized modeling. An apprentice learned much of what was to be done by observing the master and trying to imitate or replicate the observed behaviors. Today, many organizations design training programs and select initial job assignments for new employees that provide opportunities for those employees to observe the behaviors of others who have been successful in the roles that the new employees hold or aspire to in the near future.

Roles also are inferred from a combination of the focal persons' knowledge of their own products and by their perception of how they are evaluated by others. With both products and evaluations, the focal persons can imply the product-to-evaluation contingencies of others for them. That is, in the terminology of Figure 5.1, they can infer the received role. This process is a complicated one with numerous opportunities for focal persons to misperceive the intentions of others. Frequently, the role concept is based upon inaccurate and/or incomplete information. As a result, the nature of the received role often is different from that which is sent by the role senders. This fact is accepted readily by those who describe the role process, but much explication seldom is offered for the reasons or the manner of development of these discrepancies. Since the construction of product-to-evaluation contingencies on the basis of inaccurate and/or incomplete information about both products and evaluations occurs frequently, we will devote considerable attention to this process.

In most cases, the first prerequisite for the formation of product-to-evaluation contingencies is a knowledge by the focal persons of the product that they believe others think they have produced. Focal persons may believe others observed (measured) some product of theirs when, in fact, others did not. However, regardless of the accuracy of the focal person's beliefs about the products observed by others, it is the focal individual's belief that will determine the received role.

Figure 5.4 represents an elaboration of the theory as it applies to the learning of the role from other individuals. The boxes, circles, and solid lines of the figure are explicitly represented in the figure of the complete model in Chapter 2, although Figure 5.4 has rearranged the layout to some degree. For example, it begins the cycle with acts and products as inputs, whereas Figure 2.1 treated them as outputs. The top half of Figure 5.4 locates roles for the theory, and the bottom half expands upon the features of the focal person's interpersonal environment that influence the development of the cognition of a received role from others.

Figure 5.4 shows that the focal persons learn what others believe they produce (Box 4 of Figure 5.4) from two sources. First, the focal persons have their own perceptions of the set of products they produced (Box 3). From these they *infer* what they believe to be the products that others observed (line 1a in Figure 5.4). This inference represents the focal

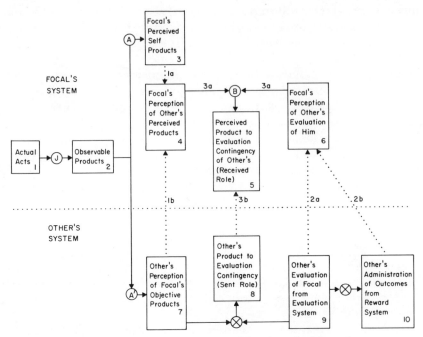

FIGURE 5.4 *Steps in the development of the role received from other.*

persons' translation of products from their own measurement systems
into the measurement systems they believe others possess. As indicated
in Figure 5.4, the focal person's actual products serve as the inputs for
the perceived products. The actual products are converted into perceived products by the focal person's own measurement system. This
process occurs in Circle A as outlined in Figure 5.4. A similar process
occurs for others and is labeled A'.

To form an impression of how others perceive their own products, the
focal persons must make inferences about what products were seen by
others. These inferences rely either upon the direct communication
from others of the products they observed (line 1b of Figure 5.4) or upon
the focal person's inferences about the measurement system used by
others. In the latter case, once focal persons have formed a concept of
what others use as a measurement system, they can translate the products they believe they themselves produced into the products they believe others perceived (line 1a of Figure 5.4).

Frequently the focal persons' perceptions of the products others perceived do not agree with the products actually perceived by others.
Anecdotal evidence abounds with such misperceptions. Yet, the theory

makes clear where these misperceptions lie. Basically, there are two possible areas for error. First, focal persons may inaccurately perceive what others see as their own products. The inaccuracy may occur because focal persons do not know the others' measurement system. Without an accurate perception of the others' measurement system, focal persons will be unable to translate the products they believe they produced into those they believe that others observed (see arrow 1a in Figure 5.4). This failure may occur because the focal persons do not understand how the others weight the products that the focal persons believe they produced, or because the others do not observe the same products as the focal persons do. In the former case, the problem is one of determining the weights assigned to elements used to form products. In the latter case, the element may not exist in the measurement system of the other, even though the focal persons believe others observed it.

Focal persons also may not perceive accurately a direct communication from others about the products the others observed (arrow 1b). For example, defense mechanisms may interfere when others attempt to communicate that they have observed products normally considered inferior. In other cases, focal persons may not have the experience to understand others' attempts to describe the products that they observed. Specifically, it may occur that the measurement system of others applied to the actual products by the process represented by A′ is different from the one applied by a focal person at point A. The results may be products that are so dissimilar that the focal person cannot form an accurate perception of the others' products simply because they do not share a common frame of reference or language. Nevertheless, for most organizational members, especially those who have had some experience on the job, the distortion of direct communication represented by arrow 1b of Figure 5.4 should occur less frequently than distortions that occur through inferences represented by arrow 1a.

Assume for a moment that a perception of others' perceived products has been formed (Box 4 of Figure 5.4). Next, focal persons must form a perception of others' evaluations of them. As indicated in Figure 5.4, this perception results from a combination of one of two sources (arrows 2a and 2b of the figure). First, others may communicate their evaluations of the focal persons directly to them (arrow 2a). Although such direct feedback is frequently recommended, individuals rarely find themselves in situations that provide reliable feedback.

In the absence of such feedback, organization members rely on many different and often invalid cues to infer an evaluation from others, especially if the other is a superior (McCall & DeVries, 1976). We are suggesting in Figure 5.4 that the more frequent cues chosen are the rewards and sanctions the others associate with their evaluations of the focal persons. These rewards or sanctions (outcomes) may be deliberately associated with evaluations, such as promotions based upon merit, or they may be more subtle and perhaps unintended such as the way a supervisor says "good morning." Regardless of the intention, most focal persons who observe such outcomes attribute some level of evaluation to them based upon their belief about the contingency between the outcomes and others' evaluation. Referring to Figure 5.4, the focal persons infer evaluations from their observation of outcomes represented by box 10 from arrow 2b. Direct feedback goes from box 9 to box 6 as indicated in line 2a. Of course, the direct feedback from box 9 may be distorted by the focal persons as the feedback is communicated from the others to the focal persons. Nevertheless, regardless of the accuracy of the evaluation, once some perception about their evaluation by others is formed, the focal persons are in a position to combine the evaluations with their product perceptions to form the concept we have labeled a role from others.

Armed with beliefs about others' perceptions of their products and with others' evaluations of those products, the focal persons have the necessary ingredients to form their received role from others. Figure 5.4 shows that these two sets of information are combined at process circle B and the result is the received role.

This perception of the contingency between a product and an evaluation more than likely develops because of some contiguity between products and evaluations that leads focal persons to attribute some causal relationship between the amount of the product and the favorability of the evaluation. Over time, focal persons have a sample of products they believe they have produced, and they have a sample of evaluations from others. Presumably, to make sense of their world, assumptions are made about how the products influenced the evaluations. The result is a belief about the extent to which each product led to some level of evaluation. That is, an inference is made about the product-to-evaluation contingency.

Phenomenologically, at any one time, each product level rarely is paired with an evaluation level by itself. Individuals generally have an idea of their role performance that represents a single point or a narrow range on the evaluation dimension. With this, they pair several products, each having various levels. For example, an employee may get a higher than average raise, which leads to his or her perception of the evaluation. To form an impression of his or her role, the employee works back from that evaluation to those products believed to be produced in the time period for which the raise represented an evaluation. This process should lead to a perception of contingencies between several products and the evaluation. Yet, to infer the contingencies for many products accurately from this small amount of fallible data is almost impossible.

The learning of roles in this fashion represents the process of multiple cue probability learning as it is frequently investigated by decision theorists. Research on multiple cue probability learning shows that people can learn the contingencies for more than one cue, but the task is not an easy one. Given that the role vector at any time may include several product elements, it is obvious that the accurate learning of such contingencies is extremely difficult.

Many factors contribute to this difficulty. First, focal persons sample a limited set of data to form their evaluation and contingency perceptions. Accurate contingencies depend upon a representative sampling of the product levels and evaluation levels or a random sampling of a relatively large number of product–evaluation pairs. In most settings, the individual gets neither.

It should be pointed out here, that for a given focal person, the number of products and evaluations is probably greater than the ones experienced directly by the individual. We noted earlier that individuals learn roles indirectly by observing others. At that point, we discussed modeling as a means of role learning. These observations of others may be combined with observations of self. That is, for product P, the individual may have one or two product levels, P_{i1} or P_{i2}, which he or she pairs with some evaluation levels. The individual may add to these pairs of product levels with evaluations from others in similar roles. In this way, the number of entries in the set of product level and evaluation couplets from which the individual infers the product-to-evaluation contingency can be greater than the specific individual's own experience. Furthermore, the variance in the product levels and in the evaluations can be greater when observations of others are included, which should improve the individual's ability to form an accurate perception of the product-to-evaluation contingency.

In addition to sampling a limited set of products and evaluations, role perceptions are limited by the fact that role performance data available to focal persons from others often is suspect in most organizations. This makes it extremely difficult to form contingency perceptions. In many settings, it is difficult for the focal persons to receive any feedback about performance. If they do receive some, it is often of poor quality. Low quality feedback has two detrimental effects. First, it makes it difficult for focal persons to form a role performance concept that in turn means that product–evaluation pairs are fewer. As a result, they are not able to form accurate contingency estimates. Second, they may accept the poor feedback or form their own self-impressions of role performance based on limited or inaccurate feedback. This creates a product–evaluation pair, but the contingency that results from it can be no better than the evaluations. Therefore, both the concept of role performance and the contingencies that constitute the role are affected adversely.

Another problem confronting the development of accurate role perceptions is that role settings are extremely fickle in the contingencies they present to individuals. When focal persons perceive that they have produced a given product, the association between that product and a given level of evaluation is not always the same even in the same setting. Consequently, even under conditions when both products and evaluations are available, the individuals have difficulty forming accurate contingencies from sampling their environment.

Regardless of the quality of their observations, the focal persons develop a set of product-to-evaluation contingencies they believe others hold for them. Presumably, this set develops early in their encounter with a new role and guides their role behavior. It remains to be discussed how focal persons use the role from others to influence their behavior on the job.

Phenomenological Role

The focal person's role from others was defined as an estimate of others' product-to-evaluation contingencies. We have implied that the cognitive process by which the role from others influences focal persons is one of weighting products by contingencies to form an evaluation perception. Yet, such a process is too complicated and time consuming to be applied every time role perceptions take place. Behling and Starke (1973) criticized a similar weighting theory of behavior, expectancy theory, for its assumptions about the complexity of human information processing. Our role process is subject to many of the same criticisms.

Perhaps phenomenologically, the individuals simplify the weighting process as they select a set of acts to perform on a day to day, moment by moment basis. But how does this simplification occur? It seems to us, individuals do this by forming sets of products, *not* product-to-evaluation contingencies, which they compare to their perceived products to infer others' evaluation of them. The set of products contains the same products that were contained in the product-to-evaluation set or vector. The difference between the two is that the entries in the set are the *amounts* of the products the focal persons feel are necessary for effective role behavior. In a sense, this vector of amounts of products can be thought of as a set of specific goals the individuals believe others hold for them if they are to perform roles effectively as others see them. We shall call this the

phenomenological role. This role most closely resembles the expected behaviors notion typically encountered in role discussions in the literature
for its elements are specific amounts of particular products.

We are suggesting that the development of the phenomenological role
follows that of the role vector composed of product-to-evaluation contingencies. The product-to-evaluation contingencies tell individuals how
important each product is for role performance. However, these contingencies do not tell them how much of each product they need to be
seen as effective role performers by others. In order to know how much
of each product is needed, focal persons need either to have been evaluated as an effective performer by others or to extrapolate beyond the
range of evaluations they believe they have received to the point where
they believe others would consider their behavior effective. In either
case, they must (*a*) establish a level of evaluation that they believe others
would see as effective; (*b*) consider the contingencies to products; then (*c*)
establish a concept of the amounts of products needed to produce the
given evaluation. Using the symbols presented in Figure 5.3 on page 122,
individuals select some evaluation level for themselves, E_s, which they
believe others do or will see as effective role behavior. They then use the
vector of weights $C_{P_1E_s}$ through $C_{P_KE_s}$ and selected amounts of products
$P_1 \cdots P_k$ that will lead to the desired E_s.

With the introduction of the phenomenological role, it is necessary to
further delineate the process by which individuals arrive at a role concept. One process has already been mentioned. That is, the individual
develops a linear model with *a* products weighted by *b* contingencies
estimating role specific *c* performance evaluation. Yet, the sequence in
which the individual develops each of the three concept sets often does
not follow the functional relationship suggested by the mathematical
nature of the model in which Y (role specific performance evaluation) is a
function of the P_{i_s} (the amounts of the products). Phenomenologically,
individuals often work from E to P rather than from P to E. This is the
case especially when the phenomenological role is developed. Recall that
this role represents a vector of products, P_{i_K}, with the specific values (*k*)
of P scaled in terms of some quantity or amount units. It seems likely that
individuals arrive at the amount of a product needed in their roles by
first having a concept of what is good role performance (that is, by having
a specific value or narrow range of values on the evaluation vector, E).
With the evaluation concept and the contingency for product *i*, they
establish an expected product level *k* for product *i* which represents good
role performance to them. The result is a configuration of products
which the focal persons believe will lead others to evaluate them positively.

Mathematically, such a process as just described is unacceptable. Functions are not transitive—the fact that E is a function of P does not imply that P is a function of E. To individuals this does not matter; they still may operate *as if* it were transitive. The implications of this are quite interesting. If people treat the relationship as transitive, for a given set of contingencies and a specific role evaluation, the phenomenological role is indeterminate. There are many configurations of the product vector that will lead to the same evaluation of role performance. This lack of precision, while disturbing to those of us who would like to predict individual behavior, fits the observed data closely. Frequently individuals on exactly the same job, with nearly identical perceptions of the contingencies between products and evaluation, hold different role expectations. Given the indeterminate nature of the way in which we are suggesting role perceptions evolve, these differing role perceptions need not reflect misperceptions of the job environment. Each can be equally valid roles for a given role setting.

Katz and Kahn's (1978) concept of equifinality is, in part, the organization analogue of what we are suggesting. They point out that equal levels of organizational effectiveness can be observed from different levels of sets of products (using our terminology). We reach the same conclusion at the individual level, although adding that this result apparently develops for focal persons because they begin with an overall evaluation from others or a desired evaluation from others and generate product levels to fit the evaluation. Thus, sets of product levels become templates of acceptable or desired role products and serve as heuristic devices that serve to guide role behavior.

Once the focal persons have a concept of the levels or amounts of products needed, they simply compare their own product levels to those of products they feel others expect. This process is probably a simple matching one that does not require the complex weighting of each product by a contingency, but is based upon some system using the extent to which actual products deviate from expected values. In fact, we would argue that once the phenomenological role vector is formed, the individuals no longer work with the role as defined by the contingenices; on a day-to-day or hour-to-hour basis they operate with their phenomenological role. The latter is conceptually simpler and more concrete. They return to the contingency role only if discrepancies occur in their environment that lead them to doubt whether their phenomenological role is still valid. Because more experience in a role often leads to habitual responses, the role demands from others may have to be quite discrepant from what the focal persons expect for these discrepancies to be noticed.

Given the phenomenological role and the contingency role, the focal persons have two bases on which to predict others' evaluations of them and to guide their acts if they desire to receive a high role evaluation from others. It is suggested that they base their prediction of others' evaluations on both roles—the role from other and the phenomenological role from other. Although the exact mix of the two cannot be specified, let us speculate for a moment. Behling and Starke (1973), among others, have criticized expectancy theory for postulating a process far too complicated to accurately describe what people do to arrive at an evaluation of courses of action. They point out that to consider all products, weight each product by its contingency, and then sum overall products is more than people are capable of or at least willing to do each time they decide on an act or in this case evaluate performance. We sympathize with Behling and Starke's position. Perhaps what focal persons do is form a phenomenological role concept early in their experience in a particular setting through the use of their product-to-evaluation contingencies. After its formation, they rely primarily upon the phenomenological role for evaluation purposes. In this case, the evaluation results from a crude matching of two product vectors to each other: one of them the phenomenological role and the other the perceived products. Such a matching process would be far simpler than the sum of the weighted products. If this were the case, it also would be consistent with the observed phenomenon that after people have been in a setting for some time, they tend to ignore changes in the actual contingencies in the job. Organizational folklore abounds with examples of employees who continue to do things the same old way long after the evaluation system has changed, making that way ineffective. Indeed, we suggest that we know very little about the factors that cause an individual to modify an established and often-used template based upon outdated contingencies. We further suggest that this question may be one of the most important questions needing to be addressed.

Self-Role

Focal persons receive work roles from many persons in their immediate environment both within and outside the organization. They also internalize a role based upon what they expect of themselves in a given setting. This internalized role provides a strong force in guiding individual acts.

The nature of the focal persons' role for themselves, hereafter referred to as the *self-role*, is in many ways the same as that of the role from others. Figure 5.5 depicts the self-role. It is evident from a comparison of

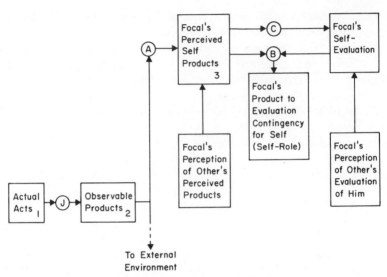

FIGURE 5.5 *Development of self-role.*

Figure 5.4 with Figure 5.5, that the nature of the self-role and the role from others is similar. The self-role represents the product-to-evaluation contingency vector for the self just as was the case for the individual's role from other.

To develop the self-role, Figure 5.5 indicates that individuals must perceive their own products and must have formed a self-evaluation of their role performance. The major input to the latter is the person's own past experience in the role. This experience is not illustrated specifically in the figure, but represents an individual difference contribution at two process points. The primary influence occurs at process circle *C*. With more experience, focal persons should form more accurate perceptions of what is or is not good role performance. Experience also influences the nature of the self-products at point A. At point A, the issue is primarily one of the individuals' measurement system converting the products they themselves produced into perceptions of these products. Experience in the role should act to influence the way in which focal persons actually perceive the results of their own actions.

Figure 5.5 illustrates that self-evaluations are not based solely upon their own internal standards or frames of reference. They also incorporate evaluation information from those external to themselves. Others' evaluations must first be perceived by focal persons as is illustrated in the figure, but once perceived, they can serve as powerful influences upon the focal persons' reliance on external agents to form their own evaluations of themselves. Such things as the credibility of others, the focal persons' past experience in the role, the specificity of the role and its influence on the concreteness of performance standards in the role, as well as individual differences typically labeled personality variables—self-esteem, internal–external control, and field dependent–field independent—are bound to influence the impact of others on self-evaluations. A full discussion of each of these is unnecessary; the only point we wish to make is that others besides the self influence self-evaluations, but the degrees to which such influence occurs is a function of many characteristics of the focal persons, the others, and the physical environment.

Similar to the role development from others, focal persons also develop a *phenomenological self-role*. We argue that their moment-by-moment self-evaluation and actions are guided by the phenomenological role just as was the case with the role from others. Furthermore, the elements in the phenomenological self-role represent the self-set product goals that each focal person intends to accomplish in order to possess a self-concept of an effective role performer. That is, to the focal persons themselves, self-roles represent the standard to which future role behaviors (more specifically, products) will be compared. The comparison will result in some self-evaluation of how well the self-role was met. Therefore, the self-role is a standard or goal to which to compare actual role behaviors through an internal comparison process.

It was pointed out early in our discussion of roles that there were two sets of role senders who, in a sense, communicate roles to focal persons. The first set was composed of all those others with whom the focal persons interact who attempt to influence their behavior. The other set contained one element—the focal person. We have now described the way in which we believe a focal person's perceptions of the roles from each of these sets develop. However, the possession of these role concepts by the focal person is only the beginning; the major concern is how these roles influence acts. In the sections that follow, several of the common concerns of role theorists will be addressed as they relate to the theory.

Role Compliance

Possession of received role concepts both from self and from others is a necessary condition for understanding the role behavior of focal persons. However, the existence of these concepts does not imply that the focal persons will act in accordance with them. In order to comply with the received role, they must possess the necessary skills to perform the acts needed to produce the products of the role, and they must want to perform in line with the role demands. For the moment, assume that the requisite ability for successful role performance exists and address the motivational aspects of role compliance.

With respect to the received role from others at the most elementary level, focal persons should desire to be seen by others as effective role performers to the extent that the focal persons value others' evaluation of them. Therefore, to understand role compliance it is necessary to consider how or under what conditions the evaluations of others become valued by focal persons.

Return for a moment to Figure 5.4. In the lower righthand portion of the figure, it shows that the reward system of others associates certain outcomes with evaluations of the focal persons. The pairing occurs in the process circle between the evaluation box and the outcomes box as drawn in the figure. The outcomes represented in the box can vary from concrete, tangible outcomes such as a raise of a certain percent to obtuse and intangible items such as inclusion as "one of the gang."

From the standpoint of the focal person, one necessary condition for role compliance is the belief that there is some degree of association between others' evaluation of the focal person's role performance and the attainment of outcomes. In other words, focal persons form some hypotheses about the distribution of reinforcements (Dulaney, 1961, 1968) that follow from others' evaluations of the focal persons. These hypotheses or beliefs about the outcomes associated with evaluations (i.e., the outcome–evaluation contingencies), influence intentions to perform the acts the focal persons believe are necessary for them to be viewed as effective performers by others. To the extent that they believe that valued outcomes follow from the evaluation (and/or negative sanctions are avoided) the more positive should be their attitude toward performing acts to produce the role products and the greater their intention to do so (Fishbein and Ajzen, 1975).

Equally as important as the perceived evaluation-to-outcome contingency is for the focal persons to value the outcomes associated with others' evaluation of them. The focal persons must want either to obtain the outcomes associated with others' evaluations or to avoid them in the case of aversive outcomes. If attainment or nonattainment of the outcomes makes no difference to the focal persons, they should not be motivated to perform acts that create products leading to the outcomes. The more the focal persons value the outcomes associated with evaluations from particular others, the more these others possess the capability to influence the behaviors of the focal persons; that is, the more power the others have with respect to the focal individuals.

The view of role behavior with respect to role compliance taken here is essentially one expressed by expectancy theory (Porter & Lawler, 1968; Vroom, 1964). Over the years, the exact formulation of the theory has taken several forms (see Mitchell, 1974, for a review), but all forms maintain as essential elements (*a*) a belief about the association between evaluations and outcomes; and (*b*) the value of those outcomes. With regard to role compliance, we suggest that focal persons attempt to comply with their received role from others to the extent that they believe a contingency exists between others' evaluations of them and the focal persons' receipt of valued outcomes.

The combination of the perceived evaluation-to-outcome contingencies and the degree to which the perceived outcomes are valued by the focal persons represents their perception of others' reward and/or coercive power over them (French & Raven, 1959). Note that the degree to which others possess this power can be determined only from the viewpoint of the focal persons. For, if the focal persons do not value the outcomes of others, these outcomes do not represent rewards or punishments to them, and their behavior will not be guided by actions that they believe will or will not lead to these outcomes. Unless they, the focal persons, believe that their own behavior influences the outcomes they receive from others, compliance with the received role from others should be minimal.

With respect to compliance with a self-role, the process is viewed in the same way. However, due to the nature of the self-role, compliance always is assumed to be the desired state. Recall that we said the self-role represented focal persons' beliefs about what products they themselves should produce. Therefore, it is assumed that this role represents the set of products believed to lead to favorable self-evaluations. The contingency between this evaluation and valued outcomes that focal persons would provide to themselves is, by definition, a strong positive one. If the focal persons believe they should perform certain acts to do what they believe is right, compliance with these beliefs should be seen as a positive or valued state. Therefore, assuming that focal persons have the necessary ability to perform a self-role, it follows that in the absence of constraints from outside the persons, focal persons should always desire to comply with their self-roles.

The final condition that needs to be discussed is the case in which focal persons comply with their own self-role and this compliance represents a conscious rejection of the role from others. For this to occur, we assume that the individuals must see the value of their own evaluation of their role behavior to be greater than the value of the outcomes they perceive they will receive from compliance with the others' role. In this situation, others would possess low power over the focal persons.

It is concluded that the amount of compliance observed to a received role is primarily a function of the degree to which a focal person sees valued rewards following compliance. In general, the greater the amount of rewards perceived to follow from role compliance, the greater the compliance with those persons and the greater their power. The same condition holds for self as an agent although such power is usually referred to as personal control (Deci, 1975) or autonomy, not self-power. However, it must be stressed that the individual is almost always faced with compliance with two or more agents—self versus another or others versus others. Therefore, the extent of compliance to any one agent is a function of the similarity or dissimilarity of role demands from various agents (the degree of compatibility among role senders) and the amount of power each agent has over self.

Role Conflict

In a general sense, role conflict exists when the individuals hold role expectations from more than one source, and they cannot mutually satisfy all expectations. Rarely are individuals confronted with a homogeneous set of role expectations from all others who send roles to them. Most frequently, multiple and often conflicting demands are placed on them. The same individual may be sent a role for productivity as high as possible by a supervisor and a role to work at a slow, steady pace by co-workers. Similarly, the supervisor may expect a report by Monday morning, which requires spending all weekend at the office, and the individual's family may send a role with markedly different expectations for his or her weekend activity.

The role conflict phenomenon has generated a considerable degree of interest because of its pervasiveness and the importance of its consequences both to individuals and to organizations. Kahn, Wolfe, Quinn, and Snoek (1964) found nearly half the work force they studied experienced some form of role conflict and approximately 15% reported that the conflict was frequently serious. There is little reason to suspect that there has been any decrease in the extensiveness of role conflict since the early 1960s; if anything, the pervasiveness of an accelerating rate of change in organizational environments should act to magnify the problem rather than to decrease it.

Important, affective, emotional, behavioral, as well as physiological responses have been found to result from role conflict. Without exception, role conflict has been found to be dissatisfying (Miles, 1975). This negative affective state often leads to or is a part of the experience of stress. Stress can have both behavioral and physiological ramifications.

Undesirable behaviors such as turnover, poor performance, and lack of ability to cope with demands have been reported. Also, physiological correlates of stress such as ulcers and hypertension have been reported (H.E.W. Report, 1972; McGrath, 1970). Frequently, the stress is attributed to role conflict present in many organizational positions (McGrath, 1976).

The model we propose addresses role conflict from the perspective of the individuals. In contrast to our earlier discussions in which the role from others (sent role) was portrayed as a single set of product-to-evaluation contingencies, we now introduce the obvious fact that multiple sets of product-to-evaluation contingencies are sent to focal persons. Often a product in a sent role from one person cannot be accomplished if the product for another person is produced by the individual.

In terms of the definition of roles presented earlier, a potential for role conflict exists when individuals perceive that they have incompatible product-to-evaluation contingencies. Frequently, the incompatible product-to-evaluation contingencies are due to conflicting demands from two or more role senders who send different role expectations to the focal persons. For example, role conflict may be experienced by those whose supervisors expect more time spent on the job and whose families expect more time at home. In this case, the product-to-evaluation contingencies of the received role from supervisors are incompatible with product-to-evaluation contingencies of the role received from the family because of limited time resources of the focal persons.

Role conflict for phenomenological roles also requires incompatibility of role demands. In such cases, focal persons believe that to produce one product would be to inhibit their possibility of being able to produce another product.

Although awareness of contingency and/or product incompatibility is a necessary condition for focal persons to experience conflict, it is not a sufficient one. In order for conflict to be experienced, the outcomes associated with each product must be known. Consider for a moment three different sets of contingencies for the example of conflict between work and family. First, assume that the report the individual's supervisor wanted by Monday is one that the supervisor feels has little value. The focal person knows if it is late, for almost any reason, the supervisor will not mind. On the other hand, his or her family has been planning the weekend outing for some time and everyone would be extremely disappointed if it had to be cancelled. In a second case, assume the same degree of pressure from the family as in the first case, but this time the report is a crucial one for which the supervisor has been waiting anxiously. If it is in by Monday, the individual is sure that his or her chances for an early promotion will be greatly enhanced; if it is late, he or she is equally certain that the promotion will be delayed, at best. Finally, assume that neither the supervisor cared about the report nor the family about the weekend activities.

In all three situations, the individual is faced with incompatible role demands. A choice must be made to select some set of actions which, in all likelihood, will not improve the probability of high evaluations from both sources. Yet, the amount of conflict experienced from the choice of action alternatives certainly is not equal for all three conditions. The second condition clearly represents greater conflict than the first and third, for only in the second condition are valued outcomes associated with failure to comply with either set of role demands. Since compliance with one role sender by definition means a lack of compliance with the other in the example, valued outcomes will be lost regardless of the alternative chosen in the second situation. Such is not as much the case in either the first or third condition.

As the example illustrates, a definition of conflict in terms of incompatible product-to-evaluation contingencies (or incompatible products in the case of phenomenological role) is not complete without some reference to the perceived consequences of role compliance from the focal persons' point of view. In order to consider consequences, focal persons must consider both the evaluation-to-outcome contingencies and the perceived value of the outcomes associated with the evaluations. As McGrath (1976) points out in his discussion of role conflict and stress, the individuals must "care about" the alternatives before the incompatible demands lead to any experienced stress. Therefore, conflict should be greatest when incompatible product-to-evaluation contingencies (or products) are each strongly associated with valued outcomes. In utility terminology, this simply means that conflict is greatest when the individual must choose between two alternatives, both of which have high utility to the individual. Conflict decreases as the utilities of the alternatives become more discrepant. When the utility of either alternative reaches zero for the individual, no conflict should exist even though the product-to-evaluation contingencies are still incompatible.

Conflict as discussed above can also be described with reference to the notion of power. Recall that other individuals were said to possess power (i.e., influence potential) over a particular focal person (a) to the extent that the others established strong contingencies between the focal person's products and the receipt of outcomes from others; and (b) to the extent that the focal person valued these outcomes. Given this view of interpersonal power, role conflict is said to be greatest when powerful others hold incompatible roles for the focal persons, and is least when powerful others hold compatible expectations or when the others differ greatly in the amount of power they hold with respect to the focal person.

Most definitions of role conflict have been limited to the degree of incongruity between product demands from different individuals in the role set and have ignored the evaluation-to-outcome contingency notion as well as the value of the outcomes to the focal person. For example, Katz and Kahn (1978) define role conflict as "the simultaneous occurrence of two or more role expectations such that compliance with one would make compliance with the other more difficult [page 204]." Since definitions of this type ignore the sanctions and rewards associated with each behavior, the lack of rewards may explain several inconsistencies in the role conflict literature.

One such inconsistency is the association between role conflict and job satisfaction. Role conflict is generally found to be associated with dissatisfaction with one or more job facets (Roos & Starke, 1980; Sales, 1969; Tosi, 1971). On the other hand, others such as Rizzo, House, and Lirtzman (1970) and Hamner and Tosi (1974) have found it uncorrelated with satisfaction. A closer look at the latter studies finds that the scale used to measure role conflict, developed by House and Rizzo (1972), defines conflict with such items as "I work under incompatible policies and guidelines," and "I receive incompatible requests from two or more people." Although these are not the only items of the scale, they definitely tap only the incompatibility of expected products of the phenomenological role. Both statements ignore the evaluation-to-outcomes contingencies as well as the value the individual places on the outcomes. According to our definition, these measures contain a necessary but not sufficient condition for role conflict. As a result, there may be situations in which such measures of conflict are uncorrelated with job satisfaction, not because role conflict and satisfaction are unrelated, but because the first measure does not tap the conflict construct sufficiently.

A second discrepancy between other definitions and the one offered here is that frequently researchers have taken both the individual's frame of reference and that of others outside the individual whereas the one offered here deals only with the individual's frame of reference. As an example of the former, Roos and Starke (1980) define role conflict as "contradictory role expectations to which the occupant of one role is exposed—[the] role occupant may or may not perceive these contradictory expectations." The definition is consistent with the typical practice of assessing a role as high or low in conflict independent of the role occupant. We are not denying that most organizations have positions which, from an objective standpoint, place heavy contradictory demands on the individual. For example, a foreman, by virtue of his or her interface between labor and management, is often in a position with high role conflict. Certainly this position has a high potential for intersender conflict. However, unless considered from the viewpoint of a particular foreman in the foreman position, one cannot say role conflict exists for that individual. It may be that a particular foreman is unaware of the conflicting demands being placed on him or her. If so, to say that high role conflict exists would be to suggest that role conflict exists for an individual even if he does not perceive it. Such a position hardly seems justifiable. Certainly, it could not exist without the individual's awareness, given the view of conflict expressed here.

Let us ignore our definition for a moment and pursue the logic of the other one, a definition that defines conflict external to the individual's perception. The latter implies that if there is at least one member of the role set who could reasonably be expected to send roles to the individual that could not be met without jeopardizing the roles sent by others, there is role conflict even (a) when the individual does not perceive the disagreement; or (b) when the other has no rewards or sanctions attached to his role expectations. We suggest that support for such definitions is found often not because the definitions are sufficient but because conditions which present contradictory role demands often are perceived by the focal person, and the conflicting others possess power over the focal person. The frequent occurrence of the latter case along with the contradictory demands from others creates the conflict in such situations. Nevertheless, if the perception of the incompatible contingencies or products and the valued outcomes associated with role compliance were not present, there would not have been role conflict, in our opinion.

We are left with a definition of role conflict that states, for conflict to exist, the individual in the conflict situation must perceive that at least one of the product-to-evaluation contingencies prescribed to his role cannot be accomplished because it is inconsistent with other role products. In addition, the magnitude of the conflict is a function of the contingency between each of the products in question and some valued outcomes. Most likely, the magnitude of the conflict experienced increases as the *difference* between the subjective expected utility of the products in question becomes smaller *and* the absolute level of the subjective expected utility of each increases. That is, conflict is highest when the competing products are both highly valued and about equal in value. It is lowest when the chosen product clearly is perceived as superior to the other or when none of the competing products is valued by the focal person.

Forms of Role Conflict

Given the two basic components described above, it is now possible to distinguish among several forms of role conflict. First, the nature of the conflict varies according to who is sending the role. For example, Katz and Kahn (1978) distinguish between intersender, intrasender, and person–role conflict. In the first case, two persons or sets of persons hold different product-to-evaluation contingencies and therefore demand different products from focal persons. In the second case, the same person in the set requires conflicting products. For example, a focal person's supervisor may require a product that can be accomplished only by going outside normal channels, and at the same time the supervisor may request that his or her subordinates always follow company policy and rules. Under such conditions, neither of the supervisor's role expectations can be met without violating the other. Finally, person–role conflict arises "when role requirements violate the needs, values, or capacities of the focal person" [Katz & Kahn, 1966, page 185]. In terms of the descriptions presented in Table 5.1, person–role conflict is conflict between the self-role and the role from the other (the received role).

Given the two major sources of role senders presented here, self and others, and the fact that conflicting products are often required within the set of sent roles from a single other, four sets of conflict situations are possible from within the perceptual framework of the individual. These are: *self versus self, self versus other,* and *other versus other.* Furthermore, the other versus other condition can be subdivided into two sets. When the same individual is the other, intrasender conflict as described exists. If the others in conflict represents two or more individuals with conflicting role demands, the focal persons are confronted with intersender conflict. Each of these will be discussed in turn. Let us first consider the ways in which contingencies or products can conflict.

Most frequently, role conflict exists because of the time constraints or limitations faced by focal persons. This form of conflict often is called role overload (McGrath, 1976). Usually, focal persons must produce given products within a limited time frame, and all products demanded by role senders cannot be accomplished within that time frame. Thus, the focal person whose job demanded that he or she work all weekend on a report, and whose family wanted to go camping, cannot satisfy both, not because the family is opposed to the behavior of working at the office or because the supervisor is opposed to family camping; it exists only because both cannot be accomplished within the time frame allowed. If the individual were able to alter the time frame (delay the report one week or change the date of the camping trip) the conflict could be resolved. However, altering the time available often is not possible and thus many individuals are overloaded with activities. This overload can be very stressful and frequently has been found to be detrimental to both physical and mental health.

A second form of conflict between products exists when the products are mutually exclusive regardless of the time frame. The supervisors' request to step-up production and the subordinates' request to maintain a steady pace represent such a conflict. Regardless of the time allowed, it is not possible to resolve both of these requests.[1]

The distinction between these two types of conflict is very important, for each implies different modes of conflict resolution. Theoretically, time-pressure conflict could be resolved by extending the time demands of the opposing products in order to meet both sets of expectations. Obviously, such extensions often are not possible, yet some variation of time manipulation is often attempted as a compromise to partially resolve the conflict. Setting priorities and other methods of distributing acts across time is one such method of resolution for role conflict due to limited time. Conflict between mutually exclusive products is more difficult to resolve. There has to be some attempt to modify the expectations of one or both of the role senders (one of which may be the focal persons themselves) or some cognitive re-evaluation on the focal person's part may distort or de-emphasize the extent of the conflict and alter the perceived contingencies or products. It is under this form of conflict that we would anticipate that individuals would be most likely to employ classical defense mechanisms such as denial of inconsistencies or rationalization to handle the conflict.

Figure 5.6 outlines types of conflict in terms of the product and person interrelationships. Each product–person combination presents the sources for and nature of the role conflict but does not reflect the amount of conflict experienced, for as was mentioned earlier, the quantitative dimension varies according to the rewards and sanctions each source brings to bear on its assessment of compliance with the role demands by the focal person. Each form of conflict is depicted in Figure 5.6.

Self versus Self

Within the self role, focal persons often experience conflict among role products they themselves would like to produce. Most frequently, this

1. It should be noted that our distinction between these two types of conflict has been described by Kahn *et al.* (1964) and others (Katz & Kahn, 1966; McGrath, 1976). However, most of the other descriptions have paired the individuals or role senders with the nature

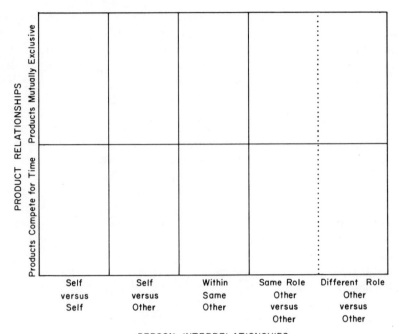

PERSON INTERRELATIONSHIPS

FIGURE 5.6 *Conditions for role conflict.*

conflict is manifested by products they would like to produce to perform their roles effectively but cannot find the time to do all of them well. The college professor who desires professional advancement and attempts to write books, direct a research program, keep up with the current litera-ture, and be an effective classroom teacher cannot maximize all. Such conflict requires that focal persons set goals and priorities that force them to evaluate products and order the products on some utility dimen-sion. Yet, it is often difficult for them to choose one alternative as more important than another. As a result, they experience conflict as they attempt to choose.

Conflict among mutually exclusive self-products is less frequent but exists. In this case, individuals may seek role accomplishment through products that are both desirable, but neither may be possible without jeopardizing the other. For example, an individual may seek to be the best performer among all his or her peers and, at the same time, may want to be well accepted by all of them. Acceptance by all may not be

---

of the conflicting behaviors rather than treat the nature of the behavioral (product) incom-patibility as a separate issue.

possible if the person also is to be seen as clearly superior to those from whom he or she desires acceptance. To the extent that the individual realizes the mutually exclusive nature of the competing products, he or she is likely to find conflict of this form quite disturbing. The ideal resolution of such conflict would be the opportunity to choose neither alternative—in a sense, to leave the field.

Self versus Other

This conflict is quite straightforward. It is what Katz and Kahn (1966) labeled person–role conflict. Again products conflict due to time constraints or their mutually exclusive relationship. Yet, the relative frequency of mutually exclusive products is potentially higher in self versus other conflict than it is in the case of internal conflict within the same person's own frames-of-reference (i.e., than with self versus self-conflict). For self versus other conflict, the value system and needs of the focal persons that shape a self-role often may not fit the role sent to them by others. Classical conflict examples of the needs of the organization for predictable role performance versus the needs of individuals to grow and develop through greater control and freedom of action fit this conflict description (Argyris, 1964).

Within Same Other

A single role sender (or a homogeneous set of role senders) may demand conflicting products from focal persons. Most frequently the products compete for time although they also may be mutually exclusive. In the latter case, the credibility of the other(s) is strained for the focal persons are being presented with contradictory demands.

Time conflict from a single role sender is common and is a frequent cause of role overload (McGrath, 1976). Organizations often define roles in which it is virtually impossible for focal persons assigned to that role to accomplish all that is being demanded to fill the role effectively. In fact, it is not uncommon for the role senders to be aware of the heavy demands of the role that they themselves are making yet they may be unwilling or unable to modify their demands to reduce the degree of role overload.

Internally inconsistent expectations from the same person or set of persons, while less frequent than overload, nevertheless are quite common (Kahn *et al.*, 1964). They occur for several reasons. For example, consider the case mentioned earlier of a supervisor who expects a set of products that only can be accomplished by violating company policy and yet expects compliance with those same policies. Such role demands may occur because the role sender is simply unaware of the fact that the inconsistency exists. Very likely the expectations were sent at different times, and the implications of one set of expectations on the other were never considered by the role sender.

Incompatible role expectations often occur when roles sent orally and behaviorally are in disagreement. Since focal persons will use both verbal and nonverbal behaviors as cues implying what role senders expect, inconsistencies often are noticed by them. The old adage, "Do as I say not as I do" attests to the fact that such inconsistencies have been long recognized in many settings. Again, the role sender often may be unaware of the inconsistency in sent roles simply because he or she may not consider both messages simultaneously.

Role senders are also inconsistent due to the lack of complete rationality on the part of human beings. Cognitive beliefs are compartmentalized, and two inconsistent ones may never be confronted by the individual. Thus, we find codes of conduct for military personnel (really prescribed role behavior) stressing the soldier's duty to evaluate orders and to refuse to follow illegal orders. Such codes evolve out of a justifiable concern for the need for ethical behavior. At the same time, the code is superimposed on a system demanding obedience to superiors (another role behavior). Both behaviors are legitimate concerns but both ignore the reality of the specific case. The line between legal and illegal, ethical and unethical, is nebulous enough that the two role demands may become contradictory. Yet, they both exist, because the role sender rarely considers both simultaneously and each alone appears extremely reasonable.

Other versus Other

The form of conflict most typically considered in an organizational setting is that which involves different members of the set of role senders who require conflicting products from focal persons. Figure 5.6 further divides intersender conflict on the basis of the overall role sent to the focal person. In the first case, both role senders (others) are interested in the same role. Katz and Kahn (1966) referred to this as intersender conflict. Conflict arises because each of the others hold different expectations for the products that will lead to effective role behavior in that given role. For example, both a foreman's supervisor and his or her subordinates are concerned about the behavior in the role of a supervisor. However, each may expect different products from an effective supervisor. As was the case in all the conflict situations discussed earlier, the products from the two sets of others may conflict due to time constraints or due to the mutually exclusive nature of the products. The magnitude of the experienced conflict is a function of the capability of each other to provide valued outcomes and the difference between the two others in their rewarding capabilities (that is, their power over focal persons).

Other versus other conflict regarding the same role is most apparent for those who hold boundary roles (Adams, 1976). Boundary roles occur in positions that require focal persons to work for the organization and yet interface with those outside the organization. A salesman's role is a typical example of a boundary role. Here both the company and the customer hold role expectations and often they conflict. Adams (1976) and his students have frequently demonstrated that these boundary role positions are high in conflict.

The second form of other versus other conflict arises when each of the others is concerned with a focal person's performance of a *different* role, and was termed interrole conflict by Kahn *et al.* (1964). A foreman's supervisor holds a set of expected products for behavior as a foreman. The foreman's spouse sends a set of behavioral expectations to him or her that concern his or her behavior in the role of spouse. In this case, conflict arises as the focal person attempts simultaneous fulfillment of two different roles. Each of the role senders may have little or no concern for how the focal person performs those roles not related to the role in which they are interested. Since every focal person fulfills multiple roles at any given time, conflict among role demands for the various roles frequently arises.

Obviously, conflict among others who hold different role expectations for the focal person can occur when products compete because of time limitations and incompatibility. The latter is more likely than it was when the other was the same person, because neither role sender is faced with any inconsistency. Each role sender may be unaware of the role demands for those concerned about a different role. Other times, both may be aware of role pressures on the focal person, but the nature of their interaction with him requires that they attempt to influence him to meet their role demands rather than someone else's.

Conflict Resolution

The classification system presented in Figure 5.6 is not only useful for descriptions of types of conflict; it also gives guidance for possible conflict resolution strategies. Recall that although role conflict has not been found always to have negative consequences, it never has been found to be a desirable state (Miles, 1975). Therefore, most organizations attempt to reduce role conflict or to create roles with a low level of role conflict.

Figure 5.6 emphasizes that different conflict resolution strategies must be undertaken depending upon the nature of the conflict. For the moment, let us assume that for any given conflict condition, the actors involved in the conflict relationship are relatively fixed; that is, the person relationships are constant. This assumption fits most organizational attempts at conflict resolution; regardless of the conflict-resolution attempt, the same individuals usually have some interest in the focal person's behavior.

The model of Figure 5.6 suggests, for any set of actors, conflict resolution must consider the nature of the product conflict. If the product conflict is time based, role conflict must either alter the time dimension in some fashion or alter the power relationship between agents sending the roles. The simplest time resolution is to expand the time allotted to produce the products making it possible for both roles to be met. In the absence of the freedom to extend deadlines, the more typical solution is the establishment of priorities for products. Obviously, all products cannot be accomplished at any given time and all products do not have the same product-to-evaluation contingencies—that is, are not equally important for successful role performance. Therefore, the conflict between role demands can be reduced by establishing a set of priorities that allow individuals to accomplish those behaviors that are most relevant to each role. The priorities rarely allow all products for every role to be completed, but they do guide behavior so that those products with the largest utility are acted upon first. Setting priorities based on the utility of the product allows for the more important behaviors in each role sender's sent role to be accomplished without expanding the time allotted to role-directed behaviors.

A second and related means for reducing time conflict is to alter the value of the outcomes associated with the sent roles. Such changes can point out more clearly to the individual which products have the highest utility. To the extent that the differences in utilities between products are great, less conflict should be felt when products with low utilities are not accomplished due to time constraints.

To reduce conflict when the products themselves are inconsistent, the options are more limited. Conflict resolution then requires that the perceived sent roles themselves be changed. The focal persons must change the product-to-evaluation contingencies they believe exist between their own products and the other's evaluation of them. This is changing the role per se as we have defined roles. For example, role conflict could be reduced by removing one of the expected products in conflict—that is, no longer requiring that product of persons in that role. Such an action merely reduces the perceived product-to-evaluation contingency to zero for that product. However, to remove expected products from the role is often difficult. The other may be unwilling to alter the contingency. The change is complicated by the fact that the person who expects the product may not be a member of the organization (e.g., the focal person's spouse). It is also difficult if the individual whose role expectation is to be changed is the focal person himself. In that case, it is necessary to change his or her perception of what the role entails. Changing one's own perceptions often is difficult, especially after the expectations have been entrenched through years of experience.

Changes in reward contingencies are subject to many of the same constraints as altering the products. The changes are difficult if not impossible when the other person is not a member of the organization or is the self. For example, those in boundary roles, such as salesmen, face conflicts between company demands for sales and customer demands for honest and open disclosure of the product's performance capabilities. Neither of these two demands can be altered given the interests of each role sender. They are also difficult to change when the person is part of the organization, but the product and/or the person are not normally considered part of the organization's domain. For example, the organization would have little influence over the rewards or sanctions administered to workers by their fellow union members for contributing to a political party.

Reagardless of the ease with which the conflict can be reduced, the model presented suggests which approaches will or will not deal with the components of the conflict. It also emphasizes that simply to label a role as high or low in conflict is of little value. Without knowledge of the nature and the magnitude of the conflict, little can be done to reduce it.

Role Ambiguity

Role ambiguity refers to the fact that the persons holding a given role are uncertain about the products to produce in that role. The uncertainty leads to two undesirable states. First, it decreases the probability that the individuals will fulfill the role by acting appropriately. From the organization's standpoint, this concern is obvious. Second, individuals often experience tension or stress to the extent that they are aware of their uncertainty about what is to be done. The tension or anxiety is increased as they perceive that valued outcomes are associated with successful role performance and realize that they are unsure what is needed in order to be perceived as successful in their role.

In terms of the contingency relationship of products, evaluations, and outcomes, role ambiguity exists when focal persons are uncertain about product-to-evaluation contingencies and are aware of their own uncertainty about them. For negative affective states to exist from this uncertainty, focal persons also need to be relatively certain of the contingency between evaluations and outcomes. They also must value the outcomes to some degree. This means that the individuals believe that some valued outcomes (rewards and/or sanctions) will be awarded by the role senders on the basis of their evaluation of focal persons, but the focal persons are uncertain about what to do to attain positive evaluations.

In general, role ambiguity is highest among new organizational members who have had little or no experience in the role or in similar roles in other organizations (Hall, 1976). With experience, the ambiguity decreases. With time they have more opportunities to learn product-to-evaluation contingencies. Role ambiguity is also correlated with levels in the organization such that higher level positions are more ambiguous than lower ones (House, 1971). In higher level positions, the product-to-evaluation contingencies are less well understood by all persons simply because the tasks are often abstract and can be accomplished in many different ways.

If focal persons are uncertain of others' product-to-evaluation contingencies (they experience role ambiguity for roles sent from others), they may or may not be uncertain as to the product-to-evaluation contingencies for their own self-role. In fact, they may be quite certain of the products needed in order to perform effectively with regard to their own view of the role. For example, they may have had considerable experience in the role and have formed firm beliefs about what is needed to do a good job. At the same time, it may be unclear to them what others expect them to do. This lack of clarity occurs because of the failure of others to communicate their role expectations to the focal person either directly or indirectly by means that were discussed earlier under the topic of the acquisition of product-to-evaluation contingencies. In any event, the focal persons in this situation experience role ambiguity with regard to others to the extent that they, the focal persons, are aware of their own lack of knowledge of what products others expect of them for effective performance. The ambiguity should arouse negative affect in the focal persons only if they value the outcomes they perceive others would administer to them if they were to perform effectively in the others' eyes. If the focal persons did not value others' rewards, they would not feel dissatisfaction assuming that they were confident of their self-roles.

Many times, conditions that create role ambiguity with respect to others' role for focal persons also lead the focal persons to be uncertain about their self-roles. If the focal persons have had little experience in the roles, they often look to others for information on which to build their perceptions of their self-roles. Therefore, uncertainty about what others expect of them makes them uncertain about what they should produce to satisfy their own self-evaluations. Ambiguity under this condition should lead to dissatisfaction because they are unable to produce products which lead to valued rewards either from others or from themselves.

To reduce role ambiguity, the organization must communicate the product-to-evaluation contingencies to focal persons. This can be done directly through feedback about the products, and through communicating the contingencies by telling the role incumbents the way the organization values certain products they have or have not produced. It also may be done indirectly through rewards for products or through modeling. All of these processes have been discussed in detail earlier as we dealt with the development of role perceptions.

Before leaving the subject of role ambiguity, it should be pointed out that individuals with the same degree of uncertainty about product-to-evaluation contingencies may experience different levels of ambiguity due to differences in tolerance for uncertainty. It has been demonstrated frequently that people differ in their tolerance for uncertainty or their need for clarity. As a result, some people may not find it unsettling to find themselves in situations in which the stakes are high but the guides for directing their behavior are few. Role ambiguity is simply a subjective state involving the interaction between the job setting and the individual in it. It cannot be defined without consideration of both.

Role Negotiation

The discussion of roles up to this point has implied that others hold certain role expectations that they send to focal persons, and the focal persons do or do not respond to their demands. The expected products or roles were considered givens and we addressed the question of how these became part of the focal person's perceptual system. The process implies that focal persons are passive recipients of the expectations of others; they merely decide whether or not to accept or reject these expectations. It is time we question and qualify such a passive view of the focal persons.

Obviously, focal persons often are anything but passive in their interaction with those who have some interest in their behavior. Graen and his colleagues (Dansereau, Graen & Haga, 1975; Graen, 1976) refer to the early stages of the encounter between focal persons and other role senders in an organizational setting as role negotiation rather than role learning to emphasize the fact that focal persons attempt to establish others' role expectations in a manner compatible with what they believe their role should be. They do not sit by and passively accept the products others want them to produce; they actively attempt to establish *others'* expectations for them so that their probability of successful role performance as seen by others is enhanced. Presumably, the individual has some idea of his or her own strengths and weaknesses and attempts to remold the role to take advantage of them.

Although we have not mentioned the dynamic interaction between focal persons and others as it influences the others' perception of roles for focal persons, support for such an interaction is frequently discussed (Graen, 1976; Hall, 1971; Hall & Schneider, 1973; Kahn *et al.*, 1964; Katz & Kahn, 1966). The model presented here does not preclude or exclude such a possibility. However, since the focus is upon the perceptions of focal persons rather than on those of others, we have been more concerned with how focal persons learn others' roles.

Obviously, the direction of influence goes both ways. Since products of the focal persons are fed back to others when they are measured by others, the others must then evaluate the products. The evaluation occurs as the others apply their evaluation system to the measured products. This process is illustrated in the model of Figure 2.1 as that of the environment because of the fact that it occurs external to the person in question. But by what standard is the behavior evaluated? Obviously, the others' evaluation is some complex mixture of an absolute standard and a relative one, the latter considering the idiosyncratic nature of the focal persons as perceived by the others. Through conscious as well as unconscious behaviors, the focal persons influence the evaluations they receive by the frame-of-reference they present to the others. For example, the product of a go-cart is evaluated differently if the focal person is an 11-year-old boy than if the focal person is his father. Likewise, if the focal person says the go-cart was made to "look good" versus to "go fast" he or she will influence the evaluation to the extent that the other now judges the product according to the focal person's intentions. Similarly, focal persons actively interact with others in most role settings to establish the others' evaluation system in a way that is consistent with their strengths. The active, purposive, interaction between focal persons and those who send them roles represents the negotiation phase of role behavior and is a part of almost all role episodes.

Although it seems likely that role negotiation behavior tapers off over time in a role, it is not clear how long such behavior persists. Most certainly the length of the negotiation phase varies for different situations and in many cases may never really cease. Yet Graen's research (Dansereau, Graen, & Haga, 1975) shows that very early in socialization of new organizational members, relatively permanent roles are established for them. They found that as early as three months after being on the job, new members were seen as active informal assistants to the supervisors with expanded roles requiring many extra products and greater responsibility, or their roles were to produce standard products with few enlightening exceptions.

Concluding Remarks

Roles have been and only can be considered cognitive structures within the belief systems of individuals. As such, it should not be surprising that a theory such as ours would view the role notion as an extremely important one. In this chapter, we have stressed the importance of roles by devoting considerable space to the development of a definition of roles, role constructs, the processes associated with the learning of roles, and the influence of roles on behavior. Of necessity, these constructs and processes were complex. However, as was done with several other processes described in this book, we offer the following qualification. While the role process as described is a complicated one, it is often simplified by individuals in their day-to-day display of role behavior. In the case of roles, phenomenological roles along with habitual responses made with little cognitive evaluation of these responses provide such a simplification process. Thus, individuals' beliefs either about expected product sets or sets of product-to-evaluation contingencies for themselves or for others provide the bases for the selection of behaviors to display in organizations.

6

Motivation

Motivation has received considerable conceptual treatment as a process fundamental to organizational psychology. There are a variety of theories of work motivation that have been proposed, and a considerable literature exists that has attempted to evaluate these theories empirically. This is appropriate if it is believed that understanding motivation is a necessary prerequisite to understanding behavior in organizations. We subscribe to the centrality of the motivation process, and have therefore attempted to develop this aspect of the theory rather fully.

In this chapter, what we mean by motivation will be defined and general conceptual issues relating to it will be discussed. We shall then show how the theory deals with the motivation process. Finally, a point that has been raised in several previous chapters, namely, that people use simplifying strategies allowing them to deal with the complicated process of allocating their resources will be further developed.

Defining Motivation

Motivation has been defined in many ways, but as Campbell and Pritchard (1976) have pointed out, motivation generally deals in an operational sense with the amplitude and direction of behavior. That is, it deals with *which* behaviors are emitted (direction) and the vigor or *intensity* (amplitude) with which these behaviors are emitted. Our approach includes the amplitude and direction components but becomes more specific. For us, *motivation is defined as the process of allocating personal resources in the form of time and energy to various acts in such a way that the anticipated affect resulting from these acts is maximized.*

159

This definition is very important, and we need to trace its components. The definition makes it clear that we are talking about *acts*. That is, motivation deals with the behaviors emitted by the person. It does not deal directly with the results of that behavior (the products) or the evaluation of that behavior (performance). In Chapter 1 we defined an act as the process of doing something. We said that an act is characterized by a direction and a level of commitment. The direction is the specific act that is being emitted such as typing, meeting with a customer, or planning a project. Commitment refers to the level (amount) of personal resources devoted to the act, and is composed of both a level of effort and a time factor. Level of effort is the energy or vigor with which the act is done and the time factor refers to how long the act is done. The combination of effort and time, then, defines the amount of the person's resources devoted to the act (i.e., the commitment devoted to the act).

It should therefore be clear from the definition of motivation that we are talking about a *resource allocation process*. The motivation process is one whereby the person takes the time and effort resources at his or her disposal and uses or distributes these resources to the various acts he or she could emit. In fact, the term resource allocation strategy might be more appropriate. We see the person as consciously committing these resources in a goal-directed manner; the resource allocation strategy is far from random. As we discussed earlier, a person has cognitive control over both the amount of time he or she devotes to a given act, and the effort or energy level with which that act is done. In addition, the person has cognitive control (choice) over which acts are actually done. What we are saying here is that the motivation process is one whereby a person more or less consciously develops and uses a strategy for committing time and energy resources to a wide variety of acts.

Turning once again to the definition, we assume that the resource allocation strategy is carried out with the objective of *maximizing anticipated affect*. This has several important implications. First, motivation is clearly a future-oriented concept. It is the anticipation of future states that is involved in the determination of the resource allocation strategy. It is only through understanding the person's expectations of the future in terms of perceived contingencies, outcomes, and the anticipated affect associated with these outcomes that we can really explain motivation. This is not to say, of course, that past history and present states are not ultimately related to motivation. Clearly, the knowledge of contingencies, awareness of potential outcomes, and the anticipated affect of outcomes all have a strong learning component based on prior experience with the environment. Furthermore, anticipated affect (i.e., valence of outcomes), is partially determined by the current level of need deprivation. These past and present events and states influence perceptions of anticipated events, and perceptions of these anticipated events are the most immediate determinants of motivation.

Anticipated affect is the criterion by which the person evolves the resource allocation strategy. Ultimately, motivational force comes from needs, and from the temporary need state. As we pointed out earlier, needs in combination with currently received outcomes lead to the temporary need state. This temporary need state is the current level of deprivation–satisfaction, and is need-specific. It is the temporary need state and the current level of affect which form the basis of the affect anticipated for future outcomes.

The definition also states that the individual will *maximize* anticipated affect. One might argue that a person rarely maximizes, but rather uses some satisficing strategy.

It is true that from an outside observer's point of view, a particular strategy might not produce maximum affect. However, it is not the outside observer's perspective that influences the person's behavior. It is the person's own perspective. From the person's point of view, given the personal cost of expending time and energy resources, it may not be worth expending resources on an act, even though expending these resources will result in more positive outcomes. It may be that cost of expending the needed resources is seen as too great for the outcome. Put more precisely, there is greater anticipated affect for engaging in some other behavior, even though engaging in the original behavior would produce some positive affect. Thus, from the person's perspective, he or she *is* maximizing the total anticipated affect that will result from behaving. Therefore, it is axiomatic that the individual always attempts to maximize affect.

There is a final issue about our definition that has been implied, but needs to be stated more clearly. This is the issue of time perspective. When we speak of the resource allocation process, we are implying a patterning of acts with their associated commitment levels over time. In the utilization of the resource allocation strategy, the person does not merely think about what he or she will do in the next few minutes. The person uses a longer time frame. This could be a morning, a day, a week, or a month. We would speculate that the more complex the job, the longer the time frame is. We suggest that the time frame variable is an ID characteristic that may be fairly stable for a given individual in a given situation and may constitute an important but not well explored motivation parameter. In any event, the person uses some time frame, fixed or variable, and the motivation process is one of allocating resources to different acts within this time frame. One major implication of this time frame is that we cannot easily predict what a person will do at any given time.[1] Whereas in theory it would be possible to do this, the amount of knowledge required by an outside observer would have to be incredibly extensive. In fact, in most situations, the person probably cannot predict it himself or herself. A simple example of this issue would be one in which a manager is sitting at her desk working on a report and intends to do so until it is completed. However, her superior asks for some information and she stops working on the report and seeks out the information.

In this example, being able to make moment-to-moment predictions about what the manager will do is essentially impossible, and probably not very important. What we do want to understand and predict is, over some time period, how much of her personal resources the manager commits to working on the report (or possibly reports in general) and how much of her resources she devotes over time to providing her superiors with needed information. Thus, this time perspective in our approach to motivation suggests that we want to predict the pattern of commitment to acts during some specified time period, not for any specific moment.

Commitment

Before turning to the motivation process as described by the theory, several points need clarification to understand our conceptualization of the process. The first issue is how commitment to acts may be conceptualized. We stated in Chapter 1 that a person rarely exerts his or her maximum effort. While a person may do this for very brief moments, such moments are atypical "emergency" situations; thus exertion of maximum effort occurs very infrequently. Thus, in the broader conceptualization of commitment that includes both effort and time, a person rarely exhibits maximum possible commitment to an act. This was implied in Chapter 1 where the notion of general level of activation was introduced as the ratio C_T/C_M where C_T is total commitment to all acts, both trivial and relevant, and C_M is maximum possible commitment. This general level of activation shows wide individual differences. Some people talk, walk, and work faster than others; they seem to operate at a higher level of energy expenditure than others. This characteristic level of arousal undoubtedly has both physiological and psychological bases, people do seem to rather reliably differ in arousal.

It is interesting to speculate on the stability of this arousal level within people and the implications of this stability. It may well be that for a

1. It is one thing to discuss how X resources will be distributed across K acts during time T. It is quite another to attempt to also predict the ordering of the K acts during T.

given person, this characteristic level of arousal or energy expenditure is rather stable, at least within a given situation. For example, if you are highly motivated to read this chapter, do you read faster than if you are not highly motivated? It may be that reading speed is rather stable within a person, and that it takes a very large change in the motivational state to alter this behavior. A more accurate view of changes in the level of motivation is that it is reflected in the level of efficiency of behavior. Specifically, the change is in the ratio C_r/C_T where $C_r + C_t = C_T$ and where C_r is the commitment to relevant acts and C_t is commitment to trivial acts. One might argue that variations in the level of motivation have their effects on commitment by altering this efficiency ratio by changes in C_r rather than by changing actual level of energy devoted to the act at a single instant in time (C_T). If you are highly motivated to read this chapter, you will not read the words faster when you read, but you will spend a higher proportion of time actually reading as opposed to daydreaming, thinking about what you are going to do for lunch, and so on. This is a subtle but important distinction. We are suggesting that the energy level (C_T) is fairly constant for a given person, and variations in motivation do not typically result in variations in the energy expended in a given moment. Further, we suggest that increases in motivation to do an act are often reflected in the elimination of trivial acts from the behavior sequence through time and an increase in the time spent on the relevant act(s). Thus, under high levels of motivation, the frequency and duration of irrelevant acts decreases. Although we cannot lose sight of the fact that variations in levels of motivation also can be reflected in the amount of time the person spends doing the act (e.g., whether he or she spends 1, 2, or 3 hours reading), the argument suggests that the other influence of variations in motivation is on the efficiency ratio, not on the momentary effort level utilized while doing the relevant act.

The implications from this line of reasoning are important. It suggests that a person's characteristic level of arousal may be quite stable in a given situation (e.g., a job context). To the extent that it is stable, increasing the motivation level of an individual does not increase speed or effort. Rather, such an increase in motivation is reflected in the person choosing to increase the proportion of relevant to irrelevant acts. While this will have the effect of increasing the total effort committed to the relevant act over a given period of time, the person has not increased his or her total effort or commitment level. The person has merely redi- rected that commitment to different, more relevant, acts. Thus, there has been a shift in the personal resource allocation pattern, but no change in the total resources committed. This suggests that often the real issue of changing motivation is one of changing *direction* of behavior, not amplitude of behavior. This is a very different conceptualization than most motivation theories. Most theories imply that by increasing motivation you increase effort on the task. While it may be true that *in a given time interval* the person has exerted more effort to task relevant acts, our position is that the overall level of time and effort commitment has not changed, but that the commitment has been reallocated in a more task-efficient manner.

We are *not* saying that overall commitment to acts will never vary. Clearly, there are daily, even hourly, variations in commitment level due to fatigue, mood, illness, distractions in the environment, and so on. One can deliberately modify the overall commitment level. The important point is that influences on the total commitment level are not typically cognitive and thus are not intentional in the sense of being deliberately "set" or established by the individual, whereas noncognitive variables influence the total commitment available to the person at a given time. They can act as a constraint on behavior much the same way as environment constraints influence the acts produced by the person. These constraints are noncognitive sources of influence on the level of commitment expressed as the amount of time spent doing the act and the proportion of relevant to irrelevant acts emitted.

There is another issue inherent in a discussion of commitment. We suggested that the characteristic arousal level (the ratio of total commitment to relevant acts to maximum possible commitment) is fairly stable. While it will vary in unusual or emergency situations, and be influenced by nonintentional factors such as illness, or mood, the cognitive or intentional factors influencing total commitment do not vary a great deal. This point applies to the momentary energy expenditure level displayed while doing an individual act, as well as to the total level (C_T) of commitment. A person has only so much energy that he or she is willing to expend throughout the day. Therefore, from the organization's point of view, it makes sense to deal with the amount of that energy devoted to organizationally relevant acts and the amount devoted to organizationally irrelevant acts during a fixed time period. We are not speaking here about behavioral efficiency at work. Although that is a manifestation of the same issue, we are speaking now of a somewhat more molar resource allocation process; of the amount of total resources the person is willing to commit to the organization. If we conceptualize the person as having a relatively fixed amount of energy resources or potential commitment, the question is what proportion of that total pool is allocated to the organization and what proportion to sources such as family, recreation, etc. The resource allocation process is one in which the total resources committed to each of these areas is related to the product-to-evaluation and evaluation-to-outcome contingencies the person perceives as characterizing the outcome allocation strategies of evaluators in these different environments, and the value of the outcomes controlled by these evaluators.

To summarize, in the motivation process, we are dealing with a resource allocation process where commitment in the form of time and effort is distributed across acts. The directional component is fairly straightforward; the person selects given acts to emit. The person has control over this choice. The level of commitment issue is more complex. The total level of commitment to all acts is seen as a function of characteristic levels of arousal (C_T/C_M), which are fairly stable for a given individual, and factors beyond the person's direct control such as illness, fatigue, and situational factors. It is possible to alter intentionally this total level of commitment, but it is probably difficult to do. Given a total pool of commitment resources, the person can choose what proportion will be expended in the work situation and what proportions will be expended elsewhere. Thus, variations in work motivation are reflected in the total amount of commitment allocated to work-related acts. The second area where variations in motivational commitment appear is related to the first. Our view implies that variations in commitment on the job will be reflected not as much in the speed or energy level expended in doing the act for a given moment, but in the efficiency of behavior as expressed by the ratio of task relevant to task irrelevant acts over a fixed time frame.[2] In essence, then, even when we speak of changes in level of commitment, we are still speaking of a choice of direction of behavior. In the first case we are speaking of choosing to devote more or less time to work as opposed to nonwork contexts. In the second case, we are speaking of choosing to engage in task-relevant as opposed to task-irrelevant acts while at work. This analysis suggests that at least within one individual, motivation does not operate to influence momentary effort level. It is entirely reflected in direction of behavior. It is only when we look at the results of these choices in direction of behavior over some specified time period, and summarize, for example, the proportion of time spent on a task relevant act that we can speak of effort, amplitude, or commitment.

In addition to this discussion of commitment, one final issue of a more general nature should be raised. This issue deals with what the person can control in the behavioral process and what he or she cannot control.

2. While we have argued that on some tasks people may not vary the momentary amount of effort they expend, it is true that in some situations individuals working on a task will vary their "speed" or their effort (i.e., they work faster or harder) from one moment to the next. However, such peaks and valleys are not particularly important and we view commitment in terms of an average performance level on the task over time.

The only things the person really controls are the levels of time and energy directed to different acts. A person can select which acts to engage in and decide the level of time and energy to devote to the acts. But in the process of performing, that is *all* the person can directly control. He or she does not have direct control over the influences involved in the translation of those products to evaluated performance. Observable products are influenced by environmental constraints and fairly fixed individual difference factors such as ability. Actual performance implies measurement and evaluation systems in which, at least for the external or objective systems, the person has little or no input. As Terborg (1978) has argued, looking at performance as a dependent variable and using measures of cognitive or affective states to predict it is adding a great deal of error variance that must, by the nature of the process involved, decrease the accuracy of predictions. The implication of this point is a simple one. If we wish to understand behavior, we should study behavior, not the consequences of behavior or the evaluation of the consequences of that behavior.

The Motivation Process

Having stated our view of the motivation process, particularly as it relates to the general notion of commitment, we will locate and describe the motivation process as proposed in the theory described in Chapter 2. The major constructs associated directly with the motivation process (Figure 2.1) are basic needs, temporary need state–arousal, and affect, all of which feed into valence of outcomes; the three sets of contingencies, plus the utility of products, utility of acts, and the resulting actual acts.

Valence or Anticipated Affect

First tracing the determinants of valance of outcomes, we stated from Chapter 2 that the perceived outcomes set is composed of all outcomes that have been received or are seen as potentially occurring in the person's environment. These represent the outcomes to which valences will be attached in process point E. The actual level of valences (i.e., anticipated affect) for a given outcome is attached to each of these outcomes at the E process point.

This level of anticipated affect for a given outcome is determined by the joint effects of the temporary need state–arousal and the level of affect. Temporary need state–arousal reflects the current level of satisfaction of the basic needs. The foundation for the motivation process comes from basic needs as they influence the temporary need state. However, this influence is moderated by a whole series of cognitive processing events before it affects behavior. The temporary need state is need specific in that it reflects the current, temporary level of satisfaction–dissatisfaction of the separate basic needs. To the extent that a basic need is not satisfied, need-specific arousal occurs, which produces a type of motivational force. The greater the dissatisfaction, the greater the force; and the more important the basic need, the greater the force. This need-specific arousal influences valence of outcomes. A given outcome satisfies certain needs and not others. That is, a given outcome such as a promotion may have the effect of increasing the satisfaction of "needs" such as self-esteem, recognition, achievement, status, and possibly financial needs.[3] Furthermore, based on past reinforcement history and verbally mediated contingencies, the person has a sense of which needs a given outcome is going to relate to. The valence of a given outcome will be related to how well that outcome is seen as satisfying different needs in terms of its influence upon the level of satisfaction–dissatisfaction of these needs. Thus, the temporary need state influences valence by making a given outcome more or less attractive due to the level of current deprivation of the needs that outcome satisfies.

The outcome component involved in the formation of valence of outcomes is affect. Recall that we are referring here to affect which is outcome-specific and is associated with outcomes that have already been received. It reflects the notion expressed previously that past experience with the affect produced by a given outcome influences the anticipated level of affect that that outcome will produce in the future. We are saying that the amount of affect ($\pm$) associated with a received outcome can influence an individual's perception of the future attractiveness of that outcome independently of its influence through the subsequent modification of the temporary need state.

Another issue becomes relevant here; one we have mentioned in earlier chapters—the concept of job satisfaction. Job satisfaction has received an enormous amount of attention in the industrial–organizational literature. Locke (1975), for example, counted several thousand studies

---

3. Although we take the position that need deprivation is need specific and for purposes of discussion, use labels such as self-esteem, or achievement for individual needs, we do not argue that some set of fixed needs that are invariant across individuals exist. Specifying and attaching labels to types and kinds of needs is an endless and often circular process. Specific needs always must be operationally defined in terms of needs for things, and these things can be any object or concept, real or imagined, on the part of an individual. We can, for convenience, group these things into categories. Such categorization processes are arbitrary and there is no adequate criterion for saying that one categorization scheme is any better than any other except the criterion of the "needs" of the user of the system.

dealing with measuring satisfaction, looking at factors which affect it, and relating it to behavior. In our view, satisfaction is included in the notion of affect. That is, it is the result of the individual taking outcomes that have been received and evaluating them on a pleasant–unpleasant continuum. The affect produced by this process is job satisfaction. It is a past-oriented concept rather than a future-oriented one.

It should be clear from the theory as stated that job satisfaction should not have a direct influence on behavior. It is true that affect (satisfaction) is one source of influence on valence of outcomes. But even valence of outcomes must be combined with the three sets of contingencies before one can even start to predict behavior.

Thus, it is not surprising that satisfaction has been found not to correlate with performance (e.g., Vroom, 1964). We would not expect satisfaction to show much relationship to actual acts because of indirect causal linkages involved. If we consider that performance is the result of an organizational measurement and evaluation process, the link is even more distant.

Thus, from the conceptual approach represented by the theory, it does not make sense to predict satisfaction–performance relationships. Using satisfaction to predict *any* behavior is bound to result in low to zero relationships. A more fruitful approach is to deal with anticipated outcomes and contingencies in the prediction of behavior.

A good example is the work done on turnover (Porter & Steers, 1973). Here we find low but significant relationships between satisfaction and turnover. We argue that this relationship occurs because, in most organizations, the reward system is fairly constant. Thus, past outcomes are a good predictor of future outcomes. Consequently, satisfaction is related to anticipated outcomes. The contingencies are relatively simple. If the person stays in the organization, he or she will receive well known levels of outcomes. If he or she leaves, he or she will not. Thus, because the contingencies are clear and strong, and past outcomes predict future outcomes, some relationship between satisfaction and turnover should appear.

However, a better strategy for exploring the relationship is to deal directly with anticipated outcomes and their associated valence and the perceived contingencies. We can also consider the resource allocation idea presented earlier, and discussed more fully later in the chapter. That is, the person is choosing between staying in the present job versus going to another job. The resource allocation notion suggests that we need to measure the valences and contingencies of this other job and compare the motivational force towards staying on the present job with the motivational force for moving to the other job. According to the theory, this should enhance our ability to predict turnover.

Temporary Need State

Before continuing our presentation of the motivation process, we need to digress to explain the operation of needs and the temporary need state. In our discussion of the underlying mechanisms of needs, we do not imply a simple deprivation model. This simple deprivation model suggests that the longer the time between rewards related to a specific need, the greater the deprivation of that need, and the greater the arousal. This model is probably a reasonable one when we speak of water or food deprivation in animals; but for humans, the experienced need deprivation is more cognitively determined.

The simple deprivation model is not descriptive of the operation of human needs in several respects. The basic point is that there is not a simple linear relationship between time of last reward and level of deprivation for the need in question. There are several ways in which this simple relationship does not hold. One way has to do with time and perception of time on the part of the person. Since people anticipate the future, and much of their behavior results from anticipation of future events, time and time sequencing of events in the future become important. One effect of this time notion is to break down the simple relationship between level of current reward and anticipated value of future reward. The simple need model discussed previously suggests that an organism which is satiated on a given need (e.g., food) would not be attracted to food. Or, more precisely, food would not serve as a reinforcer in that situation. The simple model does not hold for humans in that humans know that even though they are full at a given time, they will be hungry later. Thus, because of anticipation of future states of deprivation, a person will still value an outcome that is related to needs that are totally satisfied at a given time. For example, the manager who just received a promotion will still value the next promotion and engage in activities to obtain that promotion even when the current promotion-related needs are satisfied.

A person has a sense of anticipated time schedule of future outcomes. That is, the person anticipates that certain outcomes need to occur on some regular basis. These outcomes could be pay raises, recognition, promotion, food, or sex. The person will then behave in such a way as to keep these outcomes occurring on that more or less regular basis. Thus, even though an outcome has just occurred, and the temporary need state related to that outcome is low, the person will still have a positive valence for that outcome recurring in the future on the same schedule.

Another way in which the simple model of need deprivation does not describe the operation of complex human needs is that in some circumstances the receipt of an outcome may actually increase the strength of the need rather than decrease it. For example, as Porter and Lawler (1968) point out, increasing the level of autonomy or variety on a job may lead to stronger needs *for these outcomes.* One could argue that in this case a novel outcome is presented to the person which he or she anticipated as resulting in neutral affect but which in fact produces strong positive affect. The person then attaches a strong positive valence to this outcome. Thus, the level of need did not change, but the person sees receiving positive affect if that outcome were to be obtained where no affect would have been anticipated earlier. Whereas this is probably a more reasonable interpretation than that of changing needs, it still has the effect of complicating the simple deprivation model in that the awarding of an outcome leads to an increase in the attractiveness of that outcome rather than to a decrease.

Contingencies

The next set of constructs in the motivation process is the contingencies: act-to-product, product-to-evaluation, and evaluation-to-outcome. These three sets of perceived contingencies are formed at process point B, and are the result of cognitive processing of the basic set of perceptions. Each of these three contingencies is formed in three different ways. The first is through pairings of events. For example, when a certain evaluation is repeatedly followed by a certain outcome or set of outcomes, the contingency is formed. This environmental pairing is the most generally accepted mechanism for the forming of contingencies. In most settings, however, this mechanism may be a poor and even nonfunctional way for a person to acquire a belief or cognition about the relationship between two events. Typically, the time between such evaluations and the resulting outcomes is lengthy. Further, the evaluation may not be easily available to the individual. Similar problems exist with the lags between products and evaluations. Therefore, the formation of perceived contingency relationships through perception on the part of the individual of repeated instances in which one event is followed, or associated with, some other event, may be less frequent than we would intuitively believe.

Contingencies can also be formed through verbal mediation and through modeling. Verbally mediated contingencies are formed when a credible other formally or informally tells the person about environmental relationships. This credible other may be a coworker who informs a new employee that the supervisor demands that reports be turned in on time, but doesn't worry about what time you start work in the morning. The third way of acquiring knowledge about contingencies, modeling, can occur when, for example, the person deduces appropriate behavior from observing the behavior of others in the environment. In all three of these contingency-formation mechanisms, it is important to understand that the contingencies are formed from the person's interaction with the environment. Although a considerable amount of cognitive processing typically is going on in the person, the basic information for this processing comes from the environment.

These contingencies influence the motivation process in two ways. The first way is to influence utility of products and utility of acts. The second way is limited to product-to-evaluation contingencies, where these contingencies form the systems for self and others' evaluations.

Contingencies in the Motivation Process

Before we can proceed with the discussion of the role of contingencies in the motivation process, we must first adopt a more specific working definition of the term. In Chapter 3, we discussed the general nature of contingencies from the viewpoint of judgment. Expansion of this notion leads to the development of the notion of motivational force; and specifically, how contingencies influence the motivation process.

Contingencies typically are thought of as probabilities (Mitchell, 1974). Thus, we can speak of the probability that a given level of a product will result in a given evaluation, and the probability that a given evaluation will lead to a given level of an outcome. At first glance, this seems reasonable, but it presents a number of difficulties. The greatest is that the number of probabilities in a given situation quickly becomes large. Suppose, we wished to consider three outcomes: a pay raise with three levels (5%, 10%, 15%); feeling of personal accomplishment with three levels; and recognition with three levels. Suppose further that there are three levels of evaluation, and three levels of the product. Such a situation would call for 27 evaluation-to-outcome probabilities and nine product-to-evaluation probabilities. A more realistic situation would be 10 outcomes with five levels each, five levels of evaluation, and five levels of the product. This would result in 250 evaluation-to-outcome probabilities and 25 product-to-evaluation probabilities. The magnitude of the difficulty becomes even more apparent when we consider that this large number of probabilities would be associated with a *single* product for a *single* evaluator. If there are 20 products and four evaluators, we are rapidly drowning in a sea of probabilities. We all know how unpleasant that can be.

Another way of conceptualizing a contingency relationship between several levels of two variables is to view the total pattern of individual probabilities as an overall relationship. If we assume that both variables are continuous, not discrete (i.e., possess an underlying measurement continuum), we can describe this overall relationship in terms of (a) its form; and (b) the degree to which that form provides an adequate "fit" to the total pattern. Since the variables of concern to us at this point are indeed all continuous variables, we will define contingencies in this manner to develop our subsequent discussion of the motivational process.[4] First, clarification of a few points concerning relationships is necessary before proceeding to the theoretical development.

The Form of a Relationship

It is essential to realize that many different functions can describe the fundamental shape or trend pattern of a relationship between two variables X and Y. That is, the general equation $Y = f(x)$ can obviously take many specific mathematical forms, such as

$$Y = a + bx \qquad \text{linear}$$
$$Y = ax^b \qquad \text{parabolic–hyperbolic}$$
$$Y = ae^{bx} \qquad \text{exponential}$$
$$Y = a + bx + cx^2 \qquad \text{parabolic arc}$$

where the specifics of the function are provided by the values of the parameters a, b, and c. In subsequent sections of this chapter, we will be attending primarily if not exclusively to this characteristic of the relationships between the variables with which we are concerned. That is, our development of the motivation process will focus primarily on the underlying functions of relationships in discussing how individuals use these relationships.

The Fit of the Relationship

Contingency relationships in the theory are probabilistic. By using function forms to describe probabilistic relationships, we remove the indeterminism. Although we do this for the sake of convenience in the sections that follow, we want to point out that all these functions may be viewed as fits to probabilistic data. Thus the individual functions are probabilistic rather than deterministic and the degree of their probabilism may be expressed by a formal measure (such as least squares) of

4. The variables involved are: (a) the amount of resources an individual commits to an act; (b) the amount (and/or quality) of a product produced; (c) the degree of favorableness of a perceived evaluation judgment based upon an individual's produced products; (d) the amount of the outcome perceived as being received; (e) valence of outcomes; (f) utility of products, and (g) utility of acts.

their degree of fit to the data forming the relationship. This point is important, since we do not, in the discussion that follows, concern ourselves with the degree to which individual functions fit the data, but deal only with the forms themselves. This means that we are assuming implicitly that when individuals deal with contingencies, they do so on the basis of their perceptions of the underlying function form and are not particularly influenced by their perceptions about the amount of error or uncertainty associated with that perception. This may be a dangerous and even erroneous assumption. Although ample evidence exists that individuals can and do learn the two characteristics of form and fit of a relationship separately and perhaps at different rates (e.g., see Björkman, 1967; Naylor & Clark, 1968), there is no clear evidence that cues are utilized more on the basis of perceived function form than on degree of fit.

In short, our position is that the degree of relationship between the variables of interest is of secondary importance, and that the critical aspect of the relationship is the form of its function.

Examples

The relationship between the amount of a product and the evaluation of the product can be thought of in terms of a function relating amount of the product to favorableness of the evaluation. Figure 6.1 presents a number of examples of different functional relationships. The first set are act-to-product contingency relationships involving the relationship between the amount of personal resources (i.e., time and energy) devoted or committed to the act and the level of quantity and quality of the product produced. In example A, a positive linear relationship is shown, such that changes in the personal resources committed to the act result in large changes in the amount of the product. Example B is a situation in which a positive, linear relationship where, due to situational or task constraints, changes in resources result in smaller changes in the amount of the product. In example C, there is no functional relationship. No matter how much is committed to the act, the product will not be perceived as being produced in any quantity. This could happen due to perceived inability to produce the product, task difficulties, or extreme situational constraints. In examples A, B, and C, the function starts at zero on the product axis. This reflects the fact that when no resources are committed to the act, none of the product will be produced; a situation that will not always be the case. In many situations, (e.g., D) the person may be able to influence the level of a product by acts, but some level of the product will be produced without any commitment on his or her part.

I. Act-to-Product Relationships, Where X = Product, C = Commitment, and X = f(C)

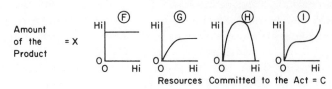

Amount
of the   = X
Product

Resources Committed to the Act = C

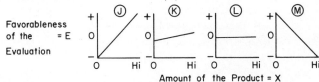

Amount
of the   = X
Product

Resources Committed to the Act = C

II. Product-to-Evaluation Relationships, Where E = Evaluation, X = Product, and E = f(X)

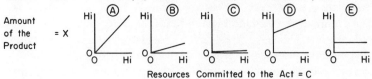

Favorableness
of the   = E
Evaluation

Amount of the Product = X

Favorableness
of the   = E
Evaluation

Amount of the Product = X

III. Evaluation-to-Outcome Relationships, Where O = Outcome, E = Evaluation, and O = f(E)

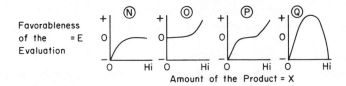

Level
of the   = O
Outcome

Favorableness of the Evaluation = E

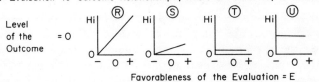

Level
of the   = O
Outcome

Favorableness of the Evaluation = E

FIGURE 6.1 *Some examples of contingency functional relationships.*

For example, in a group task where individual inputs are not separately evaluated, the group may produce some level of the product without any resources from one group member. This type of contingency may be particularly characteristic of a leader where the contingency is between the leader's acts and the products produced by subordinates.

It could also be the case that the relationship between the person's level of acts and a product is zero, but the actual level of the product may be low, as in example E, or high, as in example F. These two examples typify situations where a person's acts have no effect on the amount of the product produced. As in example D, this would frequently occur in group or leadership situations where the product produced is through some group effort. For example, the supervisor of a low performing group may feel he or she has no power to control the behavior of subordinates, is not backed up in attempts to discipline individuals, and cannot get the necessary resources to do the work. In this case, there is no relationship seen between the supervisor's acts and the level of performance of the group. Possibly, the group is a high performing group and performs at top level no matter what the supervisor does.

Examples G–I represent nonlinear contingency relationships. In example G, a person perceives that increases in personal resources have an impact on the level of the product up to some point, but beyond that point, increased commitment results in no change in the level of the product. This is a common type of contingency, particularly in more complex jobs. It is characterized by situations where a minimal level of effort or time is essential for the product, but the investment of substantial amounts of effort or time is not productive. For example, it is essential that the supervisor keep subordinates informed about decisions, but not every decision or every detail about the circumstances of a decision. The extreme form of such a contingency would be a step function, where the act must be emitted to produce the product, but once it is emitted, no variability in the level of the product results. For example, the supervisor may need to send a copy of the minutes of a meeting to a superior, but it is either done or not done. There is no variability in the quality or quantity of the product of sending the copy. Example H is a typical inverted U function relating commitment to level of product, where extreme levels of commitment (e.g., effort) result in less of the product. In most organizational settings, the likelihood of reaching a level of effort required to achieve a reduction of the quality level of the product is probably rare. A more common situation is one in which a person is so immersed in a specific task that the task becomes more complex than it really is, which has a negative effect on the product. Faculty who deal with graduate students writing papers for seminars will attest to the existence of this apparent relationship. The last example of an act-to-product contingency is situation I. Here there is a positive linear relationship between commitment to the act and the level of the product for very low levels of commitment and very high levels of commitment, but no relationship for intermediate levels of commitment. This is a common type of relationship for act-to-product relationships as well as for the other two types of contingencies. This is a situation where some minimal level of commitment of resources results in an average level of the product, but producing a higher level of the product requires a great deal of resources. For example, with a minimal level of effort, the salesperson can contact steady customers and obtain an adequate level of sales. An increase in this level of sales requires a great deal of time and effort devoted to contacting potential customers, most of whom will not buy. It is only when this contacting of new customers is done frequently and over a long period of time that any substantial increase in sales occurs.

The second set of examples in Figure 6.1 are product-to-evaluation relationships. Here the functional relationship is between the amount of the product produced and the favorableness of the evaluation. Amount of the product varies from zero to a high level of quantity and quality; favorableness varies from highly negative, through zero, to highly positive.

Examples J–M depict linear relationships. In example J, we see a positive relationship between the product and the evaluation of that product. When none of the product is produced, a highly negative evaluation results. When a large amount of the product is produced, there is a highly positive evaluation. Example K is a positive linear relationship, but it has less slope than example J. That is, in K, large variations in the product result in small variations in the evaluation. Thus the product in J is perceived as being an important product, whereas the product in K is perceived as less important. The most extreme form of low level of importance would be example L, where there is no apparent relationship between the amount of the product and the evaluation. This product is simply not evaluated, or within the range of levels of the product that could be generated by the person in that situation, no differential evaluation is perceived as occurring. In example M, a negative linear relationship exists between the level of the product and the favorableness of the evaluation.

Examples N–Q represent nonlinear relationships. In N, some level of the product must be produced to avoid a negative evaluation of that product, but producing more of the product does not result in a favorable or positive evaluation. This is a common type of perceived relationship for routine or easy tasks in a job. For example, a secretary is expected to take messages accurately; if the task is accomplished, it does not result in a favorable or positive evaluation. That is, it is atypical for a person to say that their secretary takes messages accurately. It is only when the secretary does not take messages accurately that an actual evaluation takes place. In example O, we see a situation where low levels of the product do not result in a differential evaluation, but higher levels of the product show a positive linear relationship with a favorable evaluation. This type of contingency relationship occurs for products that are not really expected by the evaluator, and while their absence does not produce a negative evaluation, their presence is considered highly desirable. For example, long-range planning by an entry-level manager may be evaluated positively, but lack of long-range planning is not seen as negative. Example P is a type of relationship that occurs frequently. It is characterized by a situation in which low levels of the product relate to the negative end of the favorableness dimension, and high levels of the product relate to the favorable end of the favorableness dimension. There is a range of intermediate product levels that exhibit little or no relationship with the evaluation. This situation would be characteristic of a product of intermediate importance to the evaluator; if little of it is done by the individual, it is seen as negative, if a great deal of it is done, this is positive, but unless these extremes are reached, no evaluation occurs. Such a situation would be likely to occur for products that are expected by the evaluator but are only moderately difficult. For example, a college professor who is a very poor teacher would be evaluated negatively; while an outstanding teacher would be evaluated positively. Most teachers fall in the large middle range, and no differential evaluation takes place. The evaluator tends to be sensitive only to substantial deviations from some normative standard.

The last example of a product-to-outcome contingency is the inverted U function in example Q. Here we have a situation where low levels of the product are evaluated negatively, intermediate levels positively, and high levels negatively. This would be the case where a certain product is desired, but too much of it is negative. For example, the supervisor may be expected to be friendly with subordinates, but extremely frequent socializing on the job is seen as negative.

The last set of sample contingencies in Figure 6.1 deals with perceived evaluation-to-outcome contingencies. Here we are relating the favorableness of the evaluation to the level of an outcome. Recall from our previous discussion that when we speak of product-to-evaluation contingencies, the evaluation in question is for that specific product. If the product is sales volume, we are speaking of the judged favorableness of a given level of sales volume. In contrast, when we speak of evaluation-to-outcome contingencies, we are referring to a more global evaluation of overall performance on a set of performance dimensions. This composite evaluation is a function of a composite of specific different products weighted according to their importance. This importance weighting may be viewed as the product-to-evaluation contingency, which may be defined more specifically in this instance in terms of the strength of the function describing that relationship.

Examples R–U depict linear relationships. In example R, large changes in the evaluation result in large changes in the level of the outcome received. In example S, there is a positive relationship in that large changes in the favorableness of the evaluation result in very small changes in the level of the outcome. A zero relationship is depicted in example T. Here none of the outcome is received no matter what the evaluation. This would be a situation in which the outcome allocator had no control over the outcome or never gives the outcome under any circumstances. The first line supervisor with no control over pay or raise level would be an example of the former case. The supervisor who never gave recognition for positive performance would be an example of the second case.

Situation U is an example in which there is no apparent relationship between favorableness of the evaluation and level of the outcome, but some minimum level of the outcome is always received. In the example, an average level of the outcome is depicted typically as being received, but the actual level could be anywhere from low to high. This type of contingency relationship is common and describes what we have previously referred to as the nonreactive characteristics of the environment. That is, the outcomes come from the environment, but the level received is not a function of the individual's behavior. Examples that typically would be nonreactive include pay levels for hourly employees, across-the-board pay raises, physical working conditions, ability of supervisors and co-workers, and physical location of the workplace. Example U would also be characteristic of a random reward system, where the level of outcome varies greatly, but is not perceived as being based on the favorableness of the evaluation. Repeated experiences where the perceived evaluation varies but the level of outcome follows no apparent pattern would lead to a perception of a random contingency.

Examples V–X depict some typical nonlinear relationships. In situation V, neutral to negative evaluations result in none of the outcome being received, but if the evaluation is above neutral, a linear relationship exists. This would represent a situation where the outcome allocator expects at least adequate performance (neutral) and only awards the outcome for performance above the adequate level. The probability of promotion to a higher position might follow such a pattern. Self-administered feelings of accomplishment would be another example if the person awarded himself or herself the outcome of a feeling of accomplishment for good performance but accurately or inaccurately attributed poorer performance to factors beyond his or her control. In that case, poor performance would not result in a feeling of personal failure. In example W, there is a positive relationship between favorableness of the evaluation and level of the outcome at the low end of the favorableness continuum, but no relationship from neutral to the positive end. This relationship would be characteristic of a situation where performance was expected to be adequate or above, and the outcome in question is removed to a greater extent as performance diminishes. An example would be one in which poor performers received the worst offices, parking places, etc., but adequate to good performers were allocated offices and parking places randomly. Example X shows a situation in which very low and very high levels of favorableness of evaluation show a positive relationship with level of outcome, but for the large middle range there is no relationship. Such a case would be the supervisor who gives feedback and recognition only to the extremely poor or extremely good performers. Another example would be promotion and demotion in organizations where both occur infrequently.

The above discussion of act-to-product, product-to-evaluation, and evaluation-outcome relationships is considerably detailed to illustrate, for each type of contingency, the variety of different functional relationships that may be present. We hope that this clarifies the nature of contingency relationships; they can and do take many different functional forms. They are frequently nonlinear and therefore form complex cognitive constructs for individuals.

The ability of people to utilize probabilistic information having different underlying functional relationships has received a substantial amount of research attention. The emerging picture is not a simple one. Complex functions have been investigated by several researchers. Wiggens and Hoffman (1968) demonstrated people's ability to use multiplicative, or interactive, cue–criterion relationships. Hammond and Summers (1965) and Summers and Hammond (1966) showed that complex (sine) functions are more difficult to learn than linear functions. Naylor and Carroll (1969) studied parabolic functions and showed that individuals first learned the lower order components of the function such as position and slope and were much slower in learning the highest order component of rate of change of slope. Brehmer (1974) has proposed a "hypothesis sampling strategy" which argues that people tend to assume the simpler (linear) functions represent reality and then substitute, or modify, this assumption with more complex functions only if necessary.

Einhorn (1970, 1971) examined the ability of people to utilize parabolic (or what he calls "disjunctive") and hyperbolic (what he calls "conjunctive") functions in making their judgments. That is, do the actual predictions of people of the amount of some Y variable based upon the known amount of some X variable conform to functions other than a simple linear one? Einhorn demonstrated that they often did. However, these results were not supported by Goldberg (1971). These findings are of some relevance to the issue of simplification strategies or "heuristics" which is dealt with later in the chapter and will be referred to again.

In summary, the apparently safe conclusions are several. First, people can learn and successfully utilize nonlinear functional relationships. Second, the more complex the function, the more difficult it is to learn and (perhaps) the more easily its use becomes disrupted under stress. Third, people appear to believe initially (or assume as if) relationships are linear, probably since a linear model (either positive, negative, or both) provides an adequate first approximation to most of the more complex functions.

This discussion, and that to follow, does not imply that the only way people learn contingencies is through repeated observations of points along the function. We have repeatedly mentioned that verbally mediated contingencies and modeling are heavily involved. In fact, we would argue that verbally mediated contingencies are probably the most common form of learning contingency relationships. A supervisor or co-worker can verbally describe even a complex, nonlinear function very easily, and the individual can learn it almost instantly.

Factors Influencing Perceptions of Contingency Relationships

We have described our notions of contingencies as functional relationships. We have not been quite as specific about the factors that influence perceptions of the shape or magnitude of these contingencies. In general terms, perceptions of contingency relationships result from a process of the person interacting with the environment. Discussion of certain specific factors that influence the actual nature of perceived contingencies is necessary at this point.

One set of factors that will influence all of the contingencies is individual differences. We pointed out in Chapter 2 that we assumed individual differences were operating at each process point in the theory. Clearly, this applies to the formation of contingencies. Such an individual difference factor influencing contingencies generally would be the level of conceptual skill of the individual. Some people make inferences about the nature of complex environments more easily than others. This could be related to abstract reasoning ability, cognitive complexity, or other abilities that enable the individual to process effectively complex information. Another factor deals with preference or ability to be analytical. More analytical individuals attempt to understand courses of events whether those events are their own behavior or that of others. A person with this sort of ability–preference would have a richer set of perceived contingencies that are probably more complex and more accurate than a person who did not have this analytical ability.

Also, personality factors probably are involved. For example, some individuals are optimistic, whereas others are pessimistic. This personality factor would increase or decrease the perceived strength of a contingency when the product, evaluation, or outcome in question was desirable. A second example of a personality factor might be locus of control. Individuals high in external locus of control would tend to see events in their environment occurring due to factors beyond their control. Such a cognitive set could lower perceived contingencies and possibly incline the individual to be less interested in learning contingencies in a complex situation. Regretably, there is not a great deal of information about the specific relationship of ID variables to the formation and utilization of contingency relationships. Carroll and Maxwell (1979), in a review of ID differences in cognitive abilities, made the following pessimistic statement about individual differences in quantitatively related behavior: "One can continue to assume that the Number factor represents degree of practice and retention of basic arithmetic skills; still largely unknown is whether individuals differ in the extent to which they can develop these skills [p. 618]."

Other factors that influence contingency perceptions are experience (Slovic & Lichtenstein, 1971) and the complexity of the environment (Dudycha & Naylor, 1966). Both of these factors influence the accuracy of perceived contingencies. The greater the experience in a situation, the larger the data base from which perceptions of contingencies are formed, and other things being equal, the more accurate the *perceptions* of contingencies.

This finding is almost universal in research related to the formation of perception of contingency relationships (Slovic & Lichtenstein, 1971). However, not so straightforward are the data concerning the way people actually use contingency relationships as they become more skilled. Certainly, most learning studies indicate that with increased experience, such as more and more trials with feedback, people substantially improve their actual performance in tasks requiring the use of contingency relationships. But there is also considerable evidence accumulating that individuals supposedly possessing highly accurate perceptions of the true contingency relationships (i.e., "experts") often perform no better—and sometimes even do worse—than nonexperts (Slovic, Fischhoff & Lichtenstein, 1977; Staël von Holstein, 1972).

The complexity of the environment is also an important factor. It is more difficult to form accurate perceptions of contingencies in more complex environments (Dudycha & Naylor, 1966; Peterson, Hammond, & Summers, 1965). A middle manager in a fast-growing organization with complex and sometimes competing role demands is in an environment where contingencies are complex and may change rapidly. This is a much more difficult environment for forming accurate contingencies than, for example, an assembler in a machine-paced operation.

In addition to the general factors that might influence people's perceptions of contingency types, there are also certain factors likely to influence perceptions of specific contingency types. It is likely that an individual's perceptions of his or her act-to-product contingencies would be markedly affected by the ability level of that individual, since ability is usually a prime determinant of the actual act-to-product contingency. In general, the greater the ability of the person, the stronger the act-to-product contingencies. People of low self-perceived ability will see that in a number of situations, increases in the personal resources of time and effort do not lead to production of more of the product or a product of better quality. Task difficulty is another such constraining factor. Tasks that are either very easy or very difficult would, in general, result in lower act-to-product contingencies. For easy tasks, only low levels of personal resources are required to do the task, and committing greater levels of resources may not result in more or better products. For difficult tasks, the reverse may be true in that low or moderate levels of personal resources do not result in the product being generated. Only when very high levels of personal resources are committed is the product generated. If the task is of intermediate difficulty, large variations in personal resources are more likely to result in large variations in the amount and quality of the product. In general, the presence of constraints either on acts or on the translation of acts to products lowers perceived act-to-product contingencies. If the person is working with faulty equipment, cannot get the resources needed, is hampered by the timeliness of others' products needed to produce his or her own products, act-to-product contingencies would be lowered.

Finally, feedback will influence act-to-product contingencies.[5] The

5. We have distinguished elsewhere between evaluative and nonevaluative feedback. Nonevaluative feedback is information about amount or quality of products that does not place these products on a normative good–bad continuum. When products are placed on a

type of feedback that would have the most effect on act-to-product contingencies is nonevaluative feedback. To develop a perceived relationship between acts and products, the individual must know how much of the product he–she produced. Without this information, it is impossible to form any accurate act-to-product contingencies.

There are also some factors likely to influence product-to-evaluation contingencies. Role clarity is one. We are referring to the knowledge the person has about tasks he or she is expected to perform or, more precisely, the products he or she is expected to produce. The person needs to know what products are expected, the priorities among these products, and expected levels of performance of these products. Without this information, accurate product-to-evaluation contingencies cannot be formed. The second factor is the presence of feedback, in this case both nonevaluative and evaluative feedback. The person needs to know both the amount of the products already produced and the evaluation that has been made of these products. Both kinds of feedback are necessary for the formation of accurate contingencies.

Evaluation-to-outcome contingencies are also affected by feedback, but in this case we are referring to evaluative feedback. Knowledge of the evaluation is necessary to be able to accurately perceive the connections between evaluation and outcome. Clarity of outcome delivery is also involved here. In some cases it may not be clear that a unique outcome has been received, or, in a comparative sense, how much of the outcome has been received. For example, the person who has been assigned to a particularly important task may not perceive that this is an outcome that is a function of a highly favorable evaluation on the part of a supervisor. Another example might be a manager who receives a pay raise but has no knowledge of what others have received. In this situation, the lack of comparison information may lead to an incorrect evaluation of how good the pay raise actually is.

Intrinsic and Extrinsic Motivation

We will digress slightly to deal with the notion of intrinsic and extrinsic motivation. This idea has been dealt with at length in the basic psychology literature (cf. Cofer & Appley, 1964) as well as in the industrial–

---

normative good–bad continuum, we speak of evaluative feedback. For example, if a keypunch operator is informed through a machine counter or other source that he or she generated 90,000 keystrokes that day, this would be nonevaluative feedback. If the supervisor told the operator that he or she felt that this level of performance was outstanding, it would be evaluative feedback.

organizational literature (e.g., Deci, 1975; Hackman & Lawler, 1972; Hackman & Oldham, 1976; Porter & Lawler, 1968; Turner & Lawrence, 1965).

Although there have been a number of conceptualizations of intrinsic and extrinsic motivation, the approach developed in our theory is based on the source of the outcome. If the outcome comes from the environment we speak of extrinsic outcomes. If it is generated by the person, we speak of intrinsic outcomes. Thus, outcomes like pay raises, working conditions, or even supervisory recognition are extrinsic because the source is the person's environment. When received, the person makes a judgment of their relative and absolute amount, and some level of affect is attached to perception of this amount.

In the case of intrinsic outcomes, the outcome is, in a sense, produced by the person. As we mentioned in Chapter 2, there are two qualitatively different processes by which these intrinsic outcomes produce affect. The first is based on the self-evaluation. When the person's own products are perceived, the person applies these to the self-role (the product-to-evaluation contingencies for self) to arrive at a self-evaluation. This self-evaluation is the person's perception of his or her performance relative to the self-role. As a result of the self-evaluation, the person gives himself or herself outcomes. Normally, we think of these outcomes as being related to a sense of accomplishment or achievement following a positive self-evaluation, and disappointment or shame following a negative self-evaluation. Thus, in the first internally mediated process, the intrinsic outcomes are contingent on the performance, as evaluated by the person.

The second process by which intrinsic outcomes are formed does not go through any self-evaluation process, but as we discussed in Chapter 2, derives fairly directly from the act itself. That is, certain acts are inherently positive or negative to a given individual. Some acts may be pleasurable, fun, exciting, interesting, or they may be painful, unpleasant, or boring. Thus, the contingency in question for this second intrinsic process is one in which the greater the amount of the act (within limits) the greater the affect that is produced.

With this distinction between intrinsic and extrinsic outcomes in mind, we can now define *extrinsic motivation* as motivational force that is ultimately tied to extrinsic outcomes and *intrinsic motivation* as motivational force that is ultimately tied to intrinsic outcomes. More precisely, the person can anticipate both intrinsic and extrinsic outcomes and these outcomes have anticipated valence associated with them. When these valences are combined with the contingencies, motivational force (which will be defined more completely later in this chapter) is produced. Motivational force that is tied to extrinsic outcomes is extrinsic motivation, whereas motivational force that is tied to intrinsic outcomes is intrinsic motivation.

It is also important to remember the distinction between the two types of intrinsic motivation. Attempts to increase performance through job enrichment or intrinsic motivation techniques (Hackman & Oldham, 1976; Herzberg, Mausner, & Snyderman, 1959; Turner & Lawrence, 1965) are essentially attempting to change the job so that the person has stronger contingencies between his or her own evaluation of performance and the affect the person awards himself or herself. For example, increasing autonomy would be predicted to raise these contingencies; giving performance feedback better enables the person to make the self-evaluation necessary to award himself or herself the outcome.

Such approaches to intrinsic motivation do not deal with the other intrinsic outcome process. That is, they do not attempt to somehow make the job fun or pleasurable. This is probably not feasible in most jobs, and even if it was, our approach implies that a person would enjoy the job more, but there would be no reason to expect an increase in performance on the job.

Valence of Outcomes

The next concept in the motivation process is valence of outcomes. We have said previously that valence of outcomes is the anticipated affect associated with potential future outcomes. The outcomes that are considered are those coming from the perceived outcome set (the heavy arrow going to process point E) which includes both outcomes received in the past and outcomes that could be received in the future. Anticipated affect is attached to or associated with these outcomes as a function of the temporary need state and the immediate affective state of the individual. The temporary need state is the source from which the outcome obtains its motivating properties. That is, the ultimate source of motivating power is the needs; these operate through the temporary need state, and the temporary need state influences the anticipated affect of a future outcome. As was pointed out earlier, the temporary need state does not operate on a simple deprivation model, particularly because of time perspective, but at any time, some level of need influences the anticipated attractiveness of outcomes. The other source of influence is immediate or present affect. The actual affect that has been experienced in the past with a given outcome will influence the anticipated attractiveness of that outcome. This source of influence also includes the social comparison process and expectation notions influencing affect.

That is, previous expectations and what others have received will influence the anticipated attractiveness of an outcome to the individual.

We need to be more specific about the meaning of valence. Typically, the valence of an outcome has been thought of as the attraction or importance of a given type of outcome. For example, one could speak of the importance or attractiveness of pay, co-worker approval, promotion, or supervisory recognition. In the example of pay, to say that pay is an attractive outcome to a person says very little, since it would be rare indeed for pay not to be positive. One could deal with pay in a comparative sense by saying that pay is more attractive to person A than to person B, or that pay for person A is more attractive than co-worker approval for that person. While this is better, it still is not particularly useful, since the attractiveness of the outcome depends on the level of the outcome received. Thus, while pay may be more attractive to person A than to person B in general, person B could easily find a pay raise of 15% more attractive than person A finds a pay raise of 8%. To make comparative statements that one type of outcome is more important to one person than to another, or that one type of outcome is more important to a given person than another type of outcome, involves calibrating or averaging attractiveness of different levels of outcome to obtain some summary value. This summary value is not particularly useful, since it gives little information about the motivational properties of the outcome for the individual.

Because of the prevalence of this type of problem, another approach dealing with specific levels of the outcome has been used. With this approach one could compare the attractiveness of pay level 1 to that of pay level 2 for a person, or pay level 1 for person A with pay level 1 for person B. However, a use of multiple levels of outcomes also has its problems. If one talks about attractiveness of different levels of the same outcome within the same person, within the range of possible outcome levels generally available, it will typically be found that more of the outcome is more attractive. How these valences of outcome levels are combined with the other constructs in the motivation model to predict behavior must be specified.

Comparing the attractiveness of a given level of an outcome for a person with the same level of outcome for another person can also be misleading. If person A finds a given level of a pay raise more attractive than does person B, one could predict that person A will be more highly motivated than will person B to obtain the raise. However, it could be the case that for person A, any level of raise is equally attractive. Person A merely wants concrete recognition from the organization. Given his–her financial situation, the actual dollar amount is not that important. For person B, the dollar amount is very important. Thus, a small raise would be much less attractive than a large raise. Therefore, if one asked the attractiveness of a small raise, person A would say it is more attractive than would person B. However, if one asked the attractiveness of a large raise, person B would indicate a greater valence than A. In this type of situation, it is clear that one could not ask the valence of a single level of the outcome, since differences in the attractiveness of different levels of the outcome is the more important issue. If person A does not have strongly differing valences for increasing levels of the raise, whereas person B does, we would expect person B to be more motivated by pay raises. That is, difference in raise levels make a real difference to person B, but not to person A.

The real issue here is: In what way do outcomes, or more specifically, valences of outcomes obtain their motivating properties? Once this is clear, implications emerge for the conceptualization of valence.

To explain this issue we must first recall that motivation is defined as a resource allocation process. That is, the individual has a set of time and energy resources that are allocated across acts. This allocation process is guided by what we will call motivational force. In defining motivation, we have stressed that anticipated affect is the guiding principle in the re- source allocation process. That is, the person will choose to expend the personal resources of time and energy on acts that will result in outcomes with maximum positive affect. However, this notion in and of itself leads to an oversimplified picture of the motivation process. It suggests that the person will engage in those acts which have the largest potential return in terms of affect. However, the complex environments we live in do not allow for simple focusing on those acts that have a high antici- pated affect. In a job situation, there are a number of different products required, and a number of different kinds of acts are related to generat- ing those products. Some of these products are more important than others, and thus some of the acts are more valuable than others. How- ever, to perform effectively on the job, there must be some level of all the products. That is, the product-to-evaluation contingencies are such that some level of less important products must often be generated for an overall favorable evaluation to occur.

Specifically, consider an example of a job we have examined before; that of a college professor in a large university. The professor may feel that the products of published scholarly work are the most important products and thus acts leading to this type of product are more valuable. If, however, the professor dedicates all his or her time to writing and does no teaching, advising of students, or departmental committee work, that professor's employment at that university will be brief. The issue is that, although some products are more valuable than others, any job must be thought of as a *pattern* of products that must be generated at some level of quantity and quality. Thus, the motivation or resource allocation process must be thought of as an allocation pattern across acts. The decision of what proportion of resources to allocate to a given act is not a decision made independently from consideration of other acts that also must have resources allocated to them.

This is one of the major problems with expectancy theory as it has been presented in the literature. The theory attempts to predict the total amount of effort the person will exert on the job. This can be in terms of predicting between people in the sense that the researcher attempts to predict the relative effort levels of different people on the same job. It can also be done within people in that predictions are made about which of several levels of overall effort the person will choose to exert.

The critical point is that predicting overall level of effort or the overall amount of personal time and energy resources the person devotes to the job ignores the way in which this total set of resources is allocated across acts. It ignores the fact that the patterning of the resource allocation process is critical to understanding behavior. This issue becomes even more critical if we accept the viewpoint expressed earlier that the total amount of personal resources committed to the job is fairly constant for a given individual. To the extent that this is the case, variation in that person's performance can be explained only in terms of the way those resources are allocated to acts.

Motivational Force

We started this discussion with the notion that motivational force is related to anticipated affect, but is not exactly the same thing. The reason that they are not the same is related to the patterning idea. Since the individual must consider the resource allocation process as distributing personal resources across a pattern of acts to achieve a pattern of products, we must be able to predict how that allocation will be achieved. To do this, we will use the construct of motivational force. It may appear that if the anticipated affect for a given act is high, the person should be willing to allocate considerable resources to that act. Writing scholarly articles would be an example for the college professor. However, as mentioned previously, it is not quite so simple. The reason that writing scholarly articles is an attractive act is that it is related to products that will result in outcomes. But more precisely, it is an act which shows a strong *relationship* between the amount of resources committed to the act and the ultimate anticipated affect. For this act, the greater the resources committed to it, the greater the anticipated affect. Thus variations in the resources committed to the act result in large variation in the anticipated affect.

This is the essential aspect of motivational force. Motivational force occurs when *different* levels of commitment to the act result in *different* levels of anticipated affect. In the example of scholarly writing, increases in the amount of scholarly writing typically result in increases in scholarly products, which result in increases in valued outcomes, which result in more positive affect. An example where motivational force would be low might be departmental committee work. Here, increases in the resources committed to acts related to committee work may result in very small increases in the favorableness of the department chair's evaluation, and thus very small increases in outcomes controlled by that evaluator. Thus, the motivational force to engage in additional committee work would be very low.

In essence, we are arguing that motivational force is present to the extent that variations in resources committed to the act are associated with variations in anticipated affect. Thus, our motivation theory must be developed so that the relationships between the amount of resources committed and the level of affect anticipated are described. If we know these relationships, we will be in a position to describe and predict the resource allocation process.

This statement emphasizes the importance of contingencies in the motivation process. That is, motivational force will be strong and the person will choose to expend resources on acts where the contingency relationship between the level of resources committed to the act and the level of the affect anticipated to derive from that act is such that an increase (or change from the present level) of resources allocated to that act will result in a large change (increase) in the amount of anticipated affect to be received as a result. That is, we propose that the ratio

$$\frac{\Delta A}{\Delta C} = MF = \text{motivational force}$$

where ΔA = change in anticipated affect and ΔC = change in commitment for that act. This means that *MF may be conceptualized as the slope of the function describing a composite contingency relationship between resources committed to an act and the amounts of affect anticipated from the committing of various levels of resources to that act.* This composite contingency is actually a composite of the three specific contingency relationships; namely, the act-to-product, product-to-evaluation, and evaluation-to-outcome contingencies.

The reader may have already recognized that the above mentioned composite contingency relationship expressing the functional relationship between resources committed to an act and the amount of anticipated affect is the utility of an act. Thus, when we speak of utility of acts, we are talking about a contingency type relationship. Here the relationship is between the amount of the act and the anticipated value or attractiveness of that amount of the act. In other words, the utility of an act is a functional relationship relating amount of resources committed to the act to the anticipated attractiveness or value that follows from that amount of committed resources. When the slope of this relationship is steep ($\Delta A/\Delta C$ = large), strong motivational force is associated with that act. If the slope is flat, in that variations in resources committed do not result in significant variations in anticipated value, little motivational force is present. As we shall see, this type of conceptualization allows us to deal with the patterning of resources across acts by using these functional relationships to predict how resources will be allocated.

Thus far we have argued that our motivation theory must ultimately provide contingencies in the form of functional relationships describing the degree to which variations in resources committed to acts result in variations in anticipated affect (i.e., functional relationships for utilities of acts). The principle of motivational force as variations in one state resulting in variations in anticipated affect is one that carries through the entire theory. We propose that the way acts, products, evaluations, and outcomes combine is based on the principle of motivational force. Therefore, the conceptualization of functional relationships relating amount of an act, product, and so on to the anticipated amount of affect associated with varying amounts of that act, product, evaluation, or outcome will be used throughout the theory.

This discussion leads to the conceptualization of valence of outcomes. We argued that to develop meaningfully a conceptualization of valence of outcomes, we needed to understand the motivational nature of valence of outcomes.

Consistent with our notion of motivational force, we would argue that the motivational nature of outcomes comes from the degree to which variations in the level of outcomes result in variations in the anticipated affect associated with those different levels of outcome. An outcome for which changes in the amount of the outcome received would result in large changes in affect experienced would have a large amount of motivational force. An outcome where differences in the level of the outcome would result in little or no difference in affect experienced would have little motivational force.

Whereas the notion of motivational force of outcomes is critical to the ultimate generation of predictors of motivational force for acts, there is another aspect of outcomes that must be considered. That is the absolute attractiveness of the outcome levels. We need to know whether a given level of the outcome would produce positive or negative affect, and how much positive or negative affect that level of the outcome will produce.

To completely describe the valence of an outcome, we must know two things. First is the relationship between changes in the levels of the outcome and changes in the anticipated affect. Second, we need to know the actual level of affect associated with different levels of the outcome. Both of these aspects are contained in our conceptualization of valence of outcomes. We view the valence of an outcome as a functional relationship relating specific levels of the outcome with specific levels of anticipated affect.

Three examples depicting this functional relationship notion are presented in Figure 6.2. For the outcomes of a pay raise, supervisory recognition, and co-worker approval, functional relationships are depicted, showing how for a given hypothetical individual, changes in the level of the various outcomes are related to changes in the level of anticipated affect. The steepness of the line indicates the degree to which changes in the level of the outcome result in changes in anticipated affect. The outcome of a pay raise shows a steeper slope than that of supervisory recognition. Thus, a pay raise has more motivational force than supervisory recognition. These functional relationships also depict the absolute level of affect associated with each level of the outcome. Thus, in these examples, the person finds high co-worker approval neutral and no co-worker approval very negative; while high supervisory recognition is highly positive but no supervisory approval is neutral.

As Figure 6.2 also indicates, these functional relationships can be nonlinear. This reflects a general characteristic of utility-type functions. This is certainly the case for utilities associated with different levels of outcomes.

These functional relationships can and should be thought of as utility functions even though we have used the term valence. Anticipated affect can be thought of as the utility associated with a given level of outcome. Utility *is* anticipated affect. The specific values of affect in the function can also be thought of as expected values. For example, the individual may perceive that if a pay raise characterized by level 4 in Figure 6.2 is received, there is a distribution of levels of affect that could possibly be experienced. That is, there is some probability that the person would experience a +1 level of affect, a +2 level of affect, or a +3 level of affect. The actual point on the figure thus represents the expected value (i.e., probability times level of affect divided by the number of levels) of a level 4 pay raise.

1. Outcome: Pay Raise

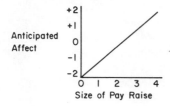

2. Outcome: Supervisory Recognition

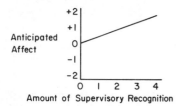

3. Outcome: Co-worker Approval

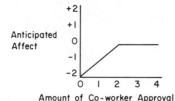

FIGURE 6.2 *Examples of valences as functional relationships.*

Regardless of whether one views these functional relationships as utility functions, viewing valence of outcomes in this way depicts the motivational force notion of valence. Furthermore, this same principle of functional relationships will be used repeatedly in the motivation theory since it enables us to better understand the resource allocation problem.

Some Implications of Defining Motivational Force as Slope

Defining motivational force as the slope of a utility function has certain behavioral implications. Consider the commitment to acts utility function as an example. Figure 6.3 shows the utility, or anticipated affect, associated with three hypothetical separate acts, A, B, and C, as a function of the degree of commitment the individual might invest in each of these behaviors.

We are proposing that the ratio $\Delta U / \Delta C$ (change in utility or antici-

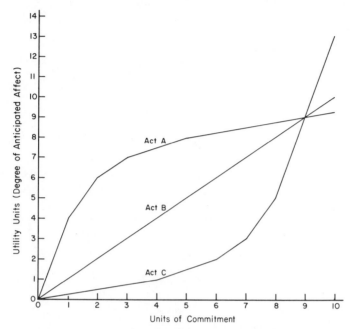

FIGURE 6.3 *Utility of acts functions for three hypothetical acts.*

pated affect divided by the associated change in anticipated commitment) is what we will call motivational force. Further, we are proposing
the fundamental principle that *a person will commit additional resources to
that act perceived as having the largest ratio (or steepest slope) for the specific
amount of additional resources that individual is willing to consider committing.*

The emphasized portion of the fundamental motivational principle
stresses two important points. First, we are talking about choosing to
commit some X amount of resources in addition to those *already* being
committed. The ΔC value always has some base which is the amount of
resources of time and effort already being spent or utilized by the individual. The second point is that the size of ΔC is set by the individual,
and its size may vary substantially from person to person, and for a given
person, from situation to situation. It may, for example, vary as a function of the base value of C. It may vary depending upon the uniqueness
of the situation (e.g., competition may lead to larger values of ΔC).

The importance of both the base value of C and the size of ΔC is
obvious, since for any nonlinear function the ratio $\Delta U/\Delta C$ will be quite
different depending upon (*a*) where one starts; and (*b*) the size of the
interval over which the slope is computed. Indeed, the size of ΔC can

affect drastically the degree to which an individual will engage in various tasks and thus can affect the total amount of received affect.

To illustrate these implications, Figure 6.3 shows three acts with different utility functions. Act A is a parabolic function of the form $Y = aX^b$ where $b > 1.0$. Act B is a linear function of the form $Y = a + bX$, and Act C is parabolic function of the form $Y = aX^b$ where $0 < b < 1.0$. Act A is, therefore, a decreasing monotonic function of X while Act C is an increasing monotonic function of X.

Suppose that we have a hypothetical individual who (a) is starting from a base of 0 commitment units; (b) "thinks" in terms of additional commitment expenditures of size 1; and (c) has a maximum of ten such units to expend across the three acts in question. How would that individual allocate resources across the acts, and what "return" in affect or utility units would the individual receive? We can easily compute the answer as follows:

Units of Size 1

Commitment Allocation	Return in Utility Units
1st Unit to A	4 units
2nd Unit to A	2 units
3rd Unit to A or B	1 unit
4th to 10th Unit to B	7 units
3 units to A, 7 to B	14 units

Now we will systematically vary the size of ΔC from 2 units to a maximum of 10 units to see what happens to the way in which resources are allocated to acts and to the return on investment.

Units of Size 2

Commitment Allocation	Return in Utility Units
1st unit of two to A	6 units
2nd through 5th units of two to B	8 units
2 units to A, 8 to B	14 units

Units of Size 3

Commitment Allocation	Return in Utility Units
1st unit of three to A	7 units
2nd & 3rd units of three to B	6 units
1 unit remainder to B	1 unit
3 units to A, 7 to B	14 units

Units of Size 4

Commitment Allocation	Return in Utility Units
1st unit of four to A	7.5 units
2nd unit of four to B	4 units
2 unit remainder to B	2 units
4 units to A, 6 to B	13.5 units

Units of Size 5

Commitment Allocation	Return in Utility Units
1st unit of five to A	8 units
2nd unit of five to B	5 units
5 units to A, 5 units to B	13 units

Units of Size 6

Commitment Allocation	Return in Utility Units
1st unit of six to A	8.25 units
4 units remainder to B	4 units
6 units to A, 4 to B	12.25 units

Units of Size 7

Commitment Allocation	Return in Utility Units
1st unit of seven to A	8.5 units
3 unit remainder to B	3 units
7 units to A, 3 to B	11.5 units

Units of Size 8

Commitment Allocation	Return in Utility Units
1st unit of eight to A	8.75 units
2 unit remainder to B	2 units
8 units to A, 2 to B	10.75 units

Units of Size 9

Commitment Allocation	Return of Utility Units
1st unit of nine to A or C	9 units
1 unit remainder to C (if C above)	4 units
or	
1 unit remainder to B (if A above)	1 units
or	
1 unit remainder to A (if B above)	4 units
9 units A and 1 B	10 units
or	or
9 units B and 1 A	13 units
or	
10 units C	13 units

Units of Size 10

Commitment Allocation	*Return in Utility Units*
1st unit of ten to C	13 units
10 units to C	13 units

Examination of the above set of results provides a clear picture of how the size of the commitment increment can influence both the pattern of resource allocation across acts and the anticipated return in utility units. Note that in the example Act C was never engaged in at all until the size of the commitment increment reached 9 basic units. Thus for any sized commitment interval less than 9, Act C will never be used. This was because the slope of B for all intervals up to and including 8 units (no matter where one is located on B) is greater than the slope of C for the same number of units with a 0 starting point. Thus Act B may be said to completely dominate Act C for all intervals up to 9.

We find for the example that the proportion of resources allocated to the various acts ranged from a high of 100% to a low of 0% for Act C, while for Acts A and B the range was from a high of 90% to a low of 0%. These rather dramatic shifts should impress the reader with the degree to which the size of ΔC is an important cognitive variable.

We also need to examine the return in utility units that occurred as a function of the change in size of ΔC.

Unit Size	Utility Units Received
1, 2, 3	14
4	13.5
5, 9, 10	13.0
6	12.25
7	11.5
8	10.75

Here the findings are less dramatic. In fact, for 7 of the 10 different interval sizes there is a total difference of only 1 utility unit, and the *entire range was only 3.25 utility units,* even for these three dramatically different utility functions.

This suggests that whereas C may be an important variable in the way in which resources are allocated to Acts, it is far less critical as a variable when measured by the effect it has on total received utility. The further implication that can then be drawn is that the actual patterning, or resource allocation, to acts that have functional relationships with antici- pated affect may not be that critical. It may be that widely divergent allocation strategies give basically the same investment return in terms of utility units received. To the extent that this is true, the more likely it is that the individual will adopt heuristic strategies which shortcut the cognitive complexity of the process we have been discussing. This point will be discussed in more length in a later section.

Utility of Products

The next concept in the motivational process is utility of products. The determinants of utility of products are valence of outcomes, product-to-evaluation contingencies, and evaluation-to-outcome contingencies. Although each of these concepts has been defined in detail in Chapter 2 and in earlier sections of Chapter 6, we must consider exactly how they combine to yield utility of products. The issue is one of combining them in a way that captures the motivational force idea discussed previously. We have conceptualized motivational force as deriving from a situation where variation in a level of a motivational element (e.g., an outcome) is associated with variation in the utility or attractiveness of that element. In the case of valence, we speak of the degree to which variation in the level or amount of the outcome results in variation in the anticipated attractiveness.

To retain the motivational force notion in utility of products, we must conceptualize it in a way that yields a description of the extent to which variability in the amount–quality of the product is associated with variability in the value, attractiveness, or utility of the product. Specifically, *the motivational force of a product is the degree to which variations in the quantity–quality of the product are accompanied by variations in amount of anticipated affect.* A product for which large changes in quantity–quality result in large changes in the perceived affect anticipated to result will have strong motivational force. A product for which large changes in quantity–quality are not associated with changes in anticipated affect will have little motivational force.

We begin with the premise that we have a series of products associated through product-to-evaluation contingencies with an evaluation. (Actually, there are multiple evaluations, since there are multiple evaluators, but for a given evaluator, there is one overall evaluation. We will consider the multiple evaluation issue later in this section. For the sake of simplicity of exposition, assume for the present that there is only one evaluator.) This overall evaluation then is associated with multiple outcomes through evaluation-to-outcomes contingencies. Finally, these outcomes have valences associated with them. This general process is depicted in Figure 6.4. As the figure indicates, the valences of the multiple outcomes converge to the overall evaluation through evaluation-to-outcome contingencies. The products obtain their utility by being associated with the overall evaluation through product-to-evaluation contingencies.

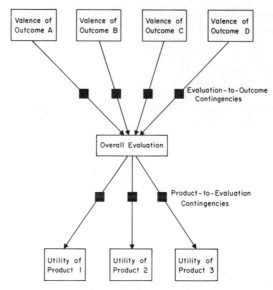

FIGURE 6.4 *Schematic representation of the formation of utility of products.*

Utility of Evaluations

With this general picture in mind, we can deal with the specific way in which these variables combine to result in utility of products such that utility of products includes the notion of motivational force. We must first develop the concept of the utility of the evaluation. The utility of an evaluation can be thought of as the functional relationship between the level of evaluation and the anticipated affect associated with those evaluations. That is, it is a functional relationship, analogous to valence, that relates the degree of favorableness or unfavorableness of the evaluation to the degree of affect anticipated to result from the outcomes that will follow that evaluation. It reflects the combination of evaluation-to-outcome contingencies and the valence of outcome functions and expresses this combination as a type of utility function.

This combination occurs in a very specific way. Specifically, *the utility of a given level of evaluation is the valence of the level of outcomes expected to be received from that level of evaluation, summed across outcomes.* The utility of a given level of evaluation can be thought of as the total anticipated attractiveness of the outcomes that will follow from that level of evaluation. To obtain this sum of valences for a given level of evaluation, the functions describing evaluation-to-outcome contingencies and the functions describing valences must be examined. Once this sum of valences is determined for each level of evaluation, a functional relationship can be developed relating level of evaluation to the utility or anticipated value of that level of evaluation.

Figure 6.5 presents an example of determining the utility of the evaluation for a hypothetical individual. In the example, three outcomes are used: pay raise, supervisory recognition, and co-worker approval. As the valence functions indicate, the pay raise shows a steep linear relationship with no raise being highly negative and a large raise being highly positive. The valence function for supervisory recognition is also linear, but not nearly as steep in slope as that for the pay raise. No supervisory recognition is seen as neutral, but very high supervisory recognition is highly positive. The coworker approval valence function is nonlinear in

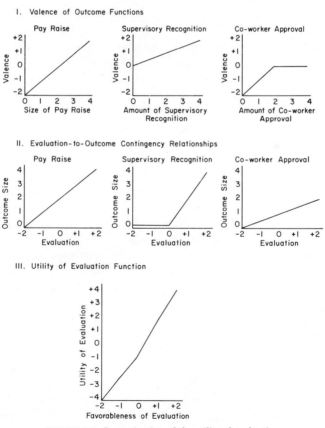

FIGURE 6.5 *Determination of the utility of evaluations.*

that low levels of co-worker approval are negative, but middle levels of approval up to high levels are seen by the person as neutral.

Evaluation-to-outcome contingencies are presented in the second part of the figure. As was indicated earlier, we are assuming for the sake of simplicity that there is only one evaluator, in this case, the supervisor. Thus, the examples reflect evaluation-to-outcome contingencies that might operate in such a situation. For the pay raise, a linear relationship exists such that the size of the pay raise is heavily determined by the evaluation of the supervisor. The contingency function for supervisory recognition indicates that no recognition will be given for neutral or negative evaluations, but when the evaluation is on the positive side, there is a steep slope between the level of the evaluation and the amount of recognition. The coworker approval contingency function indicates that there is a weak slope between the supervisor's evaluation and the approval the person gets from co-workers.

The utility of a given level of evaluation is formed by summing the valence expected from the levels of the outcomes expected to occur with that level of evaluation. Thus, based on the evaluation-to-outcome contingency functions, evaluation level -2 should result in 0 units of pay raise. The valence functions indicate that 0 units of pay raise has a valence of -2 associated with it. For supervisory recognition, an evaluation of -2 yields 0 units of recognition with an associated valence of 0. For co-worker approval, an evaluation of -2 yields 0 co-worker approval with an associated valence of -2. To obtain the utility of a -2 evaluation, we sum the valences associated with the level of evaluation across the three outcomes: $(-2) + (0) + (-2) = -4$.

This same process is carried out for each evaluation level, resulting in the values plotted in the third section of the figure. As the figure indicates, in this example there is a steep, near linear relationship between the favorableness of the evaluation and the utility of the evaluation by this evaluator. In other words, variations in the favorableness of the evaluation are associated with large variation in the anticipation of positive affect resulting from outcomes expected to be received.

Motivational Force of Evaluation

The conceptualization of utility of evaluation as a functional relationship describes the motivational force of the evaluation. This information is contained in the shape of the function. Once again, the greater the difference in the utility of different levels of favorableness of evaluation, the greater the motivational force. For example, if the functional relationship was flat with a slope, it would mean that different levels of favorableness of evaluation resulted in essentially equal levels of utility. This could come about because the evaluation-to-outcome contingencies were zero, the valence functions were flat, or some combination of these. For example, if a given evaluator had no control over any outcome, that is, his evaluation-to-outcome contingencies were flat, the utility of evaluation function for that evaluator would be flat. A more realistic example would be a case where the evaluator had no control over outcomes that were high in motivational force but had control over outcomes with little or no motivational force. Precisely, the evaluator displayed low evaluation-to-outcome contingencies for outcomes with steep valence functions, and high evaluation-to-outcome contingencies for outcomes with flat valence functions. In this case, the utility of evaluation function would be flat, and no motivational force would be associated with that evaluator's evaluation.

The utility of evaluation function also tells us the amount of *power* the evaluator has over the individual. We have said previously that power can be understood in terms of evaluation-to-outcome contingencies. That is, if an evaluator has strong evaluation-to-outcome contingencies for outcomes that are valued by the individual, that evaluator has power over the individual. We can now state this idea more precisely by bringing in our conceptualization of valence, evaluation-to-outcome contingencies, and utility of evaluation. Based on the functional relationship notion, combining valence with evaluation-to-outcome contingencies to yield the utility of evaluation function results in the function describing the degree to which changes in the evaluation result in changes in expected affect from outcomes. Thus, in addition to being an important component in the motivation process, the utility of evaluation function defines the amount of power a given evaluator has or is perceived as having over the individual.

In our discussion of the formation of utility of products, we have so far described how valence of outcomes and evaluation-to-outcome contingencies combine to produce the utility of evaluation function. We will now complete the discussion by describing how the utility of evaluation function combines with product-to-evaluation contingencies to produce utility of products.

Once again, we wish to describe the utility of products in terms of motivational force. This is fairly straightforward. We use a combination process analogous to that used for utility of evaluation. Specifically, we can define *the utility of a level of a product as the level of utility of the evaluation anticipated to occur from that level of the product.* That is, to determine the utility of a given level of a product, we determine, using the product-to-evaluation contingency relationships, the evaluation expected to follow from that level of the product. The utility of that level of evaluation is then obtained from the utility of evaluation functions. This process may be repeated across all different levels of the product resulting in a utility function relating the level of the product to the utility (degree of anticipated affect) of that level of the product.

Figure 6.6 represents an extension of the example used in Figure 6.5. Assuming a single evaluator and the previously presented valence and evaluation-to-outcome data, the utility of evaluation function produced in Figure 6.5 is presented as the first part of Figure 6.6. In the second part of the figure an individual's hypothetical product-to-evaluation contingencies for two products are shown. For product A, a steep linear relationship exists between the level (i.e., quantity–quality) of the product and the favorableness of the overall evaluation. For product B, a nonlinear relationship exists such that if none of the product is generated, a large negative evaluation occurs, but there is no difference in the

I. Utility of Evaluation Function

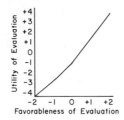

II. Product-to-Evaluation Contingencies

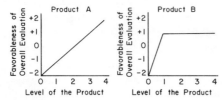

III. Utility of Products Functions

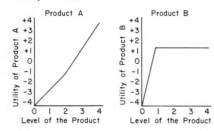

FIGURE 6.6 *Determination of the utility of products.*

evaluation if a small amount to a large amount of the product is generated.

To determine the utility of product function for product A, we determine the favorableness of the overall evaluation associated with each level of the product by examining the product-to-evaluation contingencies and then determine the utility of that level of evaluation from the utility of evaluation function. Thus, for level 0 of product A, a −2 evaluation occurs and a −2 evaluation has a utility of −4. Thus, −4 is the utility of a 0 level of product A. Level 1 of product A is associated with a −1 evaluation which has a −2.5 utility. Following this process, the utility of products functions for products A and B are generated.

The function that derives for product A shows a steep, near linear relationship between the level of the product and the utility of that level of the product. This implies that as the level of the product increases, the favorableness of the evaluation increases, as the favorableness of the evaluation increases, the amount of the outcomes increase, and the outcomes that increase in amount are outcomes where increases in amount are associated with increases in *positive affect*. Put another way, for product A, increases in the quantity–quality of the product lead to substantial increases in valued outcomes. Thus, we retain the motivational force notion as represented by the slope of the utility function.

The utility of product function for product B presents a different picture. For this product, there is a difference in utility between producing some of the product and producing none of it. Thus, there is considerable motivational force to produce some of it. However, there is no motivational force associated with producing more than a small amount of the product, since the slope of the function is zero beyond level 1 of the product.

There is a utility of product function for *each* product. It reflects the perceived importance of that product to the individual in the sense that it reflects the degree to which variations in the product result in variations in anticipated valued outcomes. As we shall see later, this conceptualization of utilities of products as functions is a crucial element in understanding the individual's allocation of personal resources.

Multiple Evaluators

It was mentioned earlier in this section and several times in previous chapters that our motivation theory must deal with the fact that for any person there are multiple evaluators who measure and evaluate the person's products and administer outcomes on the basis of this evaluation.

The different evaluators measure and evaluate different products; they use different product-to-evaluation contingencies, and they use different evaluation-to-outcome contingencies. The different evaluators have different roles for the person and they have different amounts and types of power over the person.

Given that this is the case, we must account for and describe how the process takes place. To do this, we utilize the utility of evaluation function and the utility of products functions. Recall that the utility of evaluation function describes the degree to which variations in the favorableness of the evaluation result in variations in affect anticipated to result from the outcomes. This single function incorporates all the evaluation-to-outcome contingencies and all the outcomes *for a single evaluator.* There will be one of these utility of evaluation functions for each salient evaluator in the person's environment. These functions may be radically different from one another. This difference will be due to the different levels of power the evaluators have over the person.

To the extent that evaluators have different levels of control over valued outcomes (i.e., different evaluation-to-outcome contingencies), the utility of evaluation functions will be quite different.

In addition, different evaluators may have quite different roles for the person. Certain products can have different product-to-evaluation contingencies for different evaluators. A highly important product for one evaluator may be totally irrelevant to another evaluator. That is, there is a high product-to-evaluation contingency for the product for one evaluator, but that product has a zero contingency for the other evaluator. It is also possible for the contingency to be positive for one evaluator and negative for another. For example, there may be a steep positive relationship between number of units produced and the supervisor's evaluation of the individual, but a steep negative relationship between units produced and peer evaluation. This could be the case if the peer group felt that large numbers of units produced would result in higher expectations of performance from the supervisor for all group members.

The conceptualization of the motivational process in terms of motivational force allows a straightforward resolution of the multiple evaluator issue. The utility of a given level of a product is the sum of the utilities of evaluations that that level of the product will result in, summed across all relevant evaluators. Suppose that level 0 of a product results in a -2 evaluation for evaluator A and this evaluation has a utility of -4 associated with it. For evaluator B, level 0 of the product results in a $+1$ evaluation and this evaluation has a utility of $+2$. The overall utility of level 0 of the product is then the sum of the two separate utilities or

$(-4) + (+2) = -2$. This process is carried out for each level of the product.

Implications of Multiple Evaluators

The resulting utility of product function can reflect the influence of multiple evaluators. This formulation has a number of interesting implications for situations where different evaluators agree and disagree in their product-to-evaluation functional relationships. In the case where the relationships for different evaluators are in the same direction (i.e., positive or negative), motivational force can only be increased or stay the same. For example, suppose we started with one evaluator who has a steep positive linear function between a product and his or her evaluation, and who has power over the individual. This creates substantial motivational force to produce large amounts of the product. If we add a second evaluator for whom the contingency relationship is also positive, linear, and steep for that product and his or her evaluation, the motivational force can only go up or stay the same. If the second evaluator has some power over the person, the motivational force will go up. If the second evaluator has no power over the person, the motivational force will remain unchanged. The amount of motivational force that results will obviously be a function of the importance of the product for each evaluator as expressed by the product-to-evaluation contingencies, and the power of each evaluator as expressed by the degree to which the evaluator controls the level of outcomes and the degree to which variations in those outcomes result in variations in anticipated affect for the person.[6]

The more interesting implications come about where the functional relationships between evaluators differ in direction. That is, for one

6. There is an unmentioned issue here concerning the degree to which affect (anticipated or received) is additive. That is, if an individual has +5 units of anticipated affect (utility) for product A and +6 units of anticipated affect (utility) for product B, is the anticipated affect for the combination of products A and B +11 units? The same issue relates to received affect (satisfaction). If a person who receives outcome A individually expresses +5 units of satisfaction, and who, when receiving outcome B separately, expresses +6 units of satisfaction, were to receive both outcomes simultaneously, would that person express +11 units of positive affect? This issue is one that has been of concern to utility theory for some time and is still unresolved. Even in recent work in the area of multiattribute utility theory (MAUT) it is not known whether additive or other models, such as multiplicative, are the best systems for combining utilities (Fishburn & Kenney, 1974; Huber, 1974). Svensen (1979) presents a concise discussion of the various kinds of decision rules and their properties that is applicable to this type of cognitive integration problem.

evaluator the product-to-evaluation contingency is positive for a given product, whereas for another evaluator, the contingency is negative. This is a classic example of role conflict, and the conceptualization we have proposed makes rather specific predictions of what will happen. If we assume that the product-to-evaluation contingency relationships are equally strong (have equal slopes) but are in opposite direction, *the relative amount of power* of the two evaluators will determine the utility of product function and thus how the conflict will be resolved. That is, the combination of different evaluators that we have described above will result in a positive utility of product function if the evaluator with a positive product-to-evaluation contingency is more powerful, but a negative utility of product function if the evaluator with the negative contingency is more powerful. Both have an effect, in that combining the two will decrease the steepness of the utility of product function and thus decrease motivational force. This becomes important when we deal with the translation of utility of acts into actual acts, and will be discussed further at that point.

Utility of Acts

The next component to be considered in the motivation process is utility of acts. Utilities of acts are formed by the combination of utilities of products functions with act-to-product contingencies. We need to specify how this combination takes place, and to combine the two in such a way that the motivational force notion is preserved. As is probably apparent by now, this combination is a straightforward one, analogous to the ways the other motivation constructs have been combined. Specifically, utilities of acts are viewed as utility functions relating level or amount of the act to the utility of that level of the act. The functional relationship relates level of commitment to the act in terms of time and energy resources to the utility of that level of commitment.

This utility for a given level of commitment to the act is defined as the utility of the level of the product expected to follow from that level of commitment to the act. To obtain this value, we examine the act-to-product contingencies and the utility of products functions. Figure 6.7 presents an example. We start with the utility of products functions developed in Figure 6.6, add two act-to-product contingencies, and derive the utility of act functions for the two acts. The act-to-product contingency for the first act shows a steep linear relationship between the level of commitment to the act and the amount of the product expected. The second act-to-product contingency is also linear, but has less slope.

To develop the utility of act function for act 1, we determine from the

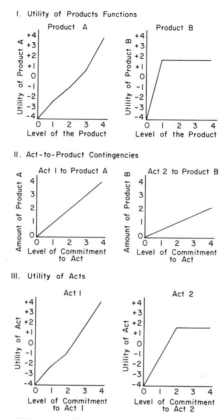

FIGURE 6.7 *Determination of the utility of acts.*

act-to-product contingency that 0 commitment to the act is associated with 0 amount of the product, and from the utility of product A function we note that 0 amount of the product results in a utility of −4. Level 1 commitment to the act results in level 1 of the product, which has a utility of −2.5. Other points in the utility function for act 1 and act 2 are derived in an analogous fashion.

This conceptualization of utility of acts as a function relating level of commitment to the act with the utility of that level of commitment can be thought of as the degree to which different levels of commitment are followed by different expected levels of valued outcomes. That is, the degree to which the different levels of commitment are related to differ-ent levels of *anticipated affect.* The conceptualization thus preserves the motivational force notion in that the steeper the slope of function, the greater the motivation of the person to exert increased levels of commitment to the act. In addition, the conceptualization clearly combines all the motivational variables: valence of outcomes, evaluation-to-outcome contingencies, product-to-evaluation contingencies, and act-to-product contingencies. Thus, as mentioned earlier, the utility of acts contingency relationship is a composite function which is constituted from (or may be decomposed into) a number of other contingency relationships.

The utility of acts function for Act 1 in Figure 6.7 shows strong motivational force for Act 1. Increases in commitment to Act 1 are associated with large increases in the utility of that act. Low levels of commitment have strongly negative utilities, whereas high levels of commitment have high positive utilities. For Act 2, there are fairly strong levels of motivational force associated with low levels of commitment, in that going from none of the act to an intermediate level of the act results in changes in utility from high negative utility to slightly positive utility. However, intermediate to high levels of commitment have no motivational force associated with them, in that going from intermediate to high levels of commitment results in no change in utility. Thus, we would predict that the individual would be willing to commit large amounts of time and energy to Act 1, but at most, only intermediate levels to Act 2. As we shall see, the allocation of time and energy resources must be done across a large number of acts. Thus, predictions of commitment must be made considering this large number of acts simultaneously.

At this point in the discussion of the motivational process, we have developed the nature of utility of acts functions. These functions are formed from specific combinations of utility of products functions and act-to-product contingencies. Utility of products functions are formed from utility of evaluation functions and product-to-evaluation contingencies. Utility of evaluation functions are in turn formed from evaluation-to-outcome contingencies and valence of outcome functions.

Actual Acts

The final step in the motivational process is the translation of utility of acts into actual acts. In other words, given that the individual has a set of utilities associated with acts, what is the process whereby these utilities influence actual behavior? To develop the description of this process, we must keep several principles in mind. First, the motivational force is associated with *differences* in utility for different levels of commitment. That is, where there are large differences in the utility of different levels of commitment to the act, motivational force will be high. Where there are small differences in the utility of different levels of commitment to the act, motivational force for the act will be low. Second, motivational force will be related to actual level of commitment to the act. That is, other things being equal, the greater the motivational force, the greater the level of time and energy resources committed to the act. However, the "other things being equal" qualification is very important. We must keep in mind that our conceptualization of the motivation process is that it is a resource allocation process where time and energy resources are allocated across acts. Thus, it is impossible to predict the level of commitment that will be directed to a given act without considering other possible acts at the same time. Current motivation theories of behavior in organizations do not really deal with this issue, but talk about overall motivation as effort that will be expended on the job. Our theory attempts to go beyond this by (a) predicting the overall level of resources the person will commit to the job; and (b) how these resources will be allocated across acts.

To do this, we start with the notion that for a given individual, the level of time and energy resources the person is willing to expend across all acts in their entire life space is fairly constant. That is, except for periods of illness, emergency, or personal crisis, the total amount of time and energy resources will be fairly constant when compared across equal time intervals. Clearly, there will be fluctuations in this level of resources for short periods of time, such as a few days, or a few hours, but over larger periods of time, such as a month, the level of resources will be fairly constant from month to month. At the very least, there is an upper limit on the level of resources that the person will commit to the acts in the life space. Furthermore, expending extreme resources is a costly process. Since expending very high levels of resources is difficult, it will be done only on the basis of extreme levels of expected or anticipated positive or negative affect resulting from the commitment of these resources. If increases in positive affect are not expected to result from an increase in resources directed toward a given act, the costliness of resource expenditure will result in lower or constant levels of commitment to the act.

In addition to the cost of time and effort that is inherent in the nature of commitment expenditure, there is another type of cost associated with committing resources to the job. Specifically, based on our resource allocation approach, we must consider the allocation of resources to the job in the context of other broader spheres in the person's life. That is, interpersonal relationships, personal development, family, recreation, and so on are other spheres requiring personal resources. The person must somehow allocate resources across all these areas including the job. Since total resources are fairly constant or at least have a fixed upper limit, expending more resources on the job results in expending less in other areas of the person's life. Thus, the second aspect of the cost of expending resources on the job is that this takes away resources from other areas of the person's life. Since motivational force is present in these other areas as well, the person must allocate resources across these areas of life. This allocation process would be based on anticipated affect in the form of motivational force, and if the appropriate acts, products, contingencies, etc., could be measured, the present theory should be able to predict this allocation to other areas as well. However, since our primary concern is job behavior, we shall deal with the issue by considering job-related behavior and combining all other aspects of the person's life into the global category of nonjob-related behavior.

Before pursuing this issue further, we need to specify how the utility of acts is translated into actual commitment to acts. We start with the utility of acts functions. Figure 6.8 presents these functions for four separate acts. Act A shows a steep linear relationship between commitment and utility, Act B, a linear relationship with moderate slope, Act C shows a zero slope, and Act D represents a nonlinear relationship such that, as long as some level of commitment is present, anticipated affect is positive. From these functions we can develop a function relating total commitment to total affect. To do this, we assume that the person will

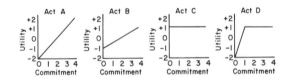

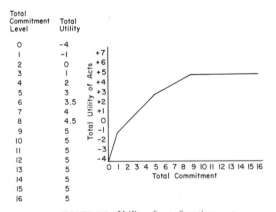

FIGURE 6.8 *Utility of acts functions.*

commit time and energy resources as a function of motivational force. That is, the greater the difference in anticipated affect between levels of commitment, the greater the force to commit the resources. Based on this assumption, we can start with the notion of zero commitment and ask where the first unit of commitment will be allocated and determine the anticipated level of affect from expending that first unit of commitment. In the example in Figure 6.8, we can determine that if zero level of commitment is expected, the total expected utility is -4. That is, if there is zero commitment to all acts, a -2 utility follows from Act A, -1 from B, $+1$ from C, and -2 from D, resulting in an overall affect of -4. This is reflected in the function at the bottom of the figure where zero commitment is associated with -4 total utility.

If the person expends 1 unit of commitment, inspection of the utility of act functions allows us to predict to which act that unit of commitment will be directed. It will be directed to that act for which adding 1 unit of commitment results in the greatest change in affect; that is, where motivational force is the highest. This would be Act D since going from 0 to 1 unit of commitment in Act D results in an increase in anticipated affect of 3 units, whereas 1 unit will result in less than 3 units of change in anticipated affect for the other three acts. Thus, exerting 1 unit of commitment will result in a total utility of -1, and that 1 unit will be allocated to Act D. If a second unit of commitment is allocated, it will be allocated to the act where the next greatest increase in utility will occur (i.e., Act A). Here there is an increase in utility of 1 unit. Thus, if a total of 2 units of commitment are allocated, the total utility will be 0, and the 2 units will be allocated one to D and one to A. This same process occurs for additional levels of commitment. In our example, the third unit of commitment would be directed toward Act A, followed by A, A, B, B, B, B. Thus, at 9 units of commitment, $+5$ units of utility would be expected. However, from 9 to 16 units of commitment, no increase in utility is present.

The issue is, however, how to go from the total commitment by total utility function to a prediction of behavior. The key to predicting behavior is to use the function to predict the level of total commitment. If we can do this, we will be able to predict both total resources committed to the job and be able to specify how much commitment will be allocated to each act. Specifically, if we can measure total commitment, we have our prediction of total effort on the job, since total commitment is by definition total effort expended on the job. Furthermore, once we know how much resources the person will commit to the job in total, we can use the utility of act functions for the individual acts to predict how much commitment will be devoted to each act. This prediction would be made in a fashion analogous to the way the total commitment—total utility—function was developed. That is, the person will direct each unit of additional commitment to the act where that increase in commitment will result in the greatest change in utility. For example, in Figure 6.8, if we were to predict that the person would exert only four units of commitment to the job, we would predict that that person would direct 1 unit of commitment to Act D, and 3 units to Act A. No commitment would be allocated to Acts B or C. If we predicted 8 units of total commitment, 1 unit would be allocated to D, 4 to A, and 3 to B.

Thus, the critical issue is how to predict total job commitment. Once this is done, we have by definition, total effort; and from this we can predict the level of resources committed to each act. We can get some information about the total commitment expended on the job from the inspection of the total commitment by total utility of acts function. We can first say that total commitment will not be higher than the point where the utility of acts function permanently flattens; that is, where increases in commitment do not yield increases in anticipated affect (utility of acts).[7] In the example in Figure 6.8, this point would be 9 units of commitment. From 10 units on, no additional increment in affect would be anticipated, and hence the motivational force would be zero.

The second thing we can say from the function is that the steeper the slope of the function, the higher the predicted total commitment. A steep slope implies large changes in anticipated affect with changes in commitment. Suppose, for example, the reward or evaluation system changed for the person depicted in Figure 6.8 so that the function showed a perfect linear relationship from 0 to 9 units of commitment, and then flatlined out at 9 units. If this were the case, we would predict that the person would be more likely to exert levels of commitment in the 5–9 range after the change since the function would be steeper in this range after the change.

Thus, consideration of where the function flattens permanently, and the steepness of the function allow us to at least make gross predictions about total commitment. We can predict what the maximum level of commitment is likely to be, and examination of the steepness and asymptotic point of the function would allow us to make relative predictions between people or for the same person with two different functions (e.g., when the reward system changed). If, for example, we had two people where Person A had a function with a fairly linear increase up to 9 units (as in Figure 6.8) and Person B had the same type of generally linear

7. It is quite possible for the total utility of acts function to exhibit plateaus, or even decreases (dips) before beginning to rise again, depending upon the shapes of the individual utility of acts curves being combined.

function with the same slope up to 12 units of commitment before asymptoting, we would predict higher overall commitment for Person B.

While this relative prediction is useful, it does not give us what we are really seeking. That is, it does not give us a point prediction of how much actual commitment the person will devote to the job. Without this point prediction we cannot go back to the individual acts and predict commitment to each act. With the relative prediction brought about by examining the functions of different people, we could make some predictions about the likelihood of different levels of commitment to different acts, but these predictions would not be precise; they would be relative. That is, we could say that person A is more likely to exert more effort on Act 1 than Person B is. This would be valuable, but we would like to make actual point predictions for a given individual.

Thus, we must be able to predict the actual level of commitment the person will devote to the job. To do this, we must go beyond the total commitment by total utility function, and recall that our basic notion of the motivation process is one of resource allocation. The person has a fixed set of personal resources which are allocated across all acts in the life space. The major domains where these resources are allocated would include work, relationships (living partners, family, on and off the job friends, etc.),personal development (health, fitness, personal growth, etc.), and maintenance (financial management, property maintenance, etc.). We have argued that our theory could be applied to any, or in principle, all of these domains, and if the variables in the theory were measured, we could predict resources allocated to each of these areas. However, since we are focusing on work behavior, we can, for the sake of simplicity, deal with the work sphere and combine all other spheres into a nonwork category.

Thus, our resource allocation notion would imply that there will be some resources allocated to work and some to the nonwork sphere. In order to make a prediction of how much of the person's resources will be devoted to the work sphere—that is, make our point prediction of total commitment—we must look at motivational force in the nonwork sphere. In essence, we are saying that the person with relatively fixed total resources makes trade-offs between different spheres of life. The most salient trade-off for our purposes is the trade-off between the work and nonwork spheres. We are arguing that we cannot predict how much of the person's resources will be committed to the job by considering the job alone. The person will allocate resources to the job as a function of the motivational force in the job *relative to* the motivational force in the nonjob sphere.

Specifically, the person will make trade-offs between these two spheres, and these trade-offs will be based on anticipated affect or motivational force. Suppose, for example, the person at some time sees that the job is going to demand an increase in expenditure of resources. Whether or not the person chooses to commit those additional resources will depend on some sense of the cost of committing those resources. That is, the additional resources will have to come from somewhere in the nonjob sphere. To the extent that shifting these resources that have been allocated to the nonjob sphere to the job sphere is in some sense costly, the person will be less likely to commit the additional resources to the job.

In this example, the increased demands on the job derive from a change in the total commitment by total utility function. That is, the slope and/or asymptotic point of the function have increased. This could come about, for example, by an added assignment. In this case, the added assignment creates a change in the contingencies between products related to the assignment and the supervisor's evaluation. Before the new assignment, the contingencies between products related to that assignment and the supervisor's evaluation were zero. After the new assignment, positive contingencies are created. In turn, positive act-to-product contingencies are created for acts related to the new products. Thus, changes occur in the utility of act functions for the acts related to the new products. Before the new assignment, these functions had zero slopes; after the assignment, they have positive slopes. This, in turn, changes the total commitment by total utility function in that it will asymptote at a higher level of total commitment. The final result is that there is an increase in motivational force for higher levels of commitment. Where the function had asymptoted prior to the assignment, we now see it still rising—thus the increase in motivational force. We will assume that the change in motivational force is of some magnitude (i.e., the difference in anticipated affect between doing the assignment and not doing it is substantial). Furthermore, given that to do the assignment requires that additional resources be committed to the job, the person must take time and/or energy resources previously committed to the nonjob sphere and redirect these personal resources to the job. This redirection is costly in the sense that committing fewer resources to the nonjob sphere typically will result in a lowering of the affect anticipated to occur in the nonjob sphere. The greater the decrease in affect, the greater the cost. Thus, the trade-off is thought of as a comparison of the gain in anticipated affect in the work sphere to the loss in anticipated affect in the nonwork sphere.

With this extended example in mind, we can now deal explicitly with the notion of the comparison between the job and nonjob spheres, and how this leads to a point-prediction of resources committed to the job.

We have said before that personal resource allocation to aspects of the person's life outside the job can be predicted by the theory in exactly the same way as job-related resource allocation. That is, by measuring contingencies, outcomes, utility of evaluations, and so on, one could develop individual utility of act functions and total commitment by total utility of act functions. This could be done separately for different spheres such as relationships, personal development, and others. An overall function that combines all nonjob areas together could also be measured. Our position is that these nonjob aspects must be considered before a point prediction of total commitment to the job can be made. That is, since we are dealing with a choice process of allocating resources across acts—specifically, allocating resources to job versus nonjob areas—we need to know something about the alternative before we can predict what will happen in the job sphere.

Specifically, we need to know the total commitment by total utility of acts function for both the job sphere and the nonjob sphere. Figure 6.9 shows two such functions for an individual. There are several features about these two functions that are noteworthy. First, the nonjob function is steeper and covers a wider range of levels of total utility (anticipated affect) than the job function. This typically will be the case since total outcomes, number of evaluators, and strength of contingencies for all nonjob areas combined will usually be greater than for the job. Second, it is reasonable to assume that these functions become negatively accelerated at high levels of commitment. The general principle of diminishing returns for very high levels of commitment to acts is probably both an intuitively appealing and a reasonable assumption to make, at least for the types of acts that would normally be of interest here. Thus, going from 75 to 80 units of commitment will produce a greater change in anticipated affect than going from 90 to 95 units of commitment. Third, while both functions start to flatten out, neither actually reaches asymptote. In the previous figure (6.8) we showed the function flattening. This was done for illustrative purposes. Realistically, the function will probably never become totally flat. The manager working 80 hours a week realizes that working 85 hours would produce more positive job outcomes. This does not mean that the person will actually commit the extra 5 hours, but there is some positive marginal utility in doing so.

Given that we have these two functions, we can predict total commitment to the job. This is done in a fashion analogous to that used for predicting commitment to individual acts. Specifically, we use a buildup process where it is assumed that the first unit of commitment will be devoted to the sphere where adding that unit of commitment produces the greatest change in total utility (i.e., anticipated affect). That unit of

A. Non-Job Sphere

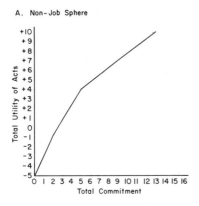

B. Job Sphere

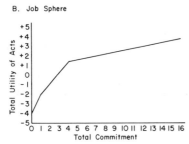

FIGURE 6.9 *Point prediction of commitment to the job.*

commitment will be directed to the sphere with the greatest motivational force. In the example in Figure 6.9, the first unit of commitment will be devoted to the nonjob sphere, since going from 0 to 1 unit of commitment results in an increase of 2 units of anticipated affect. The second through fifth units of commitment will also be devoted to the nonjob sphere, since adding each unit of commitment in this range in each case results in a greater change for the nonjob than for the job sphere. However, the sixth unit of commitment will be devoted to the job sphere, since going from 5 to 6 units in the nonjob results in a change of two-thirds of a unit of utility while going from 0 to 1 unit on the job results in a change of 1.5 units. Proceeding further, we can see that the seventh through ninth units of commitment will be devoted to the job. Thus, at 9 units of commitment, 5 will be allocated to the nonjob sphere, and 4 to the job sphere. After 9 units of commitment, all further units of commitment will be devoted to the nonjob sphere, since the change in utility is always greater for the nonjob sphere. Thus, our prediction in this case, is that the person will allocate 4 units of commitment to the job. Committing any more than 4 units would be too costly in the sense that it takes too much away from the nonjob sphere. That is, the anticipated increase in affect for committing more resources to the job is less than the anticipated decrease in affect that would result from taking one unit of commitment away from the nonjob sphere.

Thus, this approach allows us to predict exactly how much commitment will be allocated to the job. With this point prediction of total commitment we have, by definition, the total effort the person will exert on the job. In addition, by distributing the predicted total commitment across acts on the basis of change in affect (motivational force) we can predict the actual level of commitment for each act on the job.

We must recognize that this approach of comparing the job and nonjob functions to make the point prediction of total commitment to the job is based on an important assumption. The assumption is that the slope of the job function will be lower at high levels of commitment than the slope of the nonjob function. The two functions will characteristically look like those in Figure 6.9, where at higher levels of commitment, the nonjob function is rising faster than the job function. This is an important assumption in being able to make the point prediction. The problem occurs if the assumption is not true. Specifically, if the nonjob function begins to flatten out, and at high levels of commitment becomes flatter than the job function, and at the point where this occurs, the total resources that would be committed to the job and nonjob spheres together is less than the total commitment the person characteristically commits, resources will be once again committed to the job sphere. This requires a bit of explanation. We have argued previously that a person will characteristically commit a fairly constant amount of resources to living. That is, the time and energy resources committed to the job, relationships, play, loafing, and sleeping will be fairly constant over periods of time such as a month or two. This total level of resources committed will sometimes vary due to illness, mild or severe crises, etc., but by and large will be fairly constant. At the very least, there will be some level which represents an upper limit of resources expenditure that the person will commit in normal circumstances. A person will resist expending more resources than this characteristic level. However, this characteristic level is well below the maximum possible level of commitment. In situations of crisis the person will expend more resources than this characteristic upper limit, and approach the maximum level of commitment more closely, but when the crisis is over, the person will return to the characteristic level.

This characteristic level of commitment becomes important in the assumptions we are using to make our point prediction. Recall that the point prediction is that point on the job function where additional units of commitment will be directed to the nonjob sphere. That is, at the point where the nonjob function becomes steeper than the job function, additional units of commitment will be devoted to the nonjob sphere. One could argue, however, that the nonjob function will eventually flatten out and, at some point, be less steep than the job function. For example, in Figure 6.8, it could be that at 20 units of commitment the nonjob function will become flatter than the job function is in the 4–16 range of commitment. If this were the case, and the person were to be allocating more than 24 units of commitment (20 nonjob and 4 job), the commitment over 24 units would be directed to the job, and we would not predict 4 units of commitment for the job, but some value greater than 4. Thus, to be able to make our point prediction, we would need to know what the total amount of commitment will be. If we knew this value, we would still be able to make the point prediction for the job, even though the nonjob functions did become less steep than the job function at higher levels of commitment. However, as we have argued above, it would be difficult to predict what this total level of commitment would be. Thus, the assumption about the higher slope for the nonjob function at higher levels of commitment is important.

We would argue that this assumption is a reasonable one. The nonjob sphere contains many more outcomes and evaluators than the job sphere. Nonjob activities would include time with family and friends; personal development activities such as exercise, reading, hobbies; maintenance activities such as bill-paying, clean-up, maintaining the car; and even loafing and sleeping. All these in combination involve many highly valent outcomes and strong contingencies which implies that a great deal of motivational force will be present for these activities. It is reasonable to assume that, because of the many different outcomes, evaluators, and behaviors, that the nonjob function would continue to rise and would rise longer (at higher levels of commitment) than the job function.

We can look at this assumption in another way. If the assumption were not true, we would see a situation where any time the person had any free time, such as in the evening or on a weekend, the person would spend that time working. If the nonjob function flattened out more than the job function, we would predict that any increase in commitment would go to the job sphere. It is not common that people operate this way on a routine basis. This is another reason to think the assumption is a reasonable one.

It is possible, of course, for a person to devote all possible free time to work for a period of time. We see a student studying all night before a test, or the manager working late at night to finish a report. In these cases the contingencies for studying or writing the report are extremely high because of deadlines. This is not an example of violating the assumption, since such extreme forms of commitment to the job arise for fairly short time periods. Once the project is finished, the person will resort to more typical levels of commitment to the job. In fact, after such a period of time, the person typically feels that he or she deserves some time.

Even the so-called workaholic does not necessarily represent a violation of this assumption. A college professor may work from 7:30 A.M. to 6:00 P.M., eat dinner, and then work until 11:00 P.M. during the week. On the weekend, the same person works Saturday during the day and until noon on Sunday. Such extreme forms of commitment do not necessarily imply a violation of the assumption. If the person is unwilling to work Saturday night, or Sunday from noon on, he or she is saying that after exerting the commitment to the job through the week, he or she will devote all remaining commitment to the nonjob sphere. Even though the commitment to the job is very high, it has an upper limit beyond which all additional commitment will be devoted to the nonjob sphere.

By making the appropriate assumptions, we are able to compare the total commitment by total utility of acts functions for the job and nonjob spheres and make a point prediction of the total level of commitment that will be devoted to the job. By then taking that total level of commitment and distributing it across acts according to the utility of acts functions for the individual acts, we are able to make point predictions of the level of commitment devoted to each act. Thus, we have a prediction of total commitment to the job, which acts will be emitted, and the level of commitment devoted to each.

Constraints on Acts

Before completing our treatment of the basic motivation theory, we must deal with constraints issues that influence the translation of utility of acts into actual acts. Referring once again to the schematic of the full theory in Figure 2.1, it is clear that individual differences and external constraints influence actual acts. These two factors operate in a fairly straightforward way. For individual differences, we are referring to the person's actual ability to perform the act. If the person is studying financial reports and knows very little about them, the person will have a difficult time. Whereas this will clearly have an impact on the acts engaged in, the motivational aspect of ability at this stage in the theory is minor. That is, perceptions of ability will have their impact on the motivation process much earlier in the process. Specifically, abilities influence act-to-product contingencies strongly. The person who knows that he or she knows little about financial reports will perceive a very different contingency between working on the reports and coming up with meaningful conclusions than will the financial expert. We are arguing that the major source of influence of ability as it influences commitment to actual acts is to influence act-to-product contingencies. The other noncognitive source of influence occurs when the person perceives that he or she was able to emit the act but when it was attempted, found it impossible. Although this situation is possible, it will probably be rare. We should note that actual ability *will* have a direct influence on the quality of the act. With the same level of resources committed, the higher ability person will produce more and/or better products. However, this source of influence is depicted in Figure 2.1 as influencing the translation of actual acts to observable products and hence is not directly related to the motivation process.

The other source of influence between utility of acts and actual acts is the set of external constraints. These constraints operate in a straightforward fashion in that if the person is constrained so that it is not possible to engage in the intended acts, this constraint will affect the acts emitted. For example, if the person intends to perform the act but does not have the resources (tools, information, etc.) to engage in the act, the person will not commit resources to that act.

Phenomenological Simplification of the Motivation Process

It is abundantly clear that we are proposing a complex model of motivation. We have stated at several points in the book so far that people do not operate on a day-to-day basis by considering each act-to-product contingency, each product, each product-to-evaluation contingency, etc. Rather, people use simplifying strategies as heuristics to deal with the resource-allocation process. The reasons that people use heuristics have been discussed previously. We have pointed out that *simplifying behaviors are themselves acts which have their own utility functions.* Obviously the more complex the fundamental process is, the more cognitive effort is required to carry it out in all its complexity. If alternative, somewhat degraded courses of action are available that result in virtually equivalent utilities with much less total commitment, alternative behavior strategies are going to be appealing. We will now argue that at a conscious level people deal primarily with products, and discuss the circumstances when other components of the theory become salient.

We must start with an important point; whereas people use simplifying strategies and are typically only consciously aware of a subset of the elements in the theory on a day-to-day basis, people can describe all the fundamental elements of the theory. That is, if asked the appropriate questions, people can report act-to-product contingencies, product-to-evaluation contingencies, evaluation-to-outcome contingencies, who the major evaluators of their products are, what outcomes they receive and would like to receive, etc. We are not arguing that they are unaware of these elements; but rather that all the elements are not phenomenologically salient at all times. People adopt degraded versions of the fundamental process, either by choice or by necessity. These simplified strategies are often biased, or contain systematic errors in perception and information processing. Yet they typically work quite well without, it seems, much loss in effectiveness of outcomes.

A Heuristic Based on Products

Of all the elements in the theory, people are most conscious of products. When people think about what they are going to do tomorrow (i.e., how they will allocate time and energy resources), they typically think about products. A person needs to write a report, to go to a meeting, or to schedule a trip out of town. When a person describes his or her job to someone else, after the category name of professor, dancer, or cab driver, that person describes the products that are part of the job. Finally, when a person evaluates the work done at the end of the day, the quantity and quality of products completed is the focus of attention.

Thus, products are the central focus in the allocation of personal resources on the job. Products are the elements most often attended to, and are by far the most salient elements in the fundamental process. People are not nearly so continuously aware of evaluations, outcomes, and needs. In fact, one might argue that awareness of other elements in the process drops off in relation to their distance from products. That is, evaluations are less salient than products, outcomes less salient than evaluations, and needs are the least salient of all.

Acts typically are less salient than products. A secretary would rarely think about what acts must be emitted to type a report. This is particularly the case in well learned sequences of acts. When a task is being learned (i.e., when one is learning how to produce a product), acts and act-to-product contingencies are very salient. However, once the procedure is learned, the component acts are not nearly so salient to the person.

We are arguing that phenomenologically, the person attends to and deals primarily with products. We need to discuss how this represents a simplifying strategy. Specifically, products have valence or utility associated with them. There is a utility function associated with each product that relates quantity–quality of the product with the utility of that level of quantity–quality. This utility is the straightforward combination of product-to-evaluation contingencies, evaluation-to-outcome contingencies, and valence of outcomes we have described above. The shape (i.e., steepness of the utility function) determines the motivational force associated with that product. Steep slopes result in high motivational force, flat slopes result in low motivational force.

Because of the connection with evaluations and outcomes, a person can maximize positive affect by allocating resources to those products associated with the greatest motivational force. Obviously, act-to-product contingencies are also involved, in that the person has to be able to produce the product and produce it efficiently. But for most products on most jobs, the person knows how to efficiently generate the product, and this overlearned sequence is not particularly salient.

Thus, the person simplifies the resource allocation process by attempting to produce a pattern of products that will ultimately result in maximum positive affect. As long as the contingencies (act-to-product, product-to-evaluation, evaluation-to-outcome) and the valence of outcome remain fairly constant, focusing on products with their associated motivational force works rather nicely. Thus, the person is aware of the utility of different levels of the products and attempts to generate products according to this utility. For example, when the manager says that on a given day he or she must confer with a subordinate, prepare a budget, and attend three meetings, he or she is saying that these products are important, and important in the sense that they have high utility. The person typically does not think about the evaluations associated with these products, or the outcome that may result from the evaluations. It is enough that at one point in time, these links were perceived. Once they are perceived, the products take on a level utility and this utility is what is salient, not the resulting evaluation and outcomes.

This heuristic is important in that it truly does simplify the resource allocation process. Given that the acts leading to the products are fairly well learned, all one needs to do is have a sense of which products need to be emitted. With this as the guiding principle, the person does not need to be aware on a regular basis of all the other elements that enter into the resource allocation process.

However, while this phenomenological simplification process does occur, we are not arguing that people are never aware of the other elements in the resource allocation process. In fact, the other elements in the process become salient in predictable circumstances. The first circumstance is where expectations of the act-to-outcome sequence are not met. The person may find it is taking more time and energy resources to produce the products that he or she wishes to produce. This type of overload would lead to examination of act-to-product contingencies, the reasonableness of the expected levels of products, and/or the level of commitment being devoted to the job. Another type of deviation from expectation would occur when an external evaluation was different than expected or differed from the self evaluation. Finally, deviation from expectation could occur when expected outcomes were not received, or not received on the schedule the person expected. These types of deviation from expectation could result in examination of different elements of the model. For example, if an expected pay raise was not received, the person might explore product-to-evaluation and evaluation-to-outcome contingencies of the supervisor.

In addition to deviations from expectations, the person would tend to focus on elements other than products when there is a formal evaluation or reward allocation. Thus, for example, when the annual performance appraisal comes around, the contingencies, evaluations, and outcomes would become more salient. Finally, other elements become salient when the person has undergone some personal crisis, especially if the crisis is in some way related to job versus nonjob conflicts in commitment.

The motivation process is an involved one. We have stressed how it starts with needs as they are reflected by the temporary need state. These, in combination with other factors, produce valence of outcomes. Valence of outcomes are combined with contingencies to result in a series of utility-type relationships, and these relationships are the basis of the resource allocation process. The approach is very complex, even though people do use simplifying strategies. Putting all this together, it is not surprising that the motivation approaches used in the past have not been able to predict behavior very precisely. If the process is indeed as complex as we have argued, our theories and measurement procedures must deal with this complexity if we are ever going to understand and predict behavior.

Leadership: A Major Factor of the Social Environment

Environments

Although it has been acknowledged throughout the book that human behavior is a complex interaction between the individual and his or her physical and social environment, the environment was denied the degree of elaboration afforded the individual. We make no apologies for our emphasis; the theory is one of individual information processing leading to the choice of relevant acts. It is a psychological theory that looks within the individual for its primary source of explanation. Nevertheless, we do not deny the importance of the individual's environment. In this chapter we will look closely at leadership, which is an issue in the individual's environment—in particular, the social environment. However, before turning to the topic of leadership, we shall go on a brief tangent to discuss the nature of the person–environment interaction and to describe the two major subsystems within the environment—the social and the physical subsystems. Following a discussion of the last two factors, an extensive development of leadership as an organizationally relevant topic from the social environment will be presented.

Person–Environment Interaction

Our theory, presented in Chapters 2 and 3, depicts the environment as a major source of cognitions that are precursors of acts. The temporal flow of the theory is from the environment to the individual, with individual and environmental influences interacting prior to the acts. In general, this flow of events is as we intended. However, the feedback loops as well as the internal inputs into the initial processing of information recognize two important exceptions to the flow. First, the feedback loops include the fact that, although the acts are influenced by the environment, the environment is partly determined by the individual. A person's behavior may alter the environment in such a way that the environment is no longer the same due to the individual's presence in it. Second, it is possible to initiate action from internal states independent of environmental conditions. For example, a thought or an idea may lead the individual to take action. Although it is possible for a cue from the environment to trigger thoughts or ideas, they are not necessarily initiated by the environment.

It is not our intent to delineate conditions in which acts will be triggered by the environment, the individual, or some mutual condition. The two sources of stimuli were mentioned only to emphasize that the interaction between individual and environmental sources is a complex one that goes beyond the simple "mixing" of the two prior to a response. The position here is a systems view with influence going in both directions between environments and individuals.

Bandura (1978) has labeled this influence process *reciprocal determinism*. His views are worth repeating here:

> It is true that behavior is influenced by the environment, but the environment is partly of a person's own making. By their actions, people play a role in creating the social milieu and other circumstances that arise in their daily transactions. Thus, . . . psychological functioning involves a continuous reciprocal interaction between behavioral, cognitive, and environmental influences [page 345].

Physical and Social Environments

Although it must be recognized that the individual and his or her environment are not independent, the fact does not detract from the conceptual contribution of considering the environment separately. In particular, environmental stimuli are of two classes. One class includes social stimuli; the other, all remaining physical and technical stimuli. Both these sets contain extremely important organizational features. In fact, some theories of organizations have described entire organizations in one or both of these domains. Both combined represent a significant proportion of the individual's environment in an organization. Behavior variance controlled by environmental sources other than those assumed under these two systems is not of great enough significance to deserve treatment here. Let us look more closely at each system.

Physical and Technical Environment

The physical and technical system of an organization can be conceived of as thousands of stimuli that impinge upon the individual. How these stimuli are described or classified is entirely arbitrary. The classification scheme depends upon the usefulness of the constructs generated to cluster the stimuli. The usefulness must be judged against the problem or goal of the researcher or theorist. The result is a multitude of classification systems, many of which claim to be "the correct" description of the organization.

Some classification systems remain at the macro level; the level of analysis is the whole organization. Woodward (1965) focused upon the technology of the organization. Burns and Stalker (1961) and Lawrence and Lorsch (1967) also built classification systems around technological or structural variables reflecting the degree to which subparts of the organization operated in an independent or interdependent way.

At a micro level, large amounts of time and effort have been directed toward describing individuals' specific jobs. Here the focus is upon either the technological aspects of the job or the goals and behavior patterns expressed by role descriptions. In most cases, the job description is a mixture of both of these. Extensive work has been done with job descriptions by Hemphill (1959), McCormick, Jeanneret, and Mecham (1972) and many others.

It might seem advantageous to ask what are the dimensions of the physical and technical environment. However, we do not know them and, furthermore, we shall never know them. No matter what classification system is devised, another can be developed. The only solution is the development of a classification system that is useful for a particular task. Unfortunately, there is a tendency toward development of more and more "new" classification systems. The result is little consistency across investigators. Frederiksen (1972) lamented this diversity and observed that, although a major proportion of psychologists in the United States have accepted some variation or modification of the stimulus–response model of behavior, very little attention has been paid to description of the stimulus. He called for a more systematic study of the dimensions of situations. Yet, not much has changed since then. Given the nature of the problem, this is understandable. The problem has no one best solution. We hope that a comprehensive system for describing the physical and technical environment is developed eventually and that such a system will receive general acceptance, at least to the extent that considerable research can be conducted using the same structural con-

cepts. Regardless of the classification system used, one should not lose
sight of its arbitrary nature.

Social Environment

Organization are collections of two or more people. As a result, almost
every organization member works closely with others. In most cases,
these others are members of the organization. In some cases, such as that
of salespersons who spend most of their time with people not associated
with the organization, they may not be.

Whether or not the others are members of the organization, a large
proportion of behavior in organizations is shaped and influenced by
others. Our discussion of role behavior dealt explicitly with a process
through which others influence the individual's behavior. We need to
consider in greater detail the interpersonal environment.

Groups. Frequently, the others are not single individuals but collectives
of individuals. These groups are composed of a specific set of individuals
with sets of behaviors that are considered necessary to maintain membership in the group. These sets of behaviors frequently are labeled *group
norms.*

Hackman (1976), in an excellent discussion of groups and their influence on individuals, differentiates between two types of stimuli that
groups present to the individual. One type he labeled *discretionary stimuli.*
Through the use of discretionary stimuli, groups reinforce and thus
shape individuals in an attempt to influence the individual to display
some set of behaviors consistent with group goals. Note that discretionary stimuli are what we have called reactive stimuli.

Members of the group constitute a set of role senders influencing
behavior through the roles they send and the disbursement of group-
controlled rewards. Hackman points out that acceptance or rejection by
the group is the primary reinforcer available to the group for shaping
members' behavior. Group norms for behavior exist and are maintained
through the acceptance of individuals whose behavior is in line with the
norms and the rejection of those whose behavior is not. These norms,
according to our theory, serve as stimuli, which eventually influence
acts.

Hackman discusses other group stimuli, *ambient stimuli,* which influence individual behavior but are available to all members of the group
regardless of their behavior. (Earlier, we defined such stimuli as nonreactive, although we did not limit nonreactive stimuli to those from groups.)
The fact that the individual receives ambient stimuli regardless of his or

her response is interesting, for it separates this class of stimuli from those we subsumed under roles. An example of the influence of ambient stimuli on behaviors would be the amount of status or prestige one might receive for being a member of a particular department or work group. Frequently, a particular department is reputed to be the best in an area and has a well known reputation. As a result, the behaviors of group members often are influenced by the fact that they belong to that group. All members share the status equally regardless of their behavior as long as they maintain their membership in the group.

Status Differences. Identification of an individual as part of a group does not always imply that group members are of equal importance in the eyes of the group members. Obviously they are not. Research with human groups, as well as comparative research with animals, long ago discovered that relatively stable status hierarchies emerge whenever a collection of individuals exists.

Hierarchical differences among individuals are even greater in groups within organizations than within groups in other settings. In organizational settings, groups are usually established to accomplish a task or set of tasks. Groups are given a set of goals or objectives when they are formed. In order to insure control over members of groups, there is a strongly felt need for the appointment of persons who are accountable for the groups. Thus, the existence of group goals and the need for accountability lead, in almost all cases, to the appointment of people to positions of leadership in the groups. Status differences are created by fiat and are a very important influence upon the behavior of individuals in groups.

The study of interpersonal behavior in organizations has, to a large extent, concentrated upon status differences among individuals. Specifically, it has focused upon the topic of leadership. Although some have defined leadership entirely on the basis of the functions the individual provides for the group (e.g., Cartwright & Zander, 1968, Chapter 24), most have retained the status hierarchical differences among individuals. As such, the problem of leadership becomes one of understanding the nature of the behavior of persons in leadership positions as well as the effectiveness of these behaviors for influencing the other members of the group. Because of the central role of leadership in organizations, its obvious occurrence in a social setting, and the voluminous amount of theory and research that has been devoted to it, we shall examine the implications of the theory for understanding leader behavior and its effects on subordinates.

Leadership

The theory presented in Chapters 2 and 3 can address the topic of leadership from one of two perspectives. First, it can focus directly upon the behavior of the leader. In this case, the explanation of the leader's behavior is identical to the explanation for any other individual. Leaders just happen to be located in roles that require them to exert leadership behaviors. These behaviors are governed by the same processes that we have described in the earlier chapters of the book. In the discussion that follows, this orientation toward leadership will be termed the *leader's behavior* approach.

The second approach focuses upon leader behaviors as inputs into the behaviors of others to whom the leadership behaviors are directed. Leader behaviors are simply part of the inputs each of the others obtain from their environment where the environment is as diagrammed in Figure 2.1. This orientation will be termed *leader as environment* in the remainder of the chapter.

Our major concern is to describe the way in which the theory addresses leadership from each of these two perspectives. We will conclude the chapter by comparing our theory's approach to leadership to that of several other major leadership theories. Before treating these topics, it is necessary to specify more clearly what is meant by leadership and to discuss briefly leader effectiveness.

Leadership as Influence

Within the organizational context, leadership concerns focus upon the ability of those in higher status positions to influence those under them. Yet, every act of influence does not represent leadership. We side with Katz and Kahn (1978) when they define organizational influence as: "the influential increment over and above mechanical compliance with routine directives of the organization [page 528]." The incremental notion qualifies the criterion for leadership behavior; it is not sufficient to observe the degree to which one individual influences the behavior of another to evaluate the degree to which leadership is observed.

Graen and his colleagues (Dansereau, Graen, & Haga, 1975; Graen, 1976) emphasize the incremental influence notion by differentiating leadership from supervision. Supervision involves the routine application of procedures and practices bestowed upon the position in which the individual is placed. In this regard, a supervisor may recommend pay increases, evaluate subordinate performance, assign tasks under his control, and so on. Leadership, on the other hand, represents that influence over-and-above supervisory influence. Under these conditions, it is necessary to influence the subordinates to perform behaviors they technically would not have to do if they merely followed to the letter the procedures described in their position. Paying particular attention to quality, working extra hours by taking fewer breaks or shorter lunch hours, and implementing new ways to accomplish the job are a few of the behaviors that might be attributed to the leader's leadership.

In the chapter on roles, we described influence in terms of evaluation-to-outcome contingencies. Recall that the influence a role sender (other) had over the focal person was construed as the focal person's perception of (a) other's evaluation-to-outcome contingencies for the focal person; and (b) the extent to which the focal person valued the outcomes made available to him or her by the other. Within this framework, leadership becomes a subset of the role-influence concept. The other individual is that person who is in a leadership position with respect to the focal person. Leader influence is that subset of evaluation-to-outcome contingencies controlled by the leader but not automatically vested in him or her by virtue of the position that he or she occupies in the organization. As is always the case with the influence of others, the degree of influence depends upon the extent to which the subordinate perceives this subset of contingencies and the extent to which he or she values the outcomes associated with the evaluation.

Given this definition of leadership, we are assuming that the subordinate is aware of the acts that are necessary to produce certain evaluations from the leader. Technically, the degree of influence depends upon three contingencies: act-to-product, product-to-evaluation, and evaluation-to-outcome. We have concentrated on a subset of evaluation-to-outcome contingencies because it is this subset that defines the unique set of what we call leadership and because it is consistent with the existing literature.

Leader Effectiveness

If we accept that leadership is an influence process, leadership effectiveness becomes the extent to which the leader is able to influence his or her subordinates *in a way that leads to group goal accomplishment.* To evaluate leader effectiveness, some evaluation of the group's effectiveness usually is made, and leadership effectiveness is inferred from this. This is a problem. If leadership in organizations is viewed as the ability of the leader to influence behavior of those under him or her, as we have chosen to view it, then it is obvious that many factors other than leadership influence group member effectiveness. Factors within the physical and technical environments, as well as the abilities of the subordinates, affect the group's effectiveness. Thus, evaluations of leaders, that is, judgments about leadership effectiveness, may be less accurate than evaluations of others because a major proportion of the information used to make the judgments is based on the behaviors of others.

Leadership within the Theory

Leader's Behavior

In all respects, the behaviors of those in leadership positions are subject to the same influences as the behaviors of anyone else. Therefore, we can understand and explain the behavior of a leader in the same way as we would that of any other individual. Leaders as individuals receive inputs from their environment. These inputs are affected by individual differences, are subject to extensive cognitive processing, and lead to the choice of some set of acts. These acts form perceived products, which in turn are measured both by the leaders themselves and by others to form products, which, with the evaluations of the products, function as inputs to the leaders' decision process.

Inferred Products

Although it is important to realize that the behavior of leaders can be viewed in terms of the theory as previously outlined, there are several unique issues pertaining to those in leadership positions. The most critical of these is that of *inferred products*. Recall that products were defined as the result of a measurement system. With regard to leaders, the products attributed to leaders from the measurement system of others (including the self) often are based upon observed sources other than the perceived products of leaders themselves.

We are taught at an early age that leaders make things happen—they are responsible for the group's behavior. As a result, the behaviors of group members often serve as primary inputs into measurement and evaluation judgments about leader behavior. This was demonstrated most clearly by research on what is termed "implicit leadership theory" (Eden & Leviatan, 1975; Rush, Thomas, & Lord, 1977). Implicit leadership theory states that, through everyday experience, individuals develop a set of expectations about what they think leaders do and the effects of what they do (how leader behaviors are related to group members' responses and to group effectiveness). These expectations are widely shared in the population resulting in a "naive psychology" of leader behavior similar to Heider's (1958) "naive psychology" of individuals (Calder, 1977). To the extent that individuals possess some information about the responses of group members, they will infer the existence of a set of leader products that they believe influenced the group members' responses. These inferred products may bear little resemblance to the actual leader products preceding member responses. As a result, measurement systems applied to those in leadership positions, both by the leaders themselves and by others, are likely to employ information about member products. Similarly, evaluations of leaders are based upon inferences made from the evaluation of group performance. Thus, for leaders, both measurement and evaluation systems employ a subset of products inferred from the products or the evaluations of other individuals to a greater extent than occurs for nonleaders.

In our previous descriptions, the measurement system was applied to the actual products of individuals to yield perceived products. There was only one type of contingency between actual products and perceived products. For leader behavior, it is necessary to introduce second-order contingencies, which influence judgments about leader products. All the second-order contingencies represent links between the leader and other individuals that influence perceptions of leaders. First, there is the contingency between leader acts and subordinate acts. This link is the degree to which leaders influence subordinates. Second, leader products are contingent upon group member products, because judgments about leader products often are based upon judgments about group members' products.

Judgments of leaders' products also are made from knowledge about the group's performance as a whole. Although not focusing on leadership, Staw (1975) manipulated group performance and then asked group members to describe the behaviors that occurred within the group. He found that members of "successful" groups reported the occurrence of very different behaviors than did members of "unsuccessful" groups. This difference occurred in spite of the fact that group performance levels were experimentally manipulated, independently of actual group performance, and that the performance information was given after all interaction between group members had ceased but before behavior ratings were completed. Although there is some evidence suggesting that the strength of the effects of generalizations from performance are weakened by experiences in actual on-going groups (DeNisi & Pritchard, 1978), this other set of second-order contingencies does seem to exist between group products and leader products.

Individuals also carry around implicit theories of those leader behaviors associated with given evaluations of the effectiveness of groups under the leaders' jurisdiction (Calder, 1977). Translated into the language of the theory of Chapters 2 and 3, evaluations of group performance, when presented to individuals who observe leaders, serve as inputs to the individuals' measurement system and influence judgments of the leaders' products. To the extent that a priori expectations (i.e., stereotypes) are widely shared about the contingencies between leader products and group evaluations and are not overridden by specific experiences with particular leaders (e.g., DeNisi & Pritchard, 1978), the products attributed to leaders may not resemble the leaders' actual products when information about the group's performance is available. The errors in the measuring of products may occur in the leader's self-measurement system as well as in the systems of others. To the extent that the leader accepts the stereotype when presented with information about his or her group's performance, the judgment of his or her own products will be distorted in line with the expectations about the contingencies between leader products and group performance.

Although we are suggesting that the theory applies to the behavior of leaders in a similar way to the behavior of others, the existence of second-order contingencies for leaders complicates the process of translating leader acts into products. Later in the chapter we will explore some of the effects of this added complexity for leaders.

Evaluations of Leader Performance

As we have mentioned, leader effectiveness commonly refers to evaluations about the extent to which the leader contributed to the successful accomplishment of the goals of his or her group. The primary focus of the evaluator of the leader is upon the goals or mission of the group rather than upon the leader. Once an assessment of group goal accomplishments is completed, inferences are made about the contributions of the leader to the group. Presumably, evaluators take into account limiting conditions such as the extent of group member ability or the physical resources available to the group that might influence group performance independent of the leader's contributions or distractions. In practice, such considerations are extremely difficult. Knowledge about all the factors that constitute the set of limiting conditions is rarely available to any specific evaluator. Even if the evaluator consciously considered several moderators, it is unlikely that he or she could consistently weigh and use this information to evaluate the leader. Therefore, the evaluation of leader effectiveness frequently is based almost entirely upon the performance of the unit over which the leader has responsibility.

The evaluation sequence described above differs considerably from that presented in the theory for individuals other than leaders. Recall that the difference again is the addition of second-order contingencies. In this case a contingency between group evaluation and leader evaluation is added to evaluation systems applied to leaders. We stated in earlier chapters that the typical evaluation system for individuals used as its inputs the evaluator's perception of the focal person's products. Leaders also can be and are evaluated in this manner. But, evaluations of leaders are based, to a large extent, upon the evaluative judgments about the extent to which the units for which the leaders are responsible successfully meet their goals.

Perceptions of Contingencies

We have seen how the occurrence of second-order contingencies influence the nature of perceived products and perceived evaluations for leaders. Through their influence on products and evaluations, second-order contingencies also influence two of the three primary sets of contingencies in the theory. These contingencies are the ones between actual products and perceived products as well as the ones between perceived products and evaluations.

Assume that products and evaluations for leaders are more contaminated with factors beyond the leaders' control than products and evaluations for nonleaders. One of two possibilities exists for the effect of this condition on the previously mentioned contingencies. First, if the individual accepts the perceived products and evaluations as they are, both sets of contingencies are likely to reflect the objective conditions less closely than was the case for those not in leadership positions. This acknowledges the fact that the quality of two of the three elements needed to form perceptions of the contingency relationships is lowered. If both the products and the evaluations attributed to leaders are contaminated with surplus information about group products and evaluation, perceived contingencies using one or both of these two elements also are likely to be inaccurate.

Second, those observing and evaluating leaders (both the leaders themselves and others) could, in a sense, partial out the contributions of other sources to leader products and evaluations before forming contingency perceptions. In this case, the observers would need to have a sense of the degree to which the others contributed to the leader's products and evaluation. Most observers will not have a clear perception of others' contributions. Nevertheless, in conditions in which it is well known that a major portion of evaluations or product judgments usually attributed to leaders was due to factors beyond the leader's control, it is possible that some inductive partialling process occurs before actual product-to-perceived product and product-to-evaluation contingency perceptions are formed.

The most reasonable conclusion is that the contingencies of measurement and evaluation systems for leaders will be less accurate than those for nonleaders. This occurs because of the additional factors which influence inferences made about leaders but not about nonleaders. These additional factors, theoretically, often should be ignored when considering leader effectiveness. In practice, they are not ignored.

Leader as Environment

The second major orientation toward leadership treats the leader as a significant part of subordinates' environment. Leader influence is the focus of such an approach. The leader is a major part of the measurement, evaluation, and reward systems in his or her subordinates' environment and, as such, often affects the three major contingencies of the subordinates. These are the actual product-to-perceived product, perceived product-to-evaluation, and evaluation-to-outcome contingencies.[1]

Several treatises of leadership have dealt explicitly with the establishment of subordinate contingencies. The most extensive, the path–goal model of leadership (Evans, 1970; House, 1971; House & Dressler, 1974; House & Mitchell, 1974), focused upon the leader's direct influence in actively establishing contingencies. Recently indirect, more passive, influence through modeling also has been considered (see Weiss, 1977). In that case, subordinates learn contingencies for themselves by observing their superiors. For the remainder of this section, we shall describe the way in which the theory treats leadership when the leader is seen as part of the subordinates' environment. Following this, other theories of leadership will be presented and the theory presented here will be compared to them. However, it should be stated from the outset that the theory presented here owes a major intellectual debt to the notions of path–goal theory.

1. Before continuing, note should be made about terminology. Recall from the theory that actual products are those produced by the acts of individuals. However, neither individual actors themselves nor others who observe them cognitively deal with actual products. They deal with perceived products. Since perceived products are the ones most frequently of interest, unless it is necessary to distinguish actual products from perceived ones, "products" will refer to perceived products. A second terminology issue in the area of leadership deals with the fact that several leadership theories focus upon leader behavior and frequently treat leader "acts" and "behaviors" as synonymous. In terms of our theory, either acts or behaviors as used by others represent *products*. As a result, we shall convert the terminology of other theories to our term products in an attempt to avoid misinterpretation of what we mean and others mean by acts.

Actual-to-Perceived Product Contingencies

In most organizations, leaders are a major part of their subordinates' measurement system (located in the external environment area of Figure 2.1). As such, leaders establish certain actual-to-perceived product contingencies which they use to form judgments about the products produced by subordinates. These contingencies should be relatively constant across subordinates. For example, if the product is a typed letter, a judgment about the presence of a typed letter should require the same set of actual products from all subordinates.

Assuming that the actual-to-perceived product contingencies are relatively fixed, the leader influences subordinates not through changing these contingencies, but by aiding them in being able or willing to produce acts that will lead to the desired actual products. Here the leader can do at least two things. First, he can assign subordinates to subtasks within the group so that they are able to produce certain products. Assuming some variance in subordinate skills and abilities and some variance in the nature of subtasks to be assigned, judicious assignment of individuals to tasks should influence the extent to which subordinates are able to attain certain products. Second, the leader could work with subordinates to increase their skills to enable them to perform certain acts that would lead to the actual products necessary to form the desired perceived products. This again should increase the probability of attaining actual products relevant to the leader's measurement system.

One of the things implied from our discussion is that effective leaders must observe the actual products of their subordinates quite closely to be able to apply their measurement systems effectively. However, leaders often are not well informed about what their subordinates produce. Therefore, we stress that to serve as a valid measurement system, leaders must be aware of the actual products that serve as inputs into their measurement system for subordinates.

One of the advantages of a close association between leaders and subordinates that is suggested for improving the actual-to-perceived product contingencies is that leaders and subordinates are more likely to share the same measurement system. Recall that the measurement system of any perceiver converts actual products into perceived products. However, there may not be close agreement between two observers of the same actual products as to the perceived products resulting from them. For example, the bus driver and the bus rider may both have observed the same actual products of the driver along the route which would serve as inputs into their measurement system for the product of a safe ride. In spite of the same inputs entering the system, their judgments (the outputs of the measurement system) about the degree to which it was a safe ride, may differ considerably. Differences in perceptions of products between leaders and followers are quite common. Yet it is important that these differences be minimized because leaders base their evaluations of subordinates on their own perceptions of products, not on those of the subordinates. Given the fact that leaders' evaluations usually are important for most members of organizations, reducing differences between leader and subordinate perceptions of subordinate products is desirable. The process of aiding members establish contingencies between actual and perceived products deemed valuable by leaders should increase the probability of the congruence between a leader's and his or her subordinates' measurement systems.

Product-to-Evaluation Contingencies

According to the theory, the evaluation system is defined by contingencies between products and evaluations attached to those products for a given evaluator. For many individuals in organizations, their immediate superior is the primary, perhaps the only, individual who evaluates the products that they provide to the organization. Therefore, leaders are usually a major part of subordinates' evaluation system.

The evaluation system is one in which the leader may alter the contingencies to fit the individual subordinate. Leaders may take into account information about the individual (i.e., he or she is new on the job) and alter contingencies for that individual. In other words, the leader exercises influence through the application of the evaluation system both through the attachment of outcomes to evaluations, as we shall see in the next section, and through the establishment of product-to-evaluation contingencies for each subordinate that are reasonable for that person.

Evaluation-to-Outcome Contingencies

Our position is that evaluation-to-outcome contingencies represent the reward system. We have said also that these contingencies represent, in part, the leader's power and influence over subordinates. Here the leader plays a major part with respect to subordinates. With a knowledge of those outcomes that are valued by the subordinate, the leader can associate valued outcomes with particular evaluations of the subordinates. To do this effectively, the leader (a) must understand the subordinates well enough to know what are and what are not valued outcomes; (b) must have the outcomes available to make contingent upon performance; and (c) must have a good measurement and evaluation system so that the evaluations on which the rewards are based are valid. Although all three of these conditions are necessary, in most cases the last two tend to be the most important. Leaders usually are aware enough of the first, so that it provides no major concern.

Other Leadership Theories and Models

Most leadership theories accept what we have called the leader-as-environment point of view. In the discussion that follows, several leader-as-environment theories will be presented, and how these theories relate to the position we have taken will be discussed. We have separated the theories into those that have focused upon contingencies similar to our theory presented in Chapters 2 and 3 and those that use dissimilar constructs.

Contingency Focused Views of Leadership

Path–Goal Theory

According to House (House, 1971; House & Dressler, 1976; House & Mitchell, 1974) and others (Evans, 1970, 1974; Locke, 1974), leaders function primarily to motivate subordinates in such a way that the subordinates accomplish the group's and their own goal(s) simultaneously. To do this, the leader must create conditions that allow subordinates to choose courses of action (in our terminology "actual products") that will reach their goals and those of the organization.

Path–goal theory identifies two contingencies as important in this process. First, subordinates must perceive a contingency between the effort they put into their job and their performance on it. Second, valued outcomes must be contingent upon performance. The attractiveness or valence of the outcomes themselves depends upon the individual's own judgment about their value.

The leader's role in the establishment of contingencies between products and outcomes is critical from a motivational standpoint. As we have stated, these contingencies influence the attractiveness of products and, as a result, the likelihood that the products will be produced again in the future. Leaders influence contingencies by judicious *assignment* of individuals to subtasks, *training* or coaching, and the establishment of a *reward system* that associates outcomes with performance. The processes we described earlier in the chapter were entirely consistent with this position.

Our theory and path–goal theory differ on two issues. First, they differ on the degree of elaboration of both elements and contingencies of the theory. Path–goal theory focuses upon subordinates' effort as it relates to performance. Since effort is an act (i.e., it is a time and commitment issue) and performance is an evaluation in our theory, path–goal theory links acts directly to evaluations. This difference between the two positions is difficult to evaluate. From an empirical perspective, most individuals probably confuse effort (an act) with products, both actual and perceived, and as a result will report effort-to-performance contingencies that relate quite well to performance. Early work in expectancy theory by Hackman and Porter (1968) showed that ratings of effort-to-performance contingencies did quite well in predicting performance. However, from a theoretical point of view, it is more appropriate to consider the expanded interpretation that recognizes that acts are different from products, that individuals cognitively deal primarily with products, not acts, and that the measurement and evaluation systems are two distinct systems. Furthermore, keeping the distinction is useful from a diagnostic standpoint for those cases in which the measurement and evaluation systems do not co-vary in such a way as to be nearly perfectly correlated. Our preference is for the more complex elaboration of the links between acts and evaluations.

A second difference between our theory and path–goal theory is that the latter focused primarily upon two leader behaviors—initiation of structure and consideration. These behaviors have enjoyed considerable acceptance in the leadership literature area, but can be restrictive (Hammer & Dachler, 1975). They represent global behaviors which may not be of sufficient specificity to reflect what goes on in groups. The theory we presented here addresses *any* behavior of the leader. In fact, so could the basic concepts of path–goal theory. The limitation of path–goal theory to the two behavior classes was due more to preference than to the concepts of the theory per se. The focus upon initiation of structure and consideration limits the path–goal theory more than it limits what we have said.

Vertical Dyad Linkage Theory

Graen and his colleagues (Dansereau, Graen & Haga, 1975; Graen, 1976; Graen, Dansereau, & Minami, 1972) view leadership as a dyadic interaction between a leader and each of his or her subordinates. The interaction varies in quality from the routine application of policy and practice to an active sharing of the leadership role with the subordinate. At the routine level, leaders exercise their rights and responsibilities as defined by their role. They evaluate subordinates, assign jobs, and parcel out rewards to them in exchange for the subordinates' conformity to the rules and regulations and for the subordinates' performance of their work according to standard operating procedures. At this level, the leader is not exercising leadership but is supervising the behavior of others, according to Graen. At the other extreme, the leader expands subordinates' roles by giving them responsibility for greater amounts of the group's task. The expansion of the role allows selected subordinates to realize a set of outcomes usually not available to those who complete the specific requirements of a job at a minimally acceptable level. The added responsibility and involvement offered to those subordinates fortunate enough to be chosen as "informal assistants" (Graen's terminology) allows them to experience a sense of accomplishment and involvement in the work.

The essence of the vertical dyad linkage theory (VDL) is an exchange relationship between the leader and his or her subordinates. The exchange is between dyads composed of one member and the leader. This is in contrast to the view that considers the leader's behavior with respect to the group as a whole. The exchange alters the roles of leaders and subordinates as each alters and changes their roles in exchange for various parts of the group's task. The leader is primarily responsible for making final decisions about what roles subordinates will hold, but the subordinates interact and bargain with him or her to establish their own roles.

From the standpoint of the present theory, VDL, like path–goal theory, is directed toward the influence of subordinates' actual-to-perceived product contingencies as well as the two sets of contingencies affected by product-to-outcome associations (i.e., product-to-evaluations and evaluation-to-outcomes). With regard to the first, active bargaining between a leader and a subordinate to establish the subordinate's role creates the actual-to-perceived product contingencies for the subordinate. For those assigned more routine tasks, the set of products is limited and very clearly specified. The more expanded role of the informal assistant identifies ranges of products and has more flexibility about the products to be exhibited. As a result, there is more ambiguity in the actual-to-perceived product contingencies for this subordinate. The product-set is left open such that its boundaries are not known to either the leader or the subordinate when the role is established.

Concerning the association between products and outcomes, VDL sees the leader's role in a similar way to that depicted by path–goal theory. Leaders can influence the extent to which outcomes are linked to products, which affects the subordinates' motivation. At the supervisory end of the leader responses to the subordinate, path–goal theory and VDL agree completely. Therefore, these positions see the leader's function in terms of influencing both product-to-evaluation and evaluation-to-outcome contingencies.

Informal assistants are subject to much the same set of influences with two notable exceptions. First, due to the ambiguity or openness left in their roles, the product-to-evaluation contingencies may be less clear to them than they are to those not considered informal assistants. The uncertainty perhaps could create some degree of anxiety and dissatisfaction. However, the data indicate clearly that informal assistants are aware of their privileged status (Dansereau *et al.*, 1975) so this awareness may alleviate some of the anxiety. Second, informal assistants have an expanded set of outcomes available to them due to their broader, more responsible role. These outcomes are those which are seen as meeting higher-order needs, such as feelings of accomplishment and more autonomy. Therefore, the leader not only influences product-to-outcome contingencies to outcomes provided by the organization or the group; he or she can also expand the set of outcomes available to subordinates to include those related to higher-order needs.

The theoretical positions of both path–goal theory and VDL addressed one or more contingencies. However, in all cases, neither differentiated between product-to-evaluation and evaluation-to-outcome contingencies. Finally, both path–goal theory and VDL suggested that leaders could expand the outcomes available by allowing for the attainment of intrinsic outcomes by their subordinates. This could be accomplished through the assignment of tasks (or the establishment of roles) in which intrinsic outcomes are contingent upon successful task performance for those in such positions.

Three Other Theoretical Orientations

Trait Approaches

Systematic research on leadership began by focusing upon characteristics of the leader. The result was disappointing. In fact, the effects of these variables on leader effectiveness were so small and so difficult to replicate consistently that by the end of the mid to late 1950s, reviews of leadership were advocating strongly that attention be turned elsewhere (Gibb, 1954).

Recently, interest in the effects of the leader's personal traits or characteristics has increased. Stogdill's (1974) extensive compilation reflected a more favorable evaluation of traits than did previous reviews. Two possible reasons appear to have instigated this change. First, work by Ghiselli (1963, 1971) identified traits that seem to relate consistently to managerial performance for a large and diverse sample of managers. Ghiselli's research was carefully conceived and well executed so that the empirical support it provided for trait approaches was well accepted. Second, methodological limitations of the more firmly entrenched person–

situation interaction approaches turned attention back to that of traits (Korman, 1973, 1977).

Our theoretical position is not inconsistent with trait approaches to leadership. But neither is it closely related to them. First, if one focuses upon leader behavior per se, trait theories relegate the major explanatory power to individual differences. From our theory diagrammed in Chapters 2 and 3, it is obvious that we view individual differences as constraints or moderators rather than as major explanatory sources. To us, they set boundaries or limits on the cognitive processes and the response repertories of the individual.

We would argue that traits affect the leader's influence only to the extent that the traits affect some characteristics that in some way impact upon the subordinates. Trait theorists should not disagree with this position. However, we will go farther and state that most of the impact would be on the establishment of or influence on sets of contingencies between the subordinates' products and outcomes. These contingencies are those of the measurement, evaluation, and reward systems of the leader for the subordinates and are part of the external environment of the subordinates. Leader traits, from our point of view, must lead to stable behavior patterns that affect these three systems if they are to have much impact upon subordinates' behavior.

Behavior Approaches

Faced with what appeared to be little advancement in the understanding of leadership through a search for traits of leaders, researchers turned their attention to leader behavior. Leadership research involved a search for the behaviors displayed by the leader which influenced the group in such a way as to lead to effective group functioning. The quest to discover important leader behaviors utilized both laboratory and field research. Early work was concentrated at Harvard University, the University of Michigan, and Ohio State University (see Katz & Kahn, 1978; and Stogdill, 1974, for more detailed discussions of this research).

In spite of the diversity of methods, the research findings converged on two similar classes of behaviors. One set encompassed those behaviors that were directed toward task accomplishment. The other focused on the interpersonal issues in the group.

Our theory does not address directly any particular leader behaviors. Nevertheless, the underlying assumption of our theory and the behavior approach is the same. The assumption is that leaders influence members through their (leaders') behavior. The behavior approach simply described the behaviors in terms of the objects or objectives to which the behaviors were directed. None of the focus was upon contingencies or outcomes as has been discussed. In contrast, we have concentrated upon contingencies and ignored the description of behaviors, or, in our case, product classes.

Individual–Situation Interaction

Although research converged on two dimensions of leader behavior, problems arose when these behaviors were related to group effectiveness. Sometimes task behaviors were more effective and other times interpersonally oriented behaviors were. Therefore, the major focus of leadership research shifted from discovering which behaviors were most effective to examining the conditions under which specific leader behaviors were more effective.

Leadership theorists quickly discovered that it was easier to agree upon the nature of leader behavior than it was to agree upon the nature of the situation. Many taxonomic views of the leader's situation have been espoused. We have selected three. These theories frequently are identified by the individual(s) most responsible for their development.

Fiedler's Contingency Model. The mention of contingency theories of leadership immediately brings to mind the work of Fred E. Fiedler (Fielder, 1964, 1967, 1971), for he, more than anyone else, moved the focus of leadership from that of behaviors to that of behaviors in contexts. The theory itself developed inductively. From a large number of empirical studies conducted in many diverse settings, he proposed a theory that viewed leadership as an influence process. Situations in which the leader found himself or herself were said to vary in their favorability to the leader in terms of his or her ability to influence the group members. The most appropriate leader style or behavior depended upon the favorability of the situation.

With this general framework, Fiedler's model describes leader style, situational favorability, and the relationship between the two as they affect the effectiveness of the group. According to the model, leadership style varies along a continuum from person oriented to task oriented. The orientation of the leader reflects his or her preference for types of behaviors to display while working with the group in order to accomplish the group's task. Leader style is measured by a scale that asks the individual to describe the person with whom he or she has had the most difficulty working in the past (the least preferred coworker—LPC—scale). Those who score low on the scale (low LPCs) are said to be task oriented and those who score high (high LPCs) are person oriented. Fiedler believes that the leader style is a relatively permanent characteristic of the individual which is not easily changed. Furthermore, since it is a preference for a set of behaviors rather than individual behaviors, high LPCs often display task oriented behaviors and vice versa.

Fiedler concentrated upon three aspects of the leader's environment as indices of the favorability of the situation to the leader. These three are: leader–member relations, task structure, and position power. Leader–member relations refer to the extent to which the leader is accepted, linked, and respected by the members. Task structure is the extent to which there exists an agreed-upon structure for the group's task. Relatively simple tasks that can be accomplished through the step-by-step application of standard operating procedures represent highly structured tasks, whereas complex tasks with relatively unspecified means to reach some ends are considered unstructured. Finally, position power refers to the formal authority vested in the leadership position to which the leader has access by virtue of his placement in the position.

The situation's favorability to the leader is a function of all three of the above dimensions. To index it, each dimension is dichotomized, and the three are ordered in terms of importance, with leader–member relations highest on importance and position power lowest. Obviously, the most favorable situation is one in which all three situational dimensions are positive.

In Fiedler's extensive research looking at group effectiveness as a function of leader style and situational favorability, a complex interaction between the two has emerged. The model shows that task oriented leaders (low LPCs) do better in either very favorable or very unfavorable situations. Person oriented leaders (high LPCs) do better in moderately favorable situations. Therefore, it is recommended that leaders be matched with situations that fit their style (Fiedler, Chemmers, & Maher, 1976) in order to more fully utilize their abilities.

Support for the model since its inception has been mixed. Frequently it is unsupported (Graen, Alvares, Orris, & Martella, 1969) and, on other occasions, the model is supported (Chemmers & Skzypek, 1972; Csoka & Bons, 1978). However, our purpose here is not to evaluate the theory but to compare its position with our own. In that regard, the theory's assumption of leadership as influence is consistent with the position we have taken. As far as leader style is concerned, our model does not speak to this issue. According to our theory, style would be an individual difference factor that should influence the leader's response at several junctures in the theory. However, it is safe to say that the contingency model relies more heavily upon a relatively unchanging style orientation of the individual that we have posited.

We are in agreement with Fiedler's position with respect to the assumption that situations differ in the extent to which the leader can

influence group members. Although we would not argue with the belief
that leader–member relations, task structure, and position power are
important factors determining influence, we would suggest that influence would be better explored at the more direct level of managing
contingencies. This is particularly true if global concepts such as Fiedler's
three dimensions happen to encompass conflicting contingencies. Consider, for example, task structure. We would argue that as the task becomes more structured, product-to-evaluation contingencies become
clearer. Also, actual-to-perceived product contingencies may improve if
the unstructured task required more and diverse skills. As a result, assuming valued outcomes are associated with evaluations, it should be
easier for the leader to influence subordinates under conditions of high
structure. However, to the extent that high structure leads to low task
variety, autonomy, and consequently the opportunity for involvement in
the task, leader influence may decrease. In this case, the contingencies
between products and valued intrinsic outcomes would be low, at least
for some individuals. Under these conditions, more structured tasks may
decrease the leader's influence possibilities. Thus, we see that changing
tasks to make them more structured could increase leader influence in
some cases and decrease it in others.

Since some of the situational dimensions described by the contingency
model may have opposite effects on critical contingencies, we suggest
that favorability would be better addressed at the level of individual
contingencies than by clustering contingencies.[2]

Vroom and Yetton. To Vroom and Yetton (1973), leaders are decision
makers. The objective of their theory is to describe the optimal combination of leader and subordinate participation in making group decisions.

The situation enters into the model because the amount of participation that is most appropriate varies across situations. Factors that influence the amount of participation are the nature of the problem, the
knowledge of subordinates relevant to the problem, the degree to which
it is critical that subordinates accept the final decision, and so on. It is
apparent from this list that with each new problem confronted by the
leader, there is a need to evaluate the extent to which group members
should participate.

Allowing for participation among group members is not an issue of
leader style according to Vroom and Yetton. Every leader sometimes
should and sometimes should not involve group members in decisions.

2. In all fairness to Fiedler, he realized that the three proposed dimensions may not be
the best way to index favorability (Fiedler, 1964). He accepted the favorability notion but
realized that other ways to index it may be more effective.

Furthermore, the degree of participation varies; it is not an all-or-none phenomenon.

In many ways Vroom and Yetton's model of leadership is more of a flow chart for leader decision making than a theory of leadership. Based upon generalizations from a large body of research findings and from theoretical writings on participation in decision making, Vroom and Yetton (1973) constructed a set of eight questions. The questions represent branching points in the model. For example, the leader asks himself or herself the first question: "If the decision were accepted, would it make a difference which course of action were adopted?" (Vroom & Yetton, 1973, page 36). Based upon the answer to it (either yes or no), the user of the model is directed to a second question. The questions continue until the person reaches the end of a branch of the model. At this point, he or she is referred to a set of methods for reaching decisions.

The validity of the model has yet to be demonstrated. However, data from managers asked to recall successful and unsuccessful decisions, then describe these situations, do tend to support the links in the model (Vroom, 1976; Vroom & Jago, 1978). Nevertheless, these data are based upon managers' recall of past events. The extent to which they are able to recall the events accurately is unknown. Certainly the history of such techniques is not very encouraging, as Nesbett and Wilson (1977) have documented. One must keep in mind that the theory is relatively new to the leadership area; hopefully future research will clarify the issue.

When the Vroom and Yetton model is compared to the theory we have presented, we find no disagreements but neither do we find much common ground. Vroom and Yetton concentrate on a small subset of behaviors dealing with the way in which decision making is shared with group members. From our point of view, the branches in the model represent situations with known product-to-evaluation contingencies—that is, known to Vroom and Yetton based upon prior research. The user of the model may be unaware of the appropriate products to display. By telling him or her the correct response, they are explicitly stating the product(s) that have high contingencies with positive evaluations. Since we have never implied that contingencies had to be experienced to be learned, the model represents a way of presenting leaders with product-to-evaluation contingencies for a specific set of products—those products dealing with behaviors toward subordinates with regard to their participation in decision making.

Katz and Kahn. To Katz and Kahn (1978), leadership is influence. The nature of the responses of leaders depends upon the hierarchical level in the organization at which the leadership position is located. They categorize the responses of leaders in terms of whether they are cognitive or affective. For example, upper echelon leaders in the organization need cognitive responses which utilize a systems perspective. A systems perspective is the ability to conceptualize the organization as a part of the larger environment in which it operates. Top echelon leaders must consider the impact of government, labor markets, available supplies, and so on as they deal with day-to-day issues. In contrast to top echelon leaders, leaders at the lowest end of the organizational hierarchy must exercise cognitive skills that provide high levels of technical knowledge about the task. They also must understand company rules and regulations as they relate to the specific task. Note that there are more particularistic skill requirements at the lowest level than at the highest one.

With regard to the theory of Chapters 2 and 3, again there is no disagreement with Katz and Kahn's (1978) position. To place it in our framework, their theory involves the perception of sets of products that are desirable at different levels in the organization. To make such prescriptions, one assumes on the basis of past experience a set of product-to-evaluation contingencies. By stating the preferred product set, one implicitly states that those products are highly contingent upon evaluations in that setting. Katz and Kahn focus upon the products and identify those products that are most contingent at various levels of the organization.

Describing Situations

The three contingency theories accept the tenet that the behaviors displayed by a leader to achieve effective performance from the group depend upon the nature of the situation. We concur with this belief. However, it is obvious that little or no agreement exists on the issue of how the situation should be construed. Most contingency theories spin in their own descriptive worlds, not contradicting but also not integrating other positions into their own or modifying their own to fit the data from other orientations.

In our opinion, integration of the diverse contingency theories of leadership into any one of the present theories is not possible. Certainly, it cannot be done without forcing one or more positions into frameworks that they never were intended to fit. Furthermore, it does not seem likely that a new theory will emerge that will encompass all of them in situational parameters similar to the ones used here—that is, a new theory with situational descriptions in the everyday language which are commonly used to describe environments.[3]

We suggest that one approach to the contingency dilemma would be to

3. Calder (1977) calls these "first degree constructs" and criticizes them for their surplus meaning and the extent to which previous expectations cloud the ability of individuals to observe and report the effects of these variables on other variables.

focus attention closer to the behavioral phenomenon in question. In this case, the common theme is that of the leader's influence. It then could be asked what are the most salient environmental factors in influence. Our answer to this is that it is the situational factors affecting the leader's ability to influence relevant contingencies of his or her subordinates that are critical. Therefore, leadership theories wishing to incorporate situational moderators affecting leader influence should concentrate upon those situational constraints on contingency management. Such an approach is more specific than the three positions offered here and is likely to describe situations in fewer, common sense, every-day terms. But it is also likely to be able to deal with a broader range of leadership situations and encompass more of the essence of leadership.

Conclusion: A Perspective on Leadership

Calder (1977) makes the following comments on leadership:

> [R]esearchers have directly adopted the language and ideas of everyday explanation in their zeal to study the phenomenon of leadership. . . . There has been almost no attempt to define a leader in truly psychological, sociological, or anthropological terms. Instead, the reference of the construct is to our everyday conception of leadership. . . . [Our] criticism does not deny that intuition may be a source of scientific theory. It does deny that the constructs and logic of everyday language can be accepted as scientific without additional support. Leadership research has not provided that support. The paradox of leadership research is resolved by the realization that what has been attempted is not the development of scientific theory but the systematic and consistent use of everyday thought [page 182].

The theories of leadership we have reviewed all treat the leader as an important part of a subordinate's social environment. Here the commonality ceases. Each theory has developed a set of concepts and processes in the everyday language that allows for general acceptance and understanding for the scientist as well as the general public. However, the same language that encourages acceptance discourages an integration of the various theories and, more importantly, masks our understanding of the psychological processes involved in leadership due, in part, to the surplus meaning of terms from everyday language.

The theory presented in Chapters 2 and 3 offers a more general conceptual framework from which to view leadership. It accepts leadership as an influence process. The leader is simply a multi-attribute stimulus object in the subordinate's environment. The stimuli he or she presents to the subordinate obviously interact with other stimuli present to form some perceptions on the part of the subordinate. We have argued that the extent to which the leader does have influence depends upon two classes of variables. First, it depends upon the leader's control over three sets of contingencies. These are the subordinates' actual-to-perceived product, product-to-evaluation, and evaluation-to-outcome contingencies. Second, it depends upon the subordinate's perceived value of the outcomes over which the leader has some control. A better understanding of the leader's contribution to the contingencies of the measurement, evaluation, and reward systems in the subordinate's environment as well as an understanding of the subordinate's preferences for outcomes allows us to comprehend better the effects of leaders in a wide variety of settings.

8

Organizational Climate

There are few constructs in organizational psychology as confusing and as universally misunderstood as the construct of "organizational climate." The major source of this confusion centers around the extreme difficulty that has been experienced in attempting to define climate. Whereas it would seem to be unanimously agreed among organizational theorists that the basic foundation elements for the climate construct are attributes or sets of attributes of the work environment, considerable disagreement exists concerning a variety of important issues. For example, diverse opinions exist as to the nature of these attributes, the way in which these attributes themselves combine, and the way they are used by an individual to form something that one might call organizational climate. Several excellent papers have appeared in recent years in which individuals have attempted to provide some degree of clarity to many of the central issues regarding the definition of climate. In so doing, they even have raised the substantive question as to the actual worth and utility of such a construct, and whether it is indeed useful for our understanding of behavior in organizations (e.g., Campbell, Dunnette, Lawler & Weick, 1970; Guion, 1973; James & Jones, 1974, 1976; Schneider, 1975).

It seems self-evident that the construct of organizational climate is not about to disappear regardless of the admonitions and stated concerns of many who have attempted to deal with this difficult and elusive entity. It would appear to be a construct that somehow satisfies a felt need on the part of organizational theorists and for that reason we are compelled in these pages to deal with the construct as we would handle it within the boundaries of the theory developed in earlier chapters. We will provide our own definition for the construct within these boundaries in the hope

251

that it and our conceptualization of organizational climate will be as operationally useful as its predecessors. However, our final position is that the construct of organizational climate has certain restrictions that limit its usefulness as a predictor of most types of ongoing behavior in organizations, except gross approach–avoidance behaviors to a work setting (absenteeism, tenure, turnover, etc.). We will point out why we think climate may have its major usefulness as a method of learning about how individuals structure and organize their perceptions of their work environment. We will also attempt to explain why measures of fundamental climate dimensions probably should correlate highly with satisfaction measures even though they (the climate measures) are theoretically affect-free perceptions and cannot necessarily be expected to covary highly with most ongoing individual behaviors.

In examining climate, we will review and provide a brief summary of the major difficulties that have arisen in attempts to define climate to clarify the general context of the paradigm that will be provided later. This will provide a framework for understanding differences between our conceptualization and those that have been used previously. The point that needs to be impressed upon the reader from the very beginning, however, is this: *Climate is by its very nature based in some manner upon attributes of the work environment.* Therefore, its definition is operationally dependent upon the development of a formal taxonomic structure, either by the individual or by an outside source, of the attributes of the organization. Taxonomic structures of environmental attributes (or for that matter individual attributes) are fraught with all sorts of conceptual difficulties as was pointed out in Chapters 1 and 7. They are, by their very nature, arbitrary and completely dependent upon both the idiosyncrasies and whims of the individual preparing the taxonomic structure and upon the intended purposes of that structure. A universally acceptable definition of climate is perhaps an unreasonable goal. Nevertheless, with this rather dismal and bleak warning we will proceed with an examination of some major difficulties that have arisen in developing a taxonomy of work environment attributes.

True Attributes versus Perceived Attributes

One fundamental issue concerning attributes constituting the basis for the climate construct is whether these organizational or work environment attributes are measures of the actual organizational attributes that exist in a physical sense external to the individual perceiver or whether they are perceptions that exist within the cognitive structure of the individual perceiver. A strong argument for defining climate in terms of perceived attributes rather than so-called real attributes has been presented in an excellent paper by Schneider (1975). Guion (1973) also dealt quite lucidly with this issue, drawing a convenient parallel between actual measures of physical climate such as temperature and humidity and the corresponding cognitive ones consisting of human perceptions of the physical climate such as coldness and warmth, and/or dampness and dryness. These latter are psychological judgment dimensions based in a functional manner on the true physical attributes of temperature and humidity.

Although Guion presents compelling arguments about the need to validate externally any definition of climate based on perceptions, to define climate solely in terms of external environmental attributes presents certain conceptual and practical problems. Who decides, if not the focal individual, which environmental attributes are to be included in a definition of climate? Also, if the definition of climate is to be based solely on external organizational environment attributes, there must be ways of assessing or measuring these attributes independently of the responses of individuals. Any time human responses are used, these responses are perceptions of what exists rather than what actually exists. This would mean that definitions of climate based solely on physical attributes of the work environment would have to exclude any psychological characteristics of that environment such as "friendliness," "exploitativeness," and so on. The only way such psychological constructs could be included would be through the use of objective measures that could serve as operational definitions of psychological dimensions of climate. Any explanation of behavior that involves consideration of the construct of climate as a stimulus condition to the individual must deal with the way in which the external attributes of the environment are perceived by the individual or else it becomes a noncognitive explanation that is incompatible with the theory developed in earlier chapters. Johannessan (1973) has outlined in some detail the complexities involved in measuring climate.

Climate as a Judgmental Process

To be concerned over the issue of true versus perceived attributes in the definition of climate is nonproductive. We suggest that the appropriate approach is to view climate as a process that is inherently psychological in nature. This basic process is one of descriptive judgment, and the models for descriptive judgment developed in Chapters 3 and 4 provide an excellent paradigm for examining the climate construct and its importance to behavior.

We would therefore argue that a comprehensive definition of climate must be based upon the judgment process by which individuals form global perceptions of their environment from perceptions of the attributes of that environment. We would agree with Schneider (1975) to the extent that we believe the climate process is a process that begins with the individual. *The most fundamental level of dealing with climate is in terms of generalized attributions an individual makes to or about his or her environment.* These attributions are psychological constructs that imply certain general characteristics as being attributed to a particular environmental setting. These characteristics are inevitably human characteristics. That is, individuals have a tendency to attribute humanlike qualities to their work setting and to the organization in which they carry out their daily activity. Virtually all of the so-called basic climate dimensions that have been used have been labeled with terms representing attributes such as friendliness, rigidity, paternalism, exploitativeness, and so on. An anthropomorphic process therefore is basic to a representation of climate. *Climate can be viewed as the judgment process involved in attributing a class of humanlike traits to an entity outside the individual where this entity may be a work group or even an entire organization.*

One begins with a psychological construct representing an anthropomorphic attribute of an organization, then systematically moves from that construct to a definition of it in terms of observable or perceivable characteristics of that environment. Once the construct has been identified, an examination of the underlying causes, or foundation cue elements, that form the basis for the fundamental climate attribution on the part of the individual can be examined. These cue elements, which are themselves perceptions, but perceptions of specific nonpsychological environmental characteristics or attributes, may be viewed as the basis for the more general climate construct or attribution. For example, examine the construct of "friendliness" as a basic climate judgment dimension. This dimension might be defined for a particular individual in terms of such perceived environmental attributes as the number of times co-workers say "hello" in the morning, the perceived willingness of superiors to be addressed by their first names, and a variety of other types of perceived environmental attributes. Perceptions of environmental attributes must be based upon a tangible reality. Underlying the perceived amount of each attribute is the true amount of that attribute actually present in the environment. These true attribute values form a definition of climate at yet another level—one that is external to the individual.

To summarize, we are saying that the extent to which an individual perceives a given psychological climate dimension to exist in a work setting involves the degree to which specific external environmental characteristics are perceived by the individual in the environment. The degree

to which these external environmental attributes are perceived will depend upon the extent to which these external environmental attributes
actually exist in that environment. Therefore to talk about climate one
has to deal with the organization at *three different levels*. First, there are the
actual environmental characteristics that constitute the basis for the psychological climate dimension. Second, there are the individual perceptions of the degree to which these specific environmental attributes actually exist. Third, there is the perception by the individual of the amount
of a particular psychological characteristic possessed by the organization
that is based upon the individual's perception of environmental attributes.

We will refer to these three different approaches to climate as level
one, level two, and level three climate measures, respectively. Figure 8.1
illustrates all three levels schematically, illustrating how the judgment
paradigm provides a convenient frame of reference for the entire climate process. (Figure 8.1 will be discussed in a later section).

It should be apparent that a definition of climate at any of these three
levels may be developed. The first level is a definition free of individual
perceptions. On this level it should be possible theoretically to develop
measures of climate based upon examination by an independent observer of the environmental attributes that have been specified as the
basis for a particular psychological dimension of that organization. The

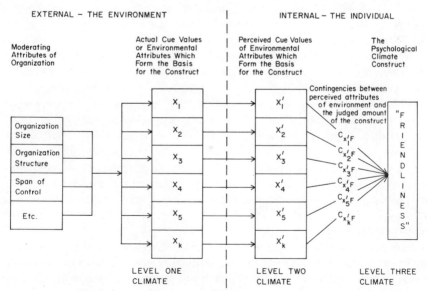

FIGURE 8.1 *A schematic representation of organizational climate.*

second and third levels would have to be based upon responses of the individual. Level two would require the individual to specify perceptions of environmental characteristics of the organization that form the basis for that individual's judgment of the degree to which a particular psychological climate construct exists in a particular work setting. On the third level of definition, judgments could be obtained directly from the individual about the exact amount of a particular psychological climate dimension perceived to be present in that setting.

We do not find it surprising that when James and Jones examined the various approaches to measuring the climate construct they found that they could be grouped into three categories that parallel the levels mentioned previously (James & Jones, 1974). They called them (a) multiple measurement—organizational attribute approach; (b) perceptual measurement—organizational attribute approach; and (c) perceptual measurement—individual attribute approach.

The organizational attribute–multiple measurement approach involved utilizing taxonomic systems based upon measurable attributes of the organization. These systems were totally free of individual perceptions or judgments and were similar to the level one climate shown in Figure 8.1. The organizational attributes–perceptual measurement approach also involved taxonomic systems, but these systems were based upon individual perceptions of specific environmental attributes (level two in Figure 8.1). Finally, there were the systems based upon perceptions of global, individual-type attributes, or judgments of climate dimension similar to the level three judgment dimension shown in Figure 8.1.

We want to emphasize again that it is the *process* by which one forms level three climate judgments that should be viewed as paramount in understanding and studying climate as opposed to a concern over which level is used to measure the construct. All three levels of approaching climate are legitimate. There are no sets of true attributes and/or psychological dimensions that can be said to constitute "the" set of attributes and/or dimensions for climate. As we have pointed out, there is no right or wrong answer to the question of whether climate is something external to the individual. A true picture of climate must consider both the external and the internal world, since climate is the result of a judgment process by which certain types of attributions are made by an individual about the environment.

Failure to clearly understand the logical difficulties arising when climate measures are based upon an indiscriminate mixture of variables from levels I, II, and III seems to be a common problem in climate research. We have already commented on the general issues inherent in any attempt to classify or to establish basic dimensions of either the true environment or the perceived environment. Attempts based upon mixtures of both are subject to even greater problems of interpretation.

Climate: Perception or Affect

A second issue that has concerned theorists dealing with the construct of organizational climate is the question of whether to treat climate as an affective response by the individual or as an affect-free cognition. (Note that both of these alternatives are phenomena residing inside the individual.) Historically, many attempts to measure climate have used questionnaire responses with items similar to satisfaction questionnaires requiring affective or "liking" responses from the individual. This made conceptual differentiation of these climate responses from more traditional types of affective questionnaire responses to organizational surroundings difficult. In particular, measures of job satisfaction are generally composed of affect-laden responses to various characteristics and attributes of the work environment.

The concept of climate seems to be one that should be kept free of affect—both theoretically and conceptually. Trying to specify climate at any of the three levels, be it exclusively in terms of external characteristics (level one) or in terms of a perception by the individual (levels two and three), means dealing with *descriptive* measures rather than with an *evaluation* of those measures. Thus we find ourselves using again the important distinction between the process of measurement (basically a descriptive type of judgment), and the process of evaluation (placing a judgment response on an affect continuum). Whereas climate may be instrumental in creating an affective response by an individual once a certain perception of climate has been formed, the perception of the amount of a given climate dimension present in the environment can and should be kept distinct from the degree of affect produced by that perception, once it has been made and evaluated, no matter how quickly that affect is produced.

Climate, then, shall be defined in terms of either an actual or a perceived amount of certain environmental characteristics. It will not constitute a measure of affect produced within the individual by an awareness of the magnitude of perceived attributes. Yet we recognize that the attempt to keep climate perceptions logically free of affect may break down in an actual attempt to measure such perceptions. As was pointed out in Chapter 3, obtaining purely descriptive judgments about stimuli having a high degree of affect associated with them is a difficult process.

Physical versus Psychological Attributes

A third difficulty in the definition of climate has been the question of what kinds of environmental attributes, be they either perceived or actual, should be included within the construct. The issue has involved such questions as whether or not to include macro attributes of the organization such as size, structure, or technology. Should climate be limited only to the psychological characteristics of an organization? Or are physical characteristics such as size, degree of structure, or span of control reasonable climate variables?

The answer to these questions has been determined by the manner in which the two previously discussed issues have been resolved. If one defines organizational climate in terms of certain anthropomorphic characteristics (a level three climate definition), that definition of climate would obviously include only psychological attributes. If one defines climate in terms of observable and measurable characteristics of the external world, which are either actual or perceived (levels one and two), then physical attributes also would be permissible.

Since we have argued that a complete picture of climate must include all three levels of conceptualization, both physical and psychological attributes must be included in the permissable attribute set. This is a view of climate similar to the definition provided by Campbell *et al.* (1970). They defined climate as:

> [A] set of attributes specific to a particular organization that may be induced from the way the organization deals with its members and its environment. For the individual member within an organization, climate takes the form of a set of attitudes and expectancies which describe the organization in terms of both static characteristics (such as degree of autonomy) and behavior–outcome and outcome–outcome contingencies [page 390].

A careful examination of this definition—which we believe to be excellent but incomplete—reveals a number of parallels with our previously stated comments concerning the need to deal with climate at various levels. For example, the first sentence defines climate as (*a*) induced attributes, which are in turn based upon; (*b*) observed organizational characteristics. The induced attributes are similar to the global personal constructs or level three climate attributions that consist of attributes such as friendliness or rigidity. The observed organizational characteristics are the initial perceptions, or level two climate variables. The second sentence of Campbell *et al.*'s definition deals with both levels simultaneously as it speaks of climate in terms of both static characteristics such as autonomy (a level three climate concept) and behavior–outcome and outcome–outcome contingencies (level two climate concepts). What is not included in the Campbell *et al.* definition are the level one climate variables (i.e., they did not recognize the fact that climate may also be defined outside of the perceptual and cognitive structure of the individual, nor did they provide any logical tie between the various characteristics). That is, the definition does not point out that their static characteristics must be at least partially based, or dependent, upon perceived contingencies.

Perhaps more importantly, the Campbell *et al.* definition fails to recognize that contingencies are actually static (to use their language) attributes. Thus they distinguish between static attributes (autonomy) and contingencies implying that contingencies are seen as nonstatic, attributes. Actually this is not the case, and since the point is important, we need to see why.

We would prefer to use the terms reactive and nonreactive attributes as opposed to static and dynamic. These terms were originally defined in Chapter 1. Reactive attributes, it will be recalled, are those characteristics of the environment that are contingent upon the measured behavior (products) of the individual. They are therefore dynamic, or nonstatic. Nonreactive attributes are stable (static) in that they are not contingent upon the individual's behavior.

Although it may seem counterintuitive to view a contingency as a nonreactive attribute, it is actually quite logical. A contingency expresses a relationship between (a) a person's behavior and an environmental attribute, such as a product-to-evaluation contingency; or (b) two separate environmental attributes, such as an evaluation-to-outcome contingency. In both instances we have reactive attributes involved in forming the contingency relationship, but the contingency itself is a nonreactive attribute. Thus all reactive attributes possess certain contingency relationships both with the individual's behavior and with other reactive attributes, but the contingency relationships themselves are nonreactive attributes of the environment. We will make use of this point again.

Probably the most interesting aspect of the Campbell *et al.* view of climate is that it is the first and only definition of climate to take the position that one class of perceptions, which are used to form climate conceptualizations, are perceptions of environmental *contingencies*. We agree with them and believe that this aspect of the Campbell *et al.* definition has been overlooked; it deserved more recognition than it has so far received.

We would suggest that climate, both at level one (the true environmental characteristics) and at level two (the perceived environmental characteristics), can be at least partially defined in terms of specific contingencies we have discussed in the preceding chapters. Specifically, we propose that the environmental role and reward contingencies play an important role in providing operational definitions of climate at levels one and two.

Thus we argue that one type of environmental characteristic that forms the foundation cues for level three climate constructs comes from the sets of contingencies which constitute the environmental evaluation systems ($C_{P \to O}$) and the environmental reward systems ($C_{E \to O}$). Note that we are not saying the evaluation and reward systems are synonymous with climate, nor are we saying that climate judgments are based solely upon contingency attributes. We are saying these contingency sets constitute one class of attributes from which climate can be partially defined. Our premise is that the individual starts with an anthropomorphic characterization of the organization that can be thought of as constituting a level three climate characteristic such as friendliness, exploitativeness, or autonomy. In forming a judgment about the degree to which the organization or subcomponent of the organization possesses a given amount of this particular attribute, the individual utilizes knowledge about various attributes in the perceived environment including the environmental contingencies between products, evaluations, and outcomes. That is, a judgment about the amount of friendliness in an organization is often predicated upon the perceptions of the individual regarding the magnitude of the contingencies which form the evaluation and reward systems of that organization. Not all the contingencies in the environmental reward and evaluation systems will necessarily be used by the individual in deciding about the amount of a global construct of friendliness present in the organization; in other words, of the total set of ($C_{P \to E}$) and ($C_{E \to O}$) contingencies perceived by the individual in the environment, only a select subset will be used in the process of making judgments about the global (level three) construct of friendliness. That subset of evaluation and reward contingencies which is used can be thought of as composing a portion of the level two definition of climate associated with the global construct of friendliness. Finally, the true environmental reward and evaluation contingencies that correspond to the perceived contingencies included in the level two definition of climate form a part of the level one or actual external operational definition of climate in the environment.

Other global, level three, climate constructs such as exploitativeness may be based on an entirely separate subset of perceived environmental variables, including contingencies. Therefore the operational definition of the construct exploitativeness at either the perceived level (level two) or the external (level one) might be totally different from the operational definitions of the construct friendliness, since the particular contingencies and other attributes involved in forming the operational definitions of the two global constructs are different and nonoverlapping. For example, the contingency between addressing a superior by his or her first name and the outcome produced by that product such as a smile, a frown, or another clear affective outcome reaction on the part of the superior is an attribute that would seem to help define for the individual a construct of friendliness. However, that same contingency would be of small value in helping the individual to arrive at a judgment concerning the degree to which the organization or subcomponent of the organization might be exploitative.

A Schematic Representation of Climate

Perhaps the points that we have attempted to make concerning the climate construct can best be illustrated by a detailed examination of Figure 8.1. This figure represents schematically the essential elements and levels of organizational climate.

For consistency, Figure 8.1 is organized in a similar manner to Figure 2.1 in that the left-handed side of the figure represents external elements to the individual and the elements to the right in the figure represent internal elements of the individual. These two broad classes of elements are separated by a vertical dotted line. In the general theory developed in previous chapters and given in detail in Figure 2.1, it has been assumed that events flow from left to right (i.e., from the external stimulus world to the internal world of the individual). To the left we have the stimulus world and to the right the organism. However, for purposes of explanation, we will reverse the normal process and examine Figure 8.1 from right to left. We do so because the most fundamental level of climate seems to us to be level three. Conceptually, we believe it is best to begin with the notion of a global climate construct on the part of a particular individual. It is this basic global construct that forms the conceptual foundation for the remainder of the element levels illustrated in Figure 8.1. For this reason we will examine Figure 8.1 from right to left rather than from left to right.

We begin with the global construct that represents an anthropomorphic attribute that the individual ascribes in some degree to the organization or to some component of the organization. This construct was defined as a level three definition of climate in the preceding pages and we consider it the most fundamental climate definition. It represents what most organizational theorists mean by the term organizational climate.

Global climate dimensions such as exploitativeness, and friendliness, are fundamental, affect-free perceptions that the individual forms about the organization. We again want to emphasize that they are affect-free perceptions. It is essential to maintain the distinction between a perception of the degree of friendliness present in a particular work environment by individual A and the amount of positive affect experienced by the individual "because" of that perception. Measuring climate at this level means dealing with measures of perceived amount of attribute as opposed to measures of perceived degree of liking or disliking.

The degree of a particular level three construct perceived to be present in a work environment is a descriptive judgment by the individual. Therefore it can best be conceptualized in terms of the judgmental process outlined in Chapters 3 and 4. The judgment of the amount of any attribute such as friendliness, if it is assumed to be a rational process, must indeed be based upon a set of cue elements perceived as existing in the work environment. The degree to which each of these perceived environmental attributes is related to the global construct of climate can be viewed as a basic contingency relationship between the attribute and the construct. Further, if one is willing for purposes of description, to assume that the formulation of a global climate construct such as friendliness is basically described by a linear additive model, the relationship between perceived environmental attributes and the global climate construct can be formalized as:

$$F = \Sigma C_{XF} X.$$

In this formulation the C_{XF} values represent the contingencies between the perceived environmental attributes and the global climate construct, F represents the amount of perceived friendliness, and X represents the amount of environmental attribute perceived by the individual. Those Xs that have contingencies greater than zero may be viewed as specifying the definition of climate at level two as shown in Figure 8.1. These Xs represent an operationalization of the friendliness construct in terms of perceived environmental attributes. For example, cues which might be employed by an individual in forming a judgment about friendliness might be the number of departmental picnics and parties, the number of times each day that the individual is greeted with a smile or a pleasant comment by coworkers, or the number of distinct cliques or social subgroups that exist within the individual's organization or department. To the individual, each of the perceived environmental attributes has a bearing on his or her judgment of how friendly the work setting is. The strength of this relationship is indicated by the size of the contingency that exists between that attribute and the construct.

Now it is important to note again that the Xs that form the level two definition of climate by having a contingency relationship with the global construct can themselves be contingencies. That is, one class of perceived environmental attributes are the product-to-evaluation and the evaluation-to-outcome contingencies existing in that environment. These are the perceived role systems and the perceived reward systems for that individual. As was pointed out earlier these role and reward contingencies are important cues that in turn have contingency relationships with global climate constructs.

We reviewed earlier the important distinction made in Chapter 1 between two kinds of environmental attributes. One class of environmental attributes was defined as nonreactive, whereas a second class of environmental attributes was defined as reactive. Nonreactive attributes, or outcomes, are those characteristics of the environment that are unrelated to the behavior of an individual as manifested by the perceived or measured products of the individual and therefore such attributes can never form the basis for either role contingencies or reward contingencies. Thus, those attributes or outcomes enter into level two climate definitions strictly in terms of their amounts or the degree to which they are or are not present in the environment. Reactive attributes or outcomes are, by definition, attributes that are related to the products of the individual, and therefore these attributes form the basis for role and reward contingencies that are perceived by the individual as existing in the environment. In the case of reactive attributes, it is the contingency, be it either the evaluation contingency or the reward contingency or both, that forms the basic cue used by the individual to form the global climate construct. In other words, if a particular environmental attribute is important to an individual in forming a global construct related to climate, we would argue that if the individual perceives that this attribute is unrelated to his or her own behavior (i.e., he or she cannot influence the amount of this product perceived as being present in the environment through his or her own behavior), it is the absolute amount of that product perceived as present in the environment that forms the cue for the level two definition of climate. On the other hand, if the attribute perceived as being important in defining the global climate construct is one that can be influenced by the behavior of the individual, the size of the overall contingency between product and evaluation or evaluation to outcome in the environment becomes the cue that is used by the individual for the level two definition of climate.

To illustrate, suppose a company had a policy of providing $5000 for tuition expenses at a state university for all children of its management personnel. This would be a static, or nonreactive, organizational attribute, and the absolute magnitude of tuition would be the critical cue variable. However, suppose only 25% of the children could receive this aid each year, and that these 25% were chosen by a random lottery. In this case the magnitude of the contingency, as represented by the magnitude of the probability (i.e., $p = .25$) becomes the critical cue variable for the individual. This is an important concept, as we will see in a moment.

Turning now to the remainder of the schematic representation presented in Figure 8.1, we move across the boundary separating the internal levels to the external world as represented by level one conceptualizations of climate. Here we have represented the actual environmental attributes. These environmental attributes are the cue values associated with the attributes employed by the individual as the basis for the global construct. Level one represents the true nature of those variables. Level one is therefore a set of actual or cue values where the Xs are composed of both contingency relationships and certain other nonreactive attributes in terms of their absolute magnitude.

The final component of Figure 8.1 is at the far left. Here are represented the moderating attributes of the organization that influence either directly or indirectly the values of the Xs found at level one. These moderating attributes often have been treated as representing a form of climate in an organization. It is probably a mistake to treat them as such since they are not perceived by the individual as being directly related with the global climate constructs. However, they may be indirectly important in the sense of having substantial influence upon the organizational attributes that form the basis for the global climate construct. Certainly variables such as size, organizational structure, and span of control are variables that can have strong effects upon the kinds and magnitudes of contingencies existing within an organization, and since these contingencies have already been said to form a critical subset of the level one and level two aspects of climate, it seemed appropriate to include these moderating attributes within our general schematic representation of climate.

Shared Climate Perceptions: What Are They?

We have presented a view of organizational climate that says climate is an individual construct and is therefore totally idiosyncratic. There is no guarantee that two individuals sharing the same environment will use the same set of anthropomorphic attributions to describe that environment. Even if they did, there is no guarantee that the judgments made on the agreed upon attribution dimension would (*a*) be similar in magnitude; or (*b*) be based upon the same set of perceived cue variables.

Some theorists have argued that for any attribute to be considered a part of organizational climate or for a particular psychological climate characteristic to exist (such as friendliness), there must be some agreement among the individuals constituting that subgroup in the organization about the amount of that characteristic present in the work setting before it can be labeled as a variable constituting climate. It is our position that such agreement is unnecessary and unrealistic. To use again Guion's analogy of heat versus perceived coldness: What is being asked is that for a geographic location to be recognized as possessing a certain climate, must all observers report the same perception of warmth? That is, what is required is not that the mean of all perceptions of temperature be at some specified value but that the variance of the perceptions be close to zero.

We feel the notion of shared climate perceptions can be a valuable and worthwhile measure. For any group of individuals, it would certainly be useful to know the average value of their climate perceptions on any particular climate dimension as well as the variability, which may or may not exist among those individual perceptions of that climate dimension. It does not, however, seem particularly useful to us to call the mean of that distribution "group climate" or to insist that the variance of that distribution be below a certain arbitrary value in order to say that the particular dimension is a useful one in specifying the climate that may or may not exist for those people. Therefore, it is our preference to use the term climate when applied to perceptions basically as an individual construct and to suggest that when climate perceptions are pooled into a composite description of groups that the resulting measures of central tendency and variability based upon those distributions may be labeled more appropriately as something other than climate.

Is Organizational Climate a Useful Construct?

Inevitably, we have finally arrived at the point where it is necessary to examine the degree to which organizational climate as a relevant construct to the psychology of behavior of people in organizations has any redeeming value. As was pointed out at the beginning of this section, the construct is an exceptionally robust one in that it seems unlikely to disappear. Somehow it seems, to fill a need on the part of people concerned with the behavior of individuals in organizations.

Obviously, there are a variety of reasons for the interest in such a construct. The notion of climate can be defended on at least two basic grounds. The first justification would be based upon the desirability of developing a taxonomic nomenclature of perceived and real environmental attributes used by individuals as the basis for the various global climate constructs that people attribute to work environments. It is certainly an inescapable fact that individuals make attributions of an anthropomorphic nature to their work setting and to the organization to which they belong. Therefore, individuals must succeed in classifying environmental attributes in a manner that is helpful in providing foundation information for the ultimate judgments made by those individuals concerning the degree of a particular anthropomorphic construct attributed to the organization. It is certainly a legitimate psychological question to ask exactly how people go about this process of clustering environmental cues into psychologically meaningful subunits.

The second logical justification for the climate construct is based on the extent to which climate constructs provide useful and reliable devices for understanding and predicting behavior of individuals in an organizational setting. This is essentially an empirical justification in that it says climate constructs are useful and helpful only if they account for some meaningful portion of the variance in behavior of individuals in organizations. This then would raise the logical subsequent question as to what kinds of behavior might be expected to be predictable from or related to climate as we have discussed it in these pages.

The Relationship of Climate to Behavior

We can look at climate within the context of the theory to see how climate constructs might relate to individual behavior. Climate as we have dealt with it here does not appear to be a construct that would normally predict most kinds of individual behavior within an organization. In fact, the only kind of organizational behaviors that one might logically expect to be significantly related to climate would be withdrawal or avoidance behaviors such as absenteeism, turnover, or tardiness. The reasons for this are interesting and, we believe, rather compelling.

First, one must keep in mind that the affect that becomes "attached" to or associated with a perceived amount of a climate dimension is itself an outcome represented by the affect box in Figure 2.1 of the theory. Thus the affect outcomes received by an individual from perceptions of the amount of various climate dimensions are no different from the affect received from other outcomes in the environment and are thus part of what we normally might call job satisfaction. We have shown previously that measures of affect based upon received outcomes (i.e., job satisfaction) cannot logically be expected to relate strongly to behavior because behavior is determined by anticipated outcomes, valence, and contingencies (see Chapter 6 for a detailed discussion).

Second, when we dealt with the question of what variables or attributes of the organization form the cues used by the individual in judging the amount of a climate dimension present in the work setting, it was pointed out that these cues were of two distinct types. The first type were nonreactive cues. They represented the amounts of specific environmental attributes perceived as being present in the organizational setting. Examples for the construct of friendliness were given such as the number of picnics and parties held by the organization, the number of pleasant greetings and smiles given to an individual by coworkers. These attributes are not typically contingent upon the behavior of the individual. Therefore, they may be assumed to exist in some finite and stable amount for any particular work setting. The second general type of climate attributes consisted of certain contingencies. These were contingencies between the behavior of the individual and the evaluations of the organization and the contingencies between the evaluations and rewards or outcomes given by the organizations. In other words, they were the product-to-evaluation and evaluation-to-outcome contingencies based upon the behavior of the individual and the degree to which the reactive attributes of the organization (evaluations and outcomes) varies as a function of the individual's behavior. But while the contingencies are predicated upon a relationship between behavior and a reactive attribute of the environment, the contingencies themselves are attributes that are nonreactive. These contingencies are nonreactive as long as the magnitude of the contingency relationship between individual behavior and the reactive attribute is not itself influenced by the individual's behavior. We propose that it is the perceived contingency associated with reactive environmental attributes that becomes a cue for judgment of the degree of the global climate construct rather than the amounts of reactive attributes themselves. We then see that *all* of the cues used to form climate constructs may be viewed as nonreactive. There is little reason then to believe that the individual is apt to behave differentially as a function of the perceived amount of the global climate construct, since his or her behavior can in no direct way influence the perceived amount of the construct present in the organization. That is, an individual cannot "make" an organization more or less friendly by varying his or her behavior. The amount of global attribute present in the work setting would seem to be a relatively static and stable characteristic of the organization, and the degree of affect produced in the individual (negative or positive) as a result of the amount of that attribute perceived as being present would also seem to be a fairly stable entity. Thus, a person can only self-administer or obtain that affect by belonging to or working in the organization and likewise can only escape receiving that affect by escaping from the organization setting.

One conclusion from this view of climate is that climate as we define it represents a collection of fairly stable actual and perceived environmental characteristics. This is particularly true if we consider only level three climate dimensions. An individual's perceptions of the amount of various global climate characteristics possessed by an organization is probably a stable perception and slow, or resistant, to change. Each judgment dimension is determined by many individual cue variables, and it is reasonable to expect that the values of the cues, whether they are contingencies or other types of attributes, will have to undergo substantial changes to produce a corresponding change in the judged amount of that global characteristic perceived by the individual.

The inevitable conclusion of this analysis is that climate as a construct in predicting the behavior of individuals within organizations does not appear to be a useful device. (The exception would be behaviors of an escape–avoidance nature.) For this reason we suggest that climate may be valuable not as a mechanism for understanding and predicting behavior of individuals in organizations but as a device for enabling us to better understand the way in which individuals organize the cues present in their environment into psychologically meaningful constructs that aid the individual in describing the environment in humanlike terms.

9

Some Concluding Comments

In the preceding chapters we have attempted to provide an integrated view of a variety of issues regarding the behavior of individuals in organizations. It is now time to look back upon this material and to summarize and highlight some of the ideas and concepts that we feel constitute the more important aspects of the theoretical viewpoint that we have presented in this book. Specifically, we will attempt here to highlight some of the important and unique aspects of the theory and point out some of the more interesting implications that are a consequence of the ideas presented.

First, we must again point out that the theory presented in this book is a general cognitive theory of behavior. Although it is addressed primarily to the problem of understanding behavior in organizational settings, it is by no means limited by that constraint. Like any theory, it is based upon certain basic premises, the most important of which is that an individual's behavior is rational. A second important premise is that the individual acts in such a way as to maximize the amount of positive affect (or to minimize the amount of negative affect) resulting in a selection of acts in which the individual will engage. These acts are selected from some larger subset of possible acts. A third basic premise is that the external environment of any individual is basically a probabilistic environment. Events and their outcomes generally have probabilities associated with them, and these probabilities are viewed as general contingency relationships between events and events and events and outcomes that are fundamental to a basic understanding of human behavior. The world is an uncertain environment, and any theory of behavior must assume that rational behavior depends upon mechanisms for dealing with uncertainty.

It must be recognized that these mechanisms can vary greatly in terms of complexity. That is, rational behavior can take place at many levels of sophistication. This theory represents an explanation of rational behavior in a complete and detailed sense. However, we have pointed out that individuals often behave rationally by using much simpler mechanisms, such as habit and other heuristic strategies.

The fundamental construct of human behavior was defined as the process of engaging in a particular act with a particular degree of commitment. Rational behavior is viewed in the theory as a resource allocation problem in which the individual is continually faced with the problem of allocating certain basic resources among some specified set of possible acts. The basic resources of an individual were defined as time resources and energy resources, and these constitute the basic behavioral units associated with an act. The extent to which an individual allocates these time and energy resources in a particular direction (engages in a particular act) is defined as the degree of total commitment that the individual has or exhibits toward that particular act. An important aspect of the theory is the distinction between the basic behavioral units of time and energy and the functional or phenomenological behavioral units, called products. Products are things that are created by or brought into existence by the commitment of time and energy to a particular process (act). It is pointed out that people tend to perceive products rather than the more basic units of commitment, and that it is the products that form the basic elements for understanding how and why people act and behave the way they do.

In dealing with the probabilistic nature of individual behavior, emphasis in the theory has been placed on the importance of contingency relationships. Contingency relationships were shown to be of several different types; these types were in turn shown to have important but at times quite different roles in determining the behavior of individuals. Specifically, three fundamental types of contingency relationships were shown to be extremely important. The first type was the act-to-product $(C_{A \to P})$ contingency, which can be either an actual or a perceived relationship between the amount of commitment that one makes to a particular act and the probability of, or amount or magnitude of, a particular product being created by that act. The second fundamental contingency class was constituted of the contingencies between the products themselves and the evaluations made of those products $(C_{P \to E})$ either by the focal individual or by evaluation entities external to the individual. These evaluation contingencies were presented as exceptionally important in that they form the foundation elements for roles. Indeed, we suggest that external roles are most appropriately seen as sets of product-to-evaluation contingencies, which are held by various entities external to the individual, and that a self-role is composed of a set of internalized product-to-evaluation contingencies held by that individual for him or herself. The third set of fundamental contingencies consists of the evaluation-to-outcome $(C_{E \to O})$ (reward) contingencies. These contingencies represent the reward systems that are operational in the environment of an individual. These reward systems can be either internal or external. They also define the construct of power as it is appropriately used in a treatment of roles. We have attempted to define explicitly the place of each of these three fundamental classes of contingencies in the explanation of behavior, at the same time recognizing that the cognitive complexity needed to deal with countless contingencies existing in the environment forces the individual to adopt various heuristic "coping" strategies.

Emphasis also has been placed upon the basic process of human judgment as a fundamental mechanism in an adequate understanding of a cognitive behavior theory. The judgment process was divided into two general types. The first type we have called *descriptive judgment,* which involves making a judgment about the amount of an attribute possessed by a stimulus object with the constraint that the judgment continuum, or attribute, is affect-free. The second judgment class was referred to as *evaluative judgment,* and again involves the process of scaling a stimulus object in terms of amount of a possessed attribute, but in this instance, the attribute is an affect-laden attribute such as like–dislike or good–bad. Each of the various process stages within the theory was shown to be a process that directly involved one or the other of these two classes of human judgment.

In Chapter 5, we developed a concept of roles, emphasizing the notion of role contingencies (defined as the product-to-evaluation contingencies) that we believe form the basic ingredients of all roles, external or internal. We elaborated on the process of role development, role conflict, and a number of other traditional role constructs all within the notion of the role contingency explanation. We pointed out that although role contingencies are the primary elements of all roles, phenomenologically, just as is the case with our earlier view of behavior, it is the products that are used to operationally define what is meant by roles for most people. When defining the construct of behavior, we took the position that the basic elements of behavior were the fundamental units of time and energy, but phenomenologically, the units of behavior employed by most people in their daily activities are the things that are produced by that behavior (products). The same thing is true of roles. Although the fundamental units of roles are the contingencies, it is the manifestation of those contingencies by an evaluator in terms of an expected level of behavior, which in turn is manifested by an expected level of product output that forms the phenomenological basis for roles on a day-to-day basis for most individuals.

The notion of affect is an important issue we have considered both in terms of its generalized function in the theory and its specific interpretation as a measure of satisfaction with the environment. The generalized affective state of the individual is important primarily for its role in determining the amount of anticipated affect associated with various future outcomes. It is anticipated affect that becomes the key element in determining future behavior; the present state of generalized affect does not necessarily show any direct relationship with future behavior. Since job satisfaction represents affect in the present, it should not be surprising that it is not closely related to behavior, which depends primarily upon anticipated affect. This is not to imply that present affect (i.e., satisfaction) cannot constitute an important end in itself. Also, we have not argued that present affect cannot correlate with behavior. What we have said is that the linkages between present affect and subsequent behavior are both multiple and distant. As a result, the relationship will rarely be strong. If one wishes to predict behavior, there are better, more direct ways of doing so than using measures of present affective state.

A popular construct with organizational theorists has been that of organizational climate, and we have reasoned that climate is best viewed as a perception by an individual person; this perception is the result of a descriptive judgment process. That is, a climate perception is not an affect-laden judgment but is a description of the amount of a certain attribute possessed by the work environment. This judgment construct is generally an anthropomorphic attribution of the degree to which some humanlike trait is characteristic of the work environment. The judgment is predicated upon perceptions of the amount of certain nonreactive environmental attributes that, for that individual, possess a contingency relationship with the judgment construct. One very important class of attributes used by the individual as a basis for such judgments are certain role and reward contingencies that the individual perceives to exist in the environment, and whose magnitudes are cues that are meaningfully connected with the climate construct—at least for that individual.

The final issue that we have attempted to define and explain within the theory is the concept of leadership. Leadership can be viewed from two different perspectives. The first perspective is to see the leader as an individual whose behavior you wish to predict. From this perspective the leader becomes an individual no different from any other individual and the explanation and prediction of the leader's behavior can be handled within the theory we have developed in these pages. However, there is one noticeable difference that should be kept in mind when predicting the behavior of an individual leader. This difference is that the products used by both the external and internal systems to evaluate a leader are usually not the actual products of the leader but are the products of the group or of the individuals forming the group directed by that leader. This introduces a set of second-level contingencies into the system. Thus, a leader must not only cope with contingencies between his or her own behavior and the products resulting from that behavior, but also between his or her behavior and the behavior of the people constituting the relevant subordinate group.

The other perspective is to view the leader as a part of the environment. In predicting the behavior of any individual, the behavior of that person's leader or superior can be seen as part of the specific environment of that person. Then the question of appropriate leader behavior becomes a question of what types of behaviors on the part of the leader produce appropriate contingencies and anticipated valences for the individual that will cause the individual to behave in a particular way. Leadership from this perspective is simply a question that is part of an even more general question relating to the issue of how one should structure the individual's environment to produce specific kinds of behaviors.

We predict that we have raised as many questions with our theory as we have answered. We hope so. Our objective is to provide a particular perspective for approaching the extremely complex issues of human behavior in an organizational setting. We think there are many fascinating questions to be asked and researched to see if the general and specific linkages and concepts developed here are empirically viable. We list some and ask the reader to create others. A few that immediately come to mind are

1. What are the relative behavioral contributions of the $C_{P \to E}$ and $C_{E \to O}$ contingencies? Are individuals actually able to discriminate between these two types of contingencies or do they tend to behave in terms of a composite "super contingency" $C_{P \to O}$? If people can distinguish between evaluation contingencies and reward contingencies, which are the most influential? If they cannot distinguish, how are the two combined into the larger contingency?

2. A related issue would involve trying to determine the degree to which evaluations of others can be or are inferred by focal individuals using observed $C_{P \to O}$ contingencies. These inferred evaluations may themselves have certain implicit outcome characteristics that produce

affect for the individual. If so, are they related to the characteristics of the evaluator, such as prestige, or power? Thus we see the role of the actual evaluation in the product $\rightarrow$ evaluation $\rightarrow$ outcome sequence as one of considerable importance and interest.

3. How do people develop simplifying strategies to cope with the complexities of uncertainty as represented by the contingencies? And even more fascinating is the question of what conditions lead to an individual revising or breaking out of a long-standing coping strategy?

4. A compelling issue of interest involves a proposition presented in the section on organizational climate. We stated that reactive environmental attributes enter into global climate perceptions only in terms of the perceived magnitude of the $C_{P \rightarrow E}$ and $C_{P \rightarrow O}$ contingencies based upon those attributes. This implies that variations in the magnitude of reactive attributes should influence only global climate perceptions to the extent that those variations produce changes in the individual's perception of the magnitudes of the contingencies involved. This proposition would seem to be amenable to empirical verification.

5. What is the role of the act-to-product contingency in the sequencing of behavior? It is a contingency based primarily upon a self-perception whereas the $C_{P \rightarrow E}$ and $C_{E \rightarrow O}$ contingencies are typical perceptions of the state of the environment. Are there systematic differences in the accuracy with which one can perceive contingencies based upon self as opposed to contingencies based upon others?

6. A subtle but *very* critical point concerning the $C_{A \rightarrow P}$ and $C_{P \rightarrow E}$ contingencies is that both contingencies have outcome characteristics. Thus a person's perceived products in the $C_{A \rightarrow P}$ contingency relationship may be viewed also as outcomes having definite affective states associated with them. Similarly, the evaluations involved in the $C_{P \rightarrow E}$ contingencies also possess definite affective states. Thus both $C_{A \rightarrow P}$ and $C_{P \rightarrow E}$ contingencies are at the same time appropriately viewed as $C_{A \rightarrow O}$ and $C_{P \rightarrow O}$ contingencies respectively. This dual character of these contingencies arises from the outcome properties of both perceived self-products and perceived evaluations of others. These contingencies may therefore influence behavior more forcefully than one might normally anticipate. An individual may engage in certain acts simply because these acts have high contingency relationships with products that in turn possess, as products, considerable positive affect, regardless of the subsequent contingency relationship these products have with evaluations of others or which these evaluations have with outcomes administered by others. This is the case when an individual engages in an act primarily for the challenge of producing a certain product (i.e., reaching a certain measurable level of achievement).

7. One of the things that should be clear in our approach is that to understand behavior we must look at acts, not performance. The major dependent variable in industrial and organizational psychology has been performance, not acts or commitment to acts. Although studying performance is worthwhile for applied purposes, it leaves much to be desired if the goal is understanding. A set of variables and processes occur between commitment to acts and evaluated products. These include whole sets of complex contingencies, individual differences, and constraints. If we are to be able to understand behavior, short-circuiting the complex process by looking at performance seems inappropriate.

8. The motivation process we have proposed may be able to explain more precisely other approaches that have been used in the motivation area. For example, intrinsic motivation as proposed by Deci (1975) argues that intrinsic motivation occurs when the person feels self-determining and competent. We would argue that, in an organization, perceptions of self-determination result when the person's own product-to-evaluation contingencies matched those of powerful evaluators. When this is the case, the person feels a sense of personal control. When the self-contingencies do not match those of an evaluator (e.g., the supervisor), and that supervisor controls valued outcomes, personal control is lowered and the feeling of self-determination is lowered. In addition, perceptions of competence occur when act-to-product contingencies are high.

As another example, goal setting has been shown to increase performance (Latham & Yuki, 1975; Locke, 1975). However, there has been little attempt to explain *why* goal setting increases performance. One possibility suggested by the theory is that when a goal is set, the slope of the product-to-evaluation contingency changes. That is, for the product and evaluator in question (usually the supervisor) the goal setting creates a large increase in the utility of the level of the product represented by the goal. At that level or amount of the product, there is a major shift in the supervisor's evaluation. That is, making the goal results in a high positive evaluation, whereas not making it results in a substantially lower evaluation, even though the level of the product is near the goal. If the person accepts the goal, the same process occurs for the self-evaluation. Thus, before the goal there may be a generally linear relationship between amount of the product and the utility of the product. After the goal there is a step-function created. Thus, in comparison to a no-goal situation, the motivational force to be above the goal is much higher than to be below the goal.

9. Our emphasis on products suggests that products, especially evaluated products, are the phenomenological focal point for the individual.

One implication of this position is that personnel systems might use evaluated products as the core of the system. For example, a job analysis would attempt to identify which products are evaluated. Performance appraisal, feedback procedures, training-need identification, and selection interviewing would be based on products.

These are simply a few of the more challenging areas for examination that are provided by the point of view presented in these pages. No doubt there are many others. We only hope that the theory we have presented will have interest, use, and value to others who are interested in behavior in work environments and who have also felt a need for some form of large theoretical scheme for dealing with the complex perceptual and cognitive processes underlying human behavior in a work setting.

References

Adams, J. S. The structure and dynamics of behavior in organizational boundary roles. In M. D. Dunnette (Ed.), *Handbook of industrial and organizational psychology*. Chicago: Rand McNally, 1976.

Argyris, C. *Integrating the individual and the organization*. New York: Wiley, 1964.

Bandura, A. The self system in reciprocal determinism. *American Psychologist*, 1978, *33*, 344–358.

Beach, L. R. Multiple regression as a model for human information utilization. *Organizational Behavior and Human Performance*, 1967, *2*, 276–289.

Behling, O., & Starke, F. A. Some limits on expectancy theories of work effort. *Proceedings of the Midwest Meeting of the American Institute of Decision Sciences*, 1973.

Biddle, B. J., & Thomas, E. J. (Eds.), *Role theory: concepts and research*. New York: Wiley, 1966.

Björkman, M. Stimulus-event learning and event learning as concurrent processes. *Organizational Behavior and Human Performance*, 1967, *2*, 219–236.

Björkman, M. Inference behavior in nonmetric ecologies. In L. Rappoport and D. A. Summers (Eds.), *Human judgment and social interaction*. New York: Holt, Rinehart and Winston, 1973, pp. 144–168.

Brehmer, B. The structure of policy conflicts. *Umeå Psychological Report 28*, 1970, The University of Umeå, Umeå, Sweden.

Brehmer, B. Hypotheses about relations between scaled variables in the learning of probabilistic inference tasks. *Organizational Behavior and Human Performance*, 1974, *11*, 1–27.

Brehmer, B. Single-cue probability learning. A general review of results. Unpublished manuscript. University of Umeå, Umeå, Sweden, 1977.

Brehmer, B. Subjects ability to find the parameters of functional rules in probabilistic inference tasks. *Organizational Behavior and Human Performance*, 1976, *17*, 388–397.

Brunswik, E. Organismic achievement and environmental probability. *Psychological Review*, 1943, *50*, 255–272.

Brunswik, E. *Perception and the representative design of psychological experiments*. Berkeley: University of California Press, 1956.

Burns, T., & Stalker, G. M. *The management of innovation*. London: Tavistock, 1961.

Calder, B. J. An attribution theory of leadership. In B. M. Staw and G. R. Salancik (Eds.), *New directions in organizational behavior.* Chicago: St. Clair Press, 1977.

Campbell, J. P., Dunnette, M. D., Lawler, E. E., III, & Weick, K. E. *Managerial behavior, performance, and effectiveness.* New York: McGraw–Hill, 1970.

Campbell, J. P., & Pritchard, R. D. Motivation theory in industrial and organizational psychology. In M. Dunnette (Ed.), *Handbook of industrial and organizational psychology.* Chicago: Rand McNally, 1976.

Carroll, John B., & Maxwell, S. E. Individual differences in cognitive abilities. *Annual Review of Psychology,* 1979, *30,* 602–640.

Cartwright, D., & Zander, A. (Eds.), *Group dynamics.* (3rd ed.). New York: Harper & Row, 1968.

Castellan, N. J., Jr. Comments on the "lens model" equation and the analysis of multiple-cue judgment tasks. *Psychometrika,* 1973, 87–100.

Chemmers, M. M., & Skzypek, G. J. Experimental test of the contingency model of leadership effectiveness. *Journal of Personality and Social Psychology,* 1972, *24,* 172–177.

Cofer, C. N., & Appley, M. H. *Motivation: theory and research.* New York: Wiley, 1964.

Csoka, L. S., & Bons, P. M. Manipulating the situation to fit the leader's style: Two validation studies of leader match. *Journal of Applied Psychology,* 1978, *63,* 295–300.

Dansereau, F., Jr., Graen, G. B., & Haga, W. J. A vertical dyad linkage approach to leadership within formal organizations: A longitudinal investigation of the role-making process. *Organizational Behavior and Human Performance,* 1975, *13,* 31–45.

Deci, E. L. *Intrinsic motivation.* New York: Plenum, 1975.

DeNisi, A. S., & Pritchard, R. D. Implicit theories of performance as artifacts in survey research: A replication and extension. *Organizational Behavior and Human Performance,* 1978, *21,* 358–366.

Dudycha, A., Dudycha, L., & Schmitt, N. W. Cue Redundancy: Some overlooked analytical relationships in MCPL. *Organizational Behavior and Human Performance,* 1974, *11,* 222–234.

Dudycha, L. W., & Naylor, J. C. Characteristics of the human inference process in complex choice behavior situations. *Organizational Behavior and Human Performance,* 1966, *1,* 110–128.

Dulany, D. E. Awareness, rules, and prepositional control: A confrontation with S–R behavior theory. In T. R. Dixon and D. L. Horton (Eds.), *Verbal behavior and general behavior theory.* Englewood Cliffs, N.J.: Prentice Hall, 1968.

Dulany, D. E. Hypotheses, habits in verbal "Operant conditioning." *Journal of Abnormal and Social Psychology,* 1961, *63,* 251–263.

Ebert, R. J., & Mitchell, T. R. *Organizational Decision Processes.* New York: Crane, Russak, 1975.

Eden, D., & Leviatan, U. Implicit leadership theory as a determinant of the factor structure underlying supervisory behavior scales. *Journal of Applied Psychology,* 1975, *60,* 736–741.

Edwards, W. Behavioral decision theory. *Annual Review of Psychology,* 1961, *12,* 473–498.

Einhorn, H. J. The use of nonlinear, noncompensatory models in decision making. *Psychological Bulletin,* 1970, *73,* 221–230.

Einhorn, H. J. Use of nonlinear, noncompensatory models as a function of task and amount of information. *Organizational Behavior and Human Performance,* 1971, *6,* 1–27.

Einhorn, H. J. Expert measurement and mechanical combination. *Organizational Behavior and Human Performance,* 1972, *7,* 86–106.

Evans, M. G. The effects of supervisory behavior on the path–goal relationship. *Organizational Behavior and Human Performance,* 1970, *5,* 277–298.

Evans, M. G. Extensions of a path–goal theory of motivation. *Journal of Applied Psychology*, 1974, *59*, 172–178.

Fiedler, F. E. A contingency model of leadership effectiveness. In L. Berkowitz (Ed.), *Advances in experimental social psychology* (Vol. 1). New York: Academic Press, 1964.

Fiedler, F. E. *A theory of leader effectiveness.* New York: McGraw–Hill, 1967.

Fiedler, F. E. Validation and extension of the contingency model of leadership effectiveness: A review of empirical findings. *Psychological Bulletin*, 1971, *76*, 128–148.

Fiedler, F. E., Chemmers, M. M., & Maher, L. L. *Improving leadership effectiveness: The leader match concept.* New York: Wiley, 1976.

Fishbein, M., & Ajzen, I. *Belief, attitude, intention and behavior: An introduction to theory and research.* Reading, Mass.: Addison–Wesley, 1975.

Fishburn, P. C., & Kenney, R. L. Seven independence concepts and continuous multiattribute utility functions. *Journal of Mathematical Psychology*, 1974, *11*, 294–327.

Fleishman, E. A. The description and prediction of perceptual-motor skill learning. In R. Glaser (Ed.), *Training research and education.* Pittsburgh: University of Pittsburgh Press, 1962.

Fleishman, E. A. Performance assessment based upon an empirically derived task taxonomy. *Human Factors*, 1967, *9*, 349–366.

Frederiksen, N. Toward a taxonomy of situations. *American Psychologist*, 1972, *27*, 114–123.

French, J. R. P., Jr. & Raven, B. H. The bases of social power. In D. Cartwright and A. Zander (Eds.), *Group dynamics: research and theory.* Ann Arbor, Mich.: Institute for Social Research, 1959.

Ghiselli, E. E. *Explorations in managerial talent.* Pacific Palisades, Calif.: Goodyear, 1971.

Ghiselli, E. E. The validity of management traits related to occupational level. *Personnel Psychology*, 1963, *16*, 109–113.

Gibb, C. A. Leadership. In G. Lindzey (Ed.), *Handbook of social psychology* (Vol. 2). Reading: Addison–Wesley, 1954, 877–920.

Goldberg, L. R. Man versus model of man: A rationale, plus some evidence, for a method of improving upon clinical inference. *Psychological Bulletin*, 1970, *73*, 422–432.

Goldberg, L. R. Five models of clinical judgment: An empirical comparison between linear and nonlinear representations of the human inference process. *Organizational Behavior and Human Performance*, 1971, *6*, 458–479.

Graen, G. B. Role-making processes within complex organizations. In M. D. Dunnette (Ed.), *Handbook of industrial and organizational psychology.* Chicago: Rand McNally, 1976.

Graen, G., Alvares, K., Orris, J. B., & Martella, J. A. Contingency model of leadership effectiveness: antecedent and evidential results. *Psychological Bulletin*, 1969, *74*, 285–296.

Graen, G., Dansereau, F., & Minami, T. Dysfunctional leadership styles. *Organizational Behavior and Human Performance*, 1972, *7*, 216–236.

Greene, N. C., & Organ, N. W. An evaluation of causal models linking the received role to job satisfaction. *Administrative Science Quarterly*, 1973, *18*, 95–103.

Guilford, J. P. The structure of intellect. *Psychological Bulletin*, 1956, *53*, 267–293.

Guilford, J. P. *The nature of human intelligence.* New York: McGraw–Hill, 1967.

Guion, R. M. A note on organizational climate. *Organizational Behavior and Human Performance*, 1973, *9*, 120–125.

Hackman, J. R. Group influences on individuals. In M. D. Dunnette (Ed.), *Handbook of industrial and organizational psychology.* Chicago: Rand McNally, 1976.

Hackman, J. R., & Lawler, E. E., III. Employee reactions to job characteristics. *Journal of Applied Psychology*, 1971, *55*, 259–286.

Hackman, J. R. & Oldham, G. R. Motivation through the design of work. *Organizational Behavior and Human Performance,* 1976, *16,* 250–279.

Hackman, J. R., & Porter, L. W. Expectancy theory predictions of work effectiveness. *Organizational Behavior and Human Performance,* 1968, *3,* 417–426.

Hall, D. T. *Careers in Organizations.* Santa Monica, CA.: Goodyear Press, 1976.

Hall, D. T., & Schneider, B. *Organizational climates and careers: The work lives of priests.* New York: Seminar Press, 1973.

Hammer, T. H., & Dachler, H. P. A test of some assumptions underlying the path–goal model of supervision: Some suggested conceptual modifications. *Organizational Behavior and Human Performance,* 1975, *14,* No. 1, 60–75.

Hammond, K. (Ed.), *The psychology of Egon Brunswick.* Holt, Rinehart & Winston, 1966.

Hammond, K. R., Hursch, C. J., & Todd, F. J. Analyzing the components of clinical inference. *Psychological Review,* 1964, *71,* 438–456.

Hammond, K. R., Stewart, T. R., Brehmer, B., & Steinmann, D. O. Social judgment theory. In M. Kaplan and S. Schwartz (Eds.), *Human judgment and decision processes: formal and mathematical approaches.* New York: Academic Press, 1975, 271–300.

Hammond, K. R., & Summers, D. A. Cognitive dependence on linear and nonlinear cues. *Psychological Review,* 1965, *72,* 215–234.

Hamner, W. C., & Tosi, H. H. Relationship of role conflict and role ambiguity to job involvement measures. *Journal of Applied Psychology,* 1974, *59,* 497–499.

Heider, F. *The psychology of interpersonal relations.* New York: Wiley, 1958.

Hemphill, J. K. Job descriptions for executives. *Harvard Business Review,* 1959, *37,* 55–67.

Herzberg, F., Mausner, B., & Snyderman, B. The motivation to work (2nd ed.). New York: Wiley, 1959.

House, R. J. A path–goal theory of leader effectiveness. *Administrative Science Quarterly,* 1971, *16,* 321–338.

House, R. J., & Dessler, G. The path–goal theory of leadership: some post hoc and priori tests. In J. G. Hunt & L. L. Larson (Eds.), *Contingency approaches to leadership.* Carbondale, Ill.: Southern Illinois University Press, 1974.

House, R. J., & Mitchell, T. R. Path–goal theory of leadership. *Journal of Contemporary Business,* 1974, *Autumn,* 81–97.

House, R. J., & Rizzo, J. R. Role conflict and ambiguity as critical variables in a model of organizational behavior. *Organizational Behavior and Human Performance,* 1972, *7,* 467–505.

Huber, G. P. Multi-attribute utility models: A review of field and field-like studies. *Management Science,* 1974, *20,* 1393–1402.

Hursch, C. J., Hammond, K. R., & Hursch, J. L. Some methodological considerations in multiple-cue probability studies. *Psychological Review,* 1964, *71,* 42–60.

James, L. R. & Jones, A. P. Organizational Climate: A review of theory and research. *Psychological Bulletin,* 1974, *83,* 1096–1112.

James, L. R., & Jones, A. P. Organizational structure: A review of structural dimensions and their conceptual relationships with individual attitudes and behavior. *Organizational Behavior and Human Performance,* 1976, *16,* 74–113.

Johanneson, R. E. Some problems in the measurement of organizational climate. *Organizational Behavior and Human Performance,* 1973, *10,* 118–144.

Kahn, R. L., Wolfe, D. M., Quinn, R. P., Snoek, J. D., & Rosenthal, R. A. *Organizational stress: studies in role conflict and ambiguity.* New York: Wiley, 1964.

Kahneman, D., & Tversky, A. Subjective probability: A judgment of representativeness. *Cognitive Psychology,* 1972, 430–454.

Katz, D., & Kahn, R. L. *The social psychology of organizations.* New York: Wiley, 1966.

Katz, D., & Kahn, R. L. *The social psychology of organizations: second edition.* New York: Wiley, 1978.

Korman, A. K. On the development of contingency theories of leadership: some methodological considerations and a possible alternative. *Journal of Applied Psychology,* 1973, *58,* 384–387.

Korman, A. K. *Organizational behavior.* Englewood Cliffs, N.J.: Prentice–Hall, 1977.

Latham, G. P., & Yukl, G. A. A review of research on the application of goal-setting in organizations. *Academy of Management Journal,* 1975, *18,* 824–845.

Lawrence, P. R., & Lorsch, J. W. *Organization and environment.* Boston: Harvard Business School, 1967.

Locke, E. A. The supervisor as "motivator": his influence on employee performance and satisfaction. In B. M. Bass, R. Cooper and J. A. Haas (Eds.), *Managing for accomplishment.* Lexington, MA.: Lexington Books, 1974.

Locke, E. A. Personnel attitudes and motivation. *Annual Review of Psychology,* 1975, *26,* 456–480.

Locke, E. A. The nature and causes of job satisfaction. In M. D. Dunnette (Ed.), *Handbook of industrial and organizational psychology.* Chicago: Rand McNally, 1976.

Marx, M. H. *Theories in contemporary psychology.* New York: MacMillan, 1963.

McCall, M. W., Jr., & DeVries, D. L. When nuts and bolts are not enough: An examination of the contextual factors surrounding performance appraisal. *Paper presented at the 84th Annual Convention of the American Psychological Association.* Washington, DC: September, 1976.

McCormick, E. J., Jeanneret, P. R., and Mecham, R. C. A study of job characteristics and job dimensions as based on the Position Analysis Questionnaire (PAQ). *Journal of Applied Psychology,* 1972, *56,* 347–368. (Monograph)

McGrath, J. E. (Ed.) *Social and psychological factors in stress.* New York: Holt, Rinehart and Winston, 1970.

McGrath, J. E. Stress and behavior in organizations. In M. D. Dunnette (Ed.), *Handbook of industrial and organizational psychology.* Chicago: Rand McNally, 1976.

Miles, R. H. An empirical test of causal inference between role perceptions of conflict and ambiguity and various personal outcomes. *Journal of Applied Psychology,* 1975, *60,* 334–339.

Mitchell, T. R. Expectancy models of job satisfaction, occupational preference, and effort: A theoretical, methodological and empirical appraisal. *Psychological Bulletin,* 1974, *81,* 1053–1077.

Montgomery, H., & Svensen, O. On decision rules and information processing strategies for choices among multiattribute alternatives. *Scandinavian Journal of Psychology,* 1976, *17,* 283–291.

Moreno, J. L. *Who shall survive?* Washington, DC: Nervous and Mental Disease Publishing Co., 1934.

Naylor, J. C. Some comments on the accuracy and validity of an information source. *Journal of Mathematical Psychology,* 1967, *4,* 154–161.

Naylor, J. C., & Schenck, E. A. ρm as an "error free" index of rates agreement. *Educational and Psychological Measurement,* 1966, *26,* 815–824.

Naylor, J. C., & Clark, R. D. Intuitive inference strategies in interval learning tasks as a function of validity magnitude and sign. *Organizational Behavior and Human Performance,* 1968, *3,* 378–399.

Naylor, J. C., & Carroll, R. M. A test of the progression–regression hypothesis in a cognitive inference task. *Organizational Behavior and Human Performance,* 1969, *4,* 337–352.

Naylor, J. C., & Wherry, R. J., Sr. Feasibility of distinguishing supervisor's policies in evaluation of subordinates using ratings of simulated job encumbents. *USAF PRL Tech. Doc. Rep.*, No. 64–25, October, 1964.

Nisbett, R. E., & Wilson, T. D. Telling more than we can know: verbal reports on mental processes. *Psychological Review*, 1977, *84* (3), 231–259.

Nystedt, L. A modified lens model: A study of the interaction between the individual and the ecology. *Perceptual and Motor Skills*, 1972, 479–498.

Nystedt, L. Consensus among judges as a function of the amount of information. *Educational and Psychological Measurement*, 1974, *34*, 91–106.

Peterson, C., Hammond, K. R., & Summers, D. A. Multiple probability learning with shifting weights of cues. *American Journal of Psychology*, 1965, *28*, 660–663.

Porter, L. W., & Lawler, E. E. III. *Managerial attitudes and performance*. Homewood, Ill: Dorsey Press, 1968.

Porter, L. W., & Steers, R. M. Organizational, work, and personal factors in employee turnover and absenteeism. *Psychological Bulletin*, 1973, *80*, 151–176.

Rizzo, J. R., House, R. J., & Lirtzman, S. I. Role conflict and ambiguity in complex organizations. *Administrative Science Quarterly*, 1970, *15*, 150–163.

Roos, L. L., Jr., & Starke, F. A. Concepts of organizational role. In W. Starbuck and P. Nystrom (Eds.) *Handbook of Organizational Design*, Oxford University Press, 1980.

Rush, M. C., Thomas, J. C., & Lord, R. G. Implicit leadership theory: A potential threat to internal validity of leader behavior questionnaires. *Organizational Behavior and Human Performance*, 1977, *20*, 93–110.

Sales, S. M. Organizational role as a risk factor in coronary disease. *Administrative Science Quarterly*, 1969, *14*, 325–336.

Schneider, B. Organizational climates: An essay. *Personnel Psychology*, 1975, *28*, 447–479.

Slovic, P. Analyzing the expert judge: A descriptive study of a stockbroker's decision process. *Journal of Applied Psychology*, 1969, *53*, 255–263.

Slovic, P., Fischhoff, B., & Lichtenstein, S. Behavioral decision theory. *Annual Review of Psychology*, 1977, *28*, 1–39.

Slovic, P., & Lichtenstein, S. C. Comparison of Bayesian and regression approaches to the study of information processing in judgment. *Organizational Behavior and Human Performance*, 1971, *6*, 649–744.

Staël von Holstein, C-A S. Probabilistic forecasting: An experiment related to the stock market. *Organizational Behavior and Human Performance*, 1972, *8*, 139–158.

Staw, B. M. Attribution of the "causes" of performance: A general alternative interpretation of cross-sectional research on organizations. *Organizational Behavior and Human Performance*, June 1975, *13*, No. 3, 414–432.

Stogdill, R. M. *Handbook of leadership*. New York: Free Press, 1974.

Summers, D. A., & Hammond, K. R. Inference behavior in multiple cue tasks involving both linear and nonlinear relations. *Journal of Experimental Psychology*, 1966, *71*, 751–757.

Svenson, O. Process descriptions of decision making. *Organizational Behavior and Human Performance*, 1979, *23*, 86–112.

Terborg, J. Employee motivation: some neglected issues. *Army Research Institute Technical Report*. July, 1978.

Tosi, H. Organizational stress as a moderator of the relationship between influences and role response. *Academy of Management Journal*, 1971, *14*, 7–20.

Tucker, L. R. A suggested formulation in the development by Hursch, Hammond, and Hursch, and by Hursch, Hammond and Todd. *Psychological Review*, 1964, *71*, 528–530.

Turner, A. N., & Lawrence, P. R. *Industrial jobs and the worker: An investigation of responses to task attributes*. Boston: Graduate School of Business Administration, Harvard University Division of Research, 1965.

Tversky, A., & Kahneman, D. Availability: A heuristic for judging frequency and probability. *Cognitive Psychology*, 1973, *5*, 207–232.

Tversky, A. & Kahneman, D. Judgment under uncertainty: heuristics and biases. *Science*, 1974, *185*, 1124–31.

Tversky, A., & Kahneman, D. Belief in the law of small numbers. *Psychological Bulletin*, 1971, *76*, 105–110.

Tyron, W. W. The test–trait fallacy. *American Psychologist*, 1979, 402–406.

U.S. Department of Health, Education and Welfare. *Work in America*. Cambridge, Mass.: MIT Press, 1973.

Vroom, V. H. *Work and motivation*. New York: Wiley, 1964.

Vroom, V. H. Leadership. In M. D. Dunnette (Ed.), *Handbook of industrial and organizational psychology*. Chicago: Rand McNally, 1976.

Vroom, V. H., & Jago, A. On the validity of the Vroom–Yetton model. *Journal of Applied Psychology*, 1978, *63*, 151–162.

Vroom, V. H., & Yetton, P. W. *Leadership and decision-making*. Pittsburgh, Pa.: University of Pittsburgh Press, 1973.

Weiss, H. M. Subordinate imitation of supervisor behavior: The role of modeling in organizational socialization. *Organizational Behavior and Human Performance*, 1977, *19*, 89–105.

Wiggens, N., & Hoffman, P. J. Three models of clinical judgment. *Journal of Abnormal Psychology*, 1968, *73*, 70–77.

Woodward, J. *Industrial organization: theory and practice*. New York: Oxford University Press, 1965.

Glossary

Act: The basic behavioral process. The fundamental unit or element of behavior. Every act has two fundamental dimensions or attributes; amplitude (the total commitment in time and effort to a particular act on the part of an individual) and direction (the specific activity being carried out).

> **Relevant Acts:** Any act of individual I that creates products entering into the evaluation system of some evaluator of I, where the evaluator may be either the self or another. Thus relevance must be defined in terms of the relevance of specific evaluators and is therefore an idiosyncratic concept that depends upon the degree to which the evaluator is perceived as having control over valued outcomes.

> **Trivial Acts:** Any act of individual I that does not create a product entering into the evaluation system of some evaluator of I who is perceived as having control over valued outcomes.

Activation Level: A ratio of the total resources committed to acts by an individual relative to the total possible (maximum) resources available for commitment. Thus Activation Level = C_T/C_M.

Affect: The degree of positive (favorable) or negative (unfavorable) feeling experienced by the individual as the result of receiving either single or multiple outcomes. When measured with respect to a defined class of received outcomes, affect is typically called satisfaction.

Amplitude (of Behavior): The quantity or amount of an individual's resources allocated to a specific act. Synonymous with commitment.

285

Attribute, nonreactive: Any definable or specifiable characteristic of the environment whose magnitude is independent of the individual's own behavior. That is, there is no contingency relationship between a person's behavior and the amount of the attribute present in the environment.

Attribute, reactive: Any definable or specifiable characteristic of the environment whose magnitude is dependent, or related to, or influenced by an individual's own behavior such that a contingency relationship exists between the behavior and the magnitude of the characteristic.

Behavior: The process of engaging in some act(s) by committing some portion of one's two basic or fundamental resources, time and effort, to the specific act.

Climate: The result of attributing human characteristics to an environmental entity such as an organization or an organizational subunit. The fundamental mechanism for these attributions is the descriptive judgment process.

Commitment (C_T): The total amount or quantity of an individual's resources (time and effort) allocated to the task of performing specific act(s). Total commitment (C_T) may be conceived as consisting of two additive components; C_r, commitment to relevant acts and C_t, commitment to trivial acts. The two fundamental resources basic to commitment are time and effort. Thus $C_T = C_r + C_t$.

Contingency: A generalized term indicating a tendency for two attributes or characteristics to exhibit some type of formal relationship. This relationship may be either causal, such that the value of X may partially determine the value of Y, or it may be simply a case of covariation of X and Y.

  Act $\rightarrow$ Product Contingencies ($C_{A \rightarrow P}$): The relationship existing between the degree of commitment to a particular act and the amount and/or quality of a particular product produced by that act.

  Product $\rightarrow$ Evaluation Contingencies ($C_{P \rightarrow E}$): The relationship existing between the amount of a particular product perceived by evaluator J as being produced by individual I and the evaluation of the product by the evaluator.

  Evaluation $\rightarrow$ Outcome Contingencies ($C_{E \rightarrow O}$): The relationship existing between the evaluation made by evaluator J of individual I's product and the amount and/or quality of the outcome (reward) given to individual I.

Descriptive Judgment: The judgment process by which an individual locates some stimulus object or stimulus attribute on an affect-free judgmental continuum.

Efficiency (of Behavior): A ratio of the amount of commitment of one's behavioral resources to relevant acts relative to the total level of resource commitment for that individual. Thus Efficiency = C_r/C_T.

Effort: A fundamental dimension of commitment, representing, along with time, a measure of the degree to which an individual is willing to devote resources to a particular act. It can be viewed as the degree to which an individual activates his or her muscular, cognitive, and perceptual systems and focuses them upon the objectives of performing a particular act.

Energy: Synonymous to effort. See **Effort.**

Evaluation (Evaluation Judgment): The judgmental process by which an individual locates some stimulus object or stimulus attribute on an affective, or good–bad, like–dislike continuum.

Evaluation System: The set of $C_{P \to E}$ product to evaluation contingencies for a given evaluator. Thus

$$\text{Evaluation system} = (C_{P_1E}, C_{P_2E}, C_{P_3E}, \cdots, C_{P_kE})$$

where P_1 to P_k are those products which have a contingency relationship with a particular evaluator's affective response system.

Judgment System: The set of contingencies that formally describe the systematic relationship existing between the judgments of an individual and the various attributes or stimulus characteristics which form the basis for those judgments. Thus

$$\text{Judgment system} = (C_{X_1J}, C_{X_2J}, \cdots, C_{X_kJ})$$

where X_1 to X_k are the stimulus attributes.

Measurement System: The set of $C_{P \to P'}$ contingencies that represent the primary perceptual, or measurement system of the individual and/or organization. These contingencies represent the relationship between the true characteristics of the products produced by an individual engaging in some act and the perceptions of these same products on the part of some perceiver (either other or self). Thus

$$\text{Measurement system} = (C_{P_1P_1'}, C_{P_2P_2'}, \cdots, C_{P_kP_k'})$$

where P_1 to P_k represent the set of products perceived by the observer.

Outcomes: Any characteristic of the environment or perceived state of being that can, either intentionally or unintentionally, have reward or reinforcement properties for the individual. Any perceived attribute of the environment is a potential outcome.

Power: The set of $C_{E\to O}$ contingencies that represent the relationships between the evaluation by some other or by self of an individual's products and the amount and/or quality of the valued outcomes given to the individual by that evaluator.

$$\text{Power} = (C_{E\to O_1}, C_{E\to O_2}, \cdots, C_{E\to O_k})$$

where O_1 to O_k represent the set of valued outcomes under the control of the evaluator.

Products: Those entities which are created by the process of an individual engaging in some act. Measurable result of acts.

Relevant Products: Any product of individual I which enters into the evaluation system of some evaluator of I, where the evaluator may be either self or other, and where the evaluator is perceived as having control over valued outcomes.

Trivial Products: Any product of individual I that does not enter into the evaluation system of some evaluator of I having control over valued outcomes.

Roles (Actual): The set of $C_{P\to E}$ contingencies describing the cognitive (belief) system of a specific evaluator of individual I's products.

$$\text{Role} = (C_{E\to O_1}, C_{E\to O_2}, \cdots, C_{E\to O_k})$$

where P_1 to P_k represent the products of individual I that evaluator J regards as important. These are the relevant products for that evaluator.

Roles (phenomenological): The set of observable products of individual I (as measured in terms of quantity and/or quality) which have contingency relationships with evaluator J's evaluation judgment.

$$\text{Role}_{\text{(Phenomenological)}} = (P_1, P_2, P_3, \cdots, P_k)$$

where P_1 to P_k are those products of individual I that evaluator J regards as important.

Index

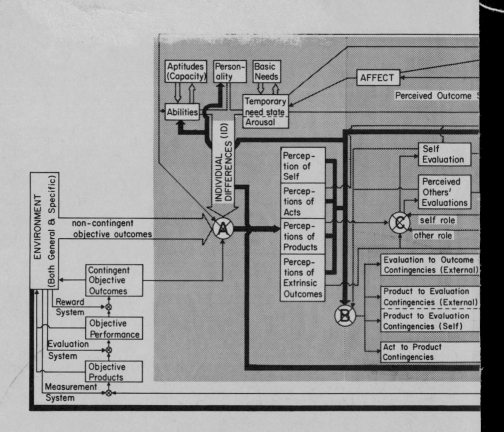